^AStroll at *Leisure* with God

A Stroll at *Leisure* with God

A Pastor's Daily Journey with Cancer

John D. Talbert

WESTBOW
PRESS
A DIVISION OF THOMAS NELSON

Library of Congress Control Number: 2012907624

WestBow Press books may be ordered through booksellers or by contacting:

WestBow Press
A Division of Thomas Nelson
1663 Liberty Drive
Bloomington, IN 47403
www.westbowpress.com
1-(866) 928-1240

ISBN: 978-1-4497-3979-9 (sc)
ISBN: 978-1-4497-3980-5 (hc)
ISBN: 978-1-4497-3978-2 (e)

Printed in the United States of America

WestBow Press rev. date: 09/04/2012

Introduction

One of the blessings of modern Internet technology is the blog. Before I got cancer, I'm not sure I even knew what a blog really was. But I'm grateful my sister Marilyn encouraged me to go to the Caring Bridge website at the recommendation of another friend, Lynda.

At first I was rather reluctant. I didn't think I'd feel like writing, not even occasionally. But was I ever wrong! And I'm so glad I was. Using this technology, I was able to get the word out about my experiences.

At the very start, that was my motivation—nothing more, nothing less. I wanted people in the church to be up to speed about my health issues without the need for multiple phone conversations. I wasn't up to that, and neither was my family.

But as I started writing, I realized I didn't want my daily blog entries to read like a doctor's report, saying things like, "Well, today I'm a little worse than yesterday. I had a headache until 10:13 A.M. Then it started to get better. I slept two and a half hours in the afternoon. My appetite wasn't as good as it was yesterday ..." I couldn't do that. No way. *Boring,* even to the patient—me!

Instead, I decided very early on I wanted the blog to be about what the Lord was teaching me through cancer. Suddenly, as I went in that direction, I found the words flowing out of me like a river.

Where did this inspiration come from? It had to come from the Lord. As the days progressed, I found that writing my daily blog entries gave me the impetus to get out of bed in the morning.

This book consists of selected material first from my journal entries and then, beginning August 17, 2010, from my daily blog postings on Caring Bridge (to find out more about this wonderful tool, please go to http://www.caringbridge.com). It charts my pilgrimage from the day I first discovered the bulge in my abdomen to the day after my sixth chemo treatment.

It is *not* the end of the story, but only the end of this leg of my stroll with God.

"A stroll at leisure with God" is a phrase I borrowed from the Message version of the Bible, the last two verses of Psalm 56. "God, you did everything you promised, and I'm thanking you with all my heart. You pulled me from the brink of death, my feet from the cliff-edge of doom. Now I stroll at leisure with God in the sunlit fields of life" (Psalm 56:12–13). I quote extensively from the Message version in this book. I so appreciate Eugene Peterson's great job on this translation, and appreciate him and his continuing ministry.

Finally, I want to thank everyone who contributed to this book. First of all, I thank my Lord Jesus because He's the one who first led me to write years ago, and empowered me through cancer to begin this book. I thank my mother and sister for all their love and support. I love you both. I praise the Lord for the congregation of the First Southern Baptist Church of Northglenn (FSBCN). I couldn't have made it this far without them. Thank you for allowing me space to go through chemotherapy and grace to embark on the journey of recovery. I also thank Laurie Stephenson for her help in editing this work, and her continuing insights and suggestions. There are no lone rangers in the Christian life. And I certainly don't walk alone on my stroll at leisure with God.

Unless otherwise noted, all Bible quotations are from Eugene H. Peterson, *The Message: The Bible in Contemporary Language,* Colorado Springs: Navpress, 2002.

List of Abbreviations

FSBCN   First Southern Baptist Church of Northglenn
KJV   King James Version
NASB   New American Standard Bible
NIV   New International Version

Chapter One: A Rather Inauspicious Beginning to the Stroll

I t is often the case that the events that have had the most impact in my life have started out in odd ways. This particular leg of my journey is certainly no exception.

I woke up early one rather average Sunday morning (of course, it had to be Sunday morning, right?), in July of 2010 with some swelling in my lower abdomen. It was strange. But it didn't seem to be all that big of a deal... at least, not at first.

July 12. A rather curious bulge appears

There's a huge difference between a grasping person and a trusting person. And it shows up in well-being. Hezekiah distinguished himself because of the priority he placed on the worship of God. This is foundational to everything. He cleaned out the temple so the people could make a priority of worship. And then they worshipped.

"Then Hezekiah the king and the leaders told the Levites to finish things off with anthems of praise to God using lyrics by David and Asaph the seer. They sang their praises with joy and reverence, kneeling in worship. Hezekiah then made this response: 'The dedication is complete—you're now consecrated to God. Now you're ready: Come forward and bring your sacrifices and Thank-Offerings to the Temple of God'" (2 Chronicles 29:30–31). Oh

Lord, I have lived a lot of my life in recent years grasping after things. Point me in a new direction, Lord. Help me.

On Saturday I discovered some swelling near my groin. I have no idea what it is, but I know I have to get it checked out. Lord, I pray the diagnosis and fix will be relatively easy. Give me wisdom in the choice of a doctor. This forces that decision. I pray I can find a doctor and get in today.

This is the first day of the mission trip to Federal Heights. Lord, all the preparation is done, and it is time to start. I'm thankful this week is finally here. I pray you will preach through me in the power of the Holy Spirit tonight. Help me and Jennifer (who's translating my sermon into Spanish) to be in sync. Help her not to be nervous. I pray the weather and all potential distractions will be put aside. Keep the skies clear and the rain away, just like you did last year. You are in charge of the wind and the waves.

On a broader scale, show me how to live so I don't kill myself with stress. I confess anger at the fact everything defaults to me. I just pray for a good pace and rhythm this week. I pray for Mother and Marilyn. Encourage both of them. I pray you will pull everything and everyone together this week.

Father, I am struggling with a lot of anger and resentment these days. Help me with this.

July 13. First night of mission trip to Federal Heights

Speaking of Hezekiah, the Bible says, "Everything he took up, whether it had to do with worship in God's Temple or the carrying out of God's Law and Commandments, he did well in a spirit of prayerful worship. He was a great success" (2 Chronicles 31:21).

Thank you Lord for helping all of us yesterday. The time went by very quickly, and even though my message wasn't quite as I planned it, thank you for helping me. Thank you for helping Jennifer. She did a great job. Thank you for the boys and girls and adults who responded. Ilamarques and Jose were there. It was off-the-charts great. Thank you for calling us to this ministry and place, Lord. Thank you for the police officers we talked with and the firemen who were there. The police made an arrest last night while they were there. Praise God.

I do lift up the Federal Heights police department. And I pray for the firemen as well.

This thing I've got is a hernia, I guess. Matt told me to avoid exercising and playing golf because it can make it worse, and to get it taken care of. Bill and Ilamarques have hernias as well. Bill is going to do nothing; Ilamarques cannot. I pray he and Edgy can have their surgeries done.

I pray for Joseph today. He's one of the children who responded to the gospel last night. I got to speak to him personally. Help this boy. Apparently his family is Catholic, and he says they go to a church in Montbello (but I doubt they go that often). Lead him to a Bible-teaching church.

I pray for the start of vacation Bible school at our church tonight. Keep us moving in a good direction. I pray everything we do will honor you, and I pray you will add people to your kingdom tonight.

I pray I can make contact with a surgeon today and get the ball rolling on this surgery. Help me with that, Lord. Pull things together for this to move quickly. But in the meantime, help me take advantage of what this forces me to do: sit and wait on you.

July 14. Referral to a surgeon

This is my paraphrase of two passages I read this morning, 2 Chronicles 32:7–8 and Proverbs 29:21 and 25.

If you let people treat you like a doormat, you'll be quite forgotten in the end. The fear of human opinion disables; trusting in God protects you from that. Be strong! Take courage! Don't be intimidated by the king of Assyria and his troops—there are more on our side than on their side. He only has a bunch of mere men; we have our God to help us and fight for us.

Father, thanks for these words. Thank you for the referral yesterday and the fact I was able to make an appointment with a surgeon for next week. Thank you for allowing me to get in to see Dr Meyer on Friday. Thank you that all of this is forcing me to move forward on some of my health issues, including a colonoscopy. Thank you for Jose last night and his words of encouragement. We didn't have many kids come in for VBS. There were a lot outside, including Tom, Eduardo, and Will. We didn't have that many folks come to eat, either. But Lord, you are in charge of all of that. Day three is here. The final day is tomorrow, and then this hurdle in the summer will be done and in the books with you. Thank you for the huge amounts of encouragement this week.

Thank you for the prayer meeting I sat in on last night. The Brazilians were praying fervently. It was very moving. I went into the room, and they prayed for me with fervency. I pray you will raise up pray-ers like this in the Anglo church.

Lord, I ask you to draw more children to you tonight. Help Susan from New Life Church, as she teaches part of my final segment to the boys and girls. Help us with this, Lord. Guide us as we share you with the kids. Thanks for all the energy and effort that went into all of this. I pray your Holy Spirit will have the freedom to work through all of us tonight.

July 21. Laying the pieces of my life before Him

Every day it's all about laying the pieces of my life before you and waiting for the fire to fall; waiting for directions to get me safely through enemy lines. Father, Psalm 5 affirms you take care of your children and you kick out the enemies.

Yesterday I learned about a hurtful thing someone in our church said to Vera. Please take care of this problem, and help Vera not to be wounded. Take care of this situation. Show Vera you are in control.

When I'm at the end of my rope, I'm at the beginning of your power and your rule. Thank you for that. Thank you for taking care of things yesterday. When I got to the office, I was told the surgeon's office had called to say the surgeon I was supposed to see had retired. Thank you that they switched me to someone else who can see me today. Thank you so much, Lord.

Yesterday I honestly felt I needed to be ready for a delay. After hearing Hope's twenty-five-year-old daughter has cancer, it sobered me up a bit. This hernia thing can be fixed. Cancer, as Hope said, is final.

I just pray for this appointment today. Lord, I pray they can get me in very soon for this surgery. I just give this to you. Help me today to ask the questions I need to ask.

Thank you for Jose taking the names of the kids who made decisions and calling them himself. This is a huge help. I pray you'll take care of all of that. I pray we can get a church planted in Federal Heights. Thank you for allowing me to go to the city council meeting in Federal Heights last night. Thank you for allowing me to see Mayor Joyce. I got to meet her husband Harold and I got to see George, who's pastor of the church at Holliday Hills. I pray for one of the council members and his family. I pray for New Life Worship Center, a church in Federal Heights. They're planning to purchase a building in town to make into a family life center. I pray we can help with that in some way.

July 23. What are the results?

Lord, I'm struggling with the gamut of emotions because of this bulge in my abdomen. Yesterday I just gave up on hearing from the doctor about the ultrasound, and of course I didn't hear anything. But today at eight o'clock I'm going to call and rattle the chain. This type of thing is just an endurance contest, and it seems to go on and on.

July 26. Reveal yourself, Lord

Psalms 9 and 10 are both about the way you bring about justice for the oppressed. When the gang lords kick us, you're there to lift us up and put the enemies in their place. As a part of my daily praying, I need to remember to pray that who you really are gets revealed to the world. And I need to pray you'll set this world right. I know you will ultimately, but use me to start doing it now.

Lord, I pray for our president. Give him wisdom and direction. Give us help as we prepare for the fiftieth anniversary weekend for FSBCN. Give us the grace to make it through a very busy weekend.

Lord, I pray you'll help this whole process with the bulge to be handled quickly and smoothly. I pray it will be taken care of quickly. I pray I can have the next step scheduled by the end of the week. I pray this surgeon will call me back quickly. I pray you'll help me when I go eat at Betty's on Thursday night. I'm very tired and I just can't seem to get over my fatigue.

August 4. Craziness

These last few days have been absolutely crazy with the fiftieth anniversary. On Friday night several people stood up to testify that God had healed them of cancer. Saturday evening we had a great music service. Les Gilmore, who was saved and baptized at FSBCN, led worship with his group, the Ambassadors. Before the service he handed me a stack of all the CDs his group has produced. What a gift! April Jackson sang and did a fantastic job, and so did Dan Tracy.

Sunday's service was at the Ramada Inn. We had over 400 folks in attendance, including the mayor of Northglenn! It was great to see the crowd. After the service we went back to the church for a catered meal. The day and the weekend were great, but I'm very tired.

In spite of the fact that Dr Schatz is convinced I have cancer, I don't think I've ever felt more at peace than I did yesterday. I didn't sleep very well on Monday night, but I woke up yesterday refreshed and relaxed. Even though I was delayed almost an hour, the whole process of surgery was fantastic. Mother and Marilyn were there with me. All the folks were praying for me—all over the country and all over the world—and more prayer warriors tried to call yesterday, including Dan, Mike, and Sam, along with Brent and Holly who live next door to my mother. People from all over are praying.

Ilamarques sent me Isaiah 26:3: "You will keep in perfect peace him whose mind is steadfast, because he trusts in you" (NIV). This is so true.

Last night I talked with a special couple from our church. I'm so thankful for them, Lord. They're special friends. Both are extraordinary. The man reminded me to wait for a woman who, besides her relationship with the Lord, will make me her top priority. I appreciated this reminder, and it will have to be your doing, Lord.

Lord, I ask you to make the report come back saying I don't have cancer. I ask this in the name of Jesus. But Father, if you choose to allow me to walk through this, I trust your grace and know I can't do it without your people praying for me. If I do, I want to give you more glory.

Whatever the outcome of this biopsy, I must change the way I'm living. Father, I need wisdom and direction more than ever.

August 6. Waiting to hear from the surgeon

I might hear from the surgeon today. It makes me a little nervous. This thing is so weird ... you wake up one day and everything is different. The whole course of my life has changed over the past few weeks.

One of the things I realize today (and I don't know if it will last or not) is it's difficult, if not impossible, to think about things at church. I'm just too preoccupied. I need to be careful because right now I still have a job, and I need one. But Lord, had this not happened, I probably would have continued exactly the way I was going—no changes, nothing different. I just can't keep up this pace and work as many hours as I've been working. It's crazy.

How do your prepare to hear you have cancer? How do you get ready for that? This is one of those things that goes on your health record. It's there forever. Just like Gary going in for a checkup. Take care of him and that exam, Lord. Father, this has always been so remote, and I made it that way on purpose after Daddy's illness and death—I just don't want to think about it. (My dad got colon cancer. The doctors operated on it. They thought they got it all, but two years later they discovered it had spread to his liver, and eight months after that diagnosis he was dead.)

My mother and sister and I have decided even if we hear news today, we're not going to tell anyone until next week. I don't want to let the cat out of the bag until I'm around to communicate it myself (unless it's good news). And Lord, I pray it is. I pray once again you will confound the doctors. Help Dr Schatz to see a miracle and to believe you are God. I know she's convinced I have cancer. Blow her away with your grace and power. I include Dr Meyer in that loop as well.

Lord, show me what you want me to do.

Chapter Two: The Stroll Begins in Earnest

August 7. Psalm 21 and Matthew 10; I have cancer

It's hard to believe and very hard to swallow. I'm not sure the full impact of it has totally hit me yet. Mantle cell lymphoma—that's the name the surgeon used. I got a call late in the afternoon from someone at a Dr Jotte's office. When she realized I didn't even know I had cancer yet, she hung up quickly. How bad is that?

Then Dr Schatz called me to tell me I have a low-grade lymphoma. What does that mean? Cancer is cancer. It's just hard to get it in my mind. I forget about it for a while and then it comes crashing in on me. I had to schedule a PET scan and an appointment with the oncologist. It's scary. And I don't want to go through this. I don't want cancer and cancer treatments and this sledgehammer hanging over my head for the rest of my life. And I don't have a lot of confidence anyone ever gets over it. I guess some people do—Lance Armstrong, Paul Azinger, and others come to mind. Maybe I need to read their stories. Lord, I know you can do anything, but it all seems so bleak right now.

Listening to the Word helped last night. Marilyn downloaded the Message version of the Psalms on my phone. Maxwell, one of our cats, comes into this room a lot and sits here with me. Animals can sense when something's going on.

Father, I know some people have to go through this alone, and I don't see how they do it. I'm so thankful for Mother and Marilyn. Last night they sat with me and were there for me. Thank you so much for them. I know this is hard on them, and I know they're trying to avoid losing it for my sake. Help them.

I'm glad I have a couple days before I let this cat out of the bag. I don't know if I can handle it or not. Sometimes I think I want people around me and other times I think I don't care if I ever see another person again.

Help me with anger, Lord. I'm angry when I think about all the stress I've put myself under the past few months. That's one emotion, and then I revert to thinking something I've done has caused this.

But Lord, I pray for wisdom when it comes to my job at the church. Again, what do you want me to do? I'm struggling with so many things. All this makes me feel like an even older man. Now I'm a fifty-two-year-old man with cancer. If I really let this sink in, I think I'll start to cry and never stop. Lord, I don't want this. I don't want to go through this.

"Show your strength, God, so no one can miss it" (Psalm 21:13).

August 9. Torture

Welcome to the longest weekend of my life. I just sat around all day Saturday. That wasn't good. Sunday I took two walks. That seemed to help a little. The hardest thing about this is the agonizing waiting—the sitting, the waiting, and the thinking. It's torture. I decided not to let the cat out of the bag until today. Mother and Marilyn told a couple people. They have to deal with this in their own way, but I wasn't ready. I just wasn't ready to talk to everyone before I announce it to the church, and I didn't want to leave it for JJ to share this news.

But the other issue in all of this is I'm angry. I'm mad I had to get cancer and mad at everything that caused it. And I'm not even sure what that is at this point. But what a waste! What do I have to show for all the effort and the energy I poured out? Nothing.

Matthew 11 has a perfect word for me today, Lord. Why should I doubt you would speak to me directly, when you have all these years? Here's John who spoke up for you and what did it get him? He ended up in prison, doubting. Then because of some frivolous party promise by some flaky ruler, he had his head chopped off. And this is all an indication of the fickleness of the people who rejected John, who lived and preached one extreme, and rejected you because you lived and preached another.

Was this rejection and failure the ministry's fault? No! It was judgment against the places that rejected their opportunity—Chorazin and Capernaum, two places where you spent a lot of time, but they rejected you anyway.

Lord, I'm tired. I'm burned out on religion. Lord, I'm struggling with doubt and fear. And I don't know why. As Mother said yesterday, you've taken care of us in amazing ways. She's never had a job for one day since Daddy died, and yet you've allowed us to do just about whatever we wanted to do. We haven't lacked one thing.

In the meantime, help me through today. Show me how to tell everyone. Marilyn is right. Who cares? I'm just going to do it. I pray for help as I talk with folks and share this today. I pray you'll help me through another two days of inactivity and prepare me for that test tomorrow. Beyond this, I'm going to turn it all over to you.

I pray for Sharon, JP, and Hope's daughter Kari. I pray you'll comfort them and heal them.

There's a song called "Were It Not for Grace" on the CDs Les Gilmer gave me. Without your grace, I'd be headed down the road to nowhere—running down some dead-end street. But Lord, I thank you for your grace that gives me the strength to run this leg of the race. Help me to learn the unforced rhythms of grace. But I'm tired, so tired of feeling as if I have to explain myself to everyone. Those days are *over*. Take me or leave me.

"Are you tired? Worn out? Burned out on religion? Come to me. Get away with me and you'll recover your life. I'll show you how to take a real rest. Walk with me and work with me—watch how I do it. Learn the unforced rhythms of grace. I won't lay anything heavy

11

or ill-fitting on you. Keep company with me and you'll learn to live freely and lightly" (Matthew 11:28–30).

What makes the passage I read today so difficult is you say you won't lay anything heavy or ill-fitting on me. Does this include cancer? I'm struggling with this, Lord.

August 10. A pregnant pause

Here are the parts of today's passages that caught my eye and my heart. Psalm 23:3 says, "True to your word, you let me catch my breath and send me in the right direction."

Lord, I thank you that this is a stop, a pregnant pause, where I'm forced to sit and do nothing. Because of the PET scan today, I was told to exert little or no physical activity. So for another day, here I am—sitting here before you. I've been this way for a week now. I haven't felt like doing anything anyway.

But I know the pause is purposeful—to send me in the right direction. Father, with all my heart, that's what I want. I want to go in the right direction.

Here's what I heard yesterday from more than one person: "Whenever you need me, I'll come. However you need me." And Lord, I do need people. I do need to be with them. I'm so thankful for Andy and Jen, who make me laugh. I'm thankful for Walt and Beth. Steve and Bethany are good friends. Rob is with his daughter in North Carolina. Bill and Melba are still here. ER and Jackie are available. Bob organized a prayer meeting for today. Rick was encouraging.

The whole scene this past week and particularly yesterday was just so quiet and peaceful. I took another walk yesterday. I walked down Happy Canyon to Quincy and then back up and down the street the other way to Ivy and around to the athletic fields, the track at Thomas Jefferson High School. I took a picture of it. Here's my metaphor for this track that overlooks the city of Denver: here's the next lap for my life that will require more discipline and energy and focus than anything I've ever done. Cancer. And I don't even know what I'm facing yet.

This neighborhood is so sedate and serene. This is my home. I've lived my whole life (except four years) in this area. For the most part, the houses and yards are well-manicured. I didn't see much evidence of anyone yesterday at 12:30.

I walked by the Wests' house, down the street from where Gordon lived. Then I turned the corner at Hillcrest and made my way up our street, past the doctor's house. He died a few years ago and now his wife lives there alone. The Ericksons have moved away. The Johnsons lived across the street from us—that's where my friend Bill in the wheelchair lived. He was my best friend until he died in seventh grade.

Shortly after, I met Gary on the golf course. We're the last of the originals still in this neighborhood—forty-eight years. I honestly can't imagine driving by this house of ours and seeing someone else living here. I don't think I could handle it.

One of the greatest things about these days is the way it clouds up and rains in the late afternoon and early evening. It makes sitting on the porch so comforting. I don't know why. Everything cools down when it rains, and Mother and Marilyn and I have to cover ourselves with blankets. We've sat on that porch until dark. Yesterday at sunset the sky was spectacular, with veins of orange and white stretching out across the panoply of our view. Lord, you painted a masterpiece last night. I have pictures of it as well.

But going back to the passage I read yesterday at the end of Matthew 11, here's what I noticed today: "Get away with me ... walk with me and work with me ... and keep company with me" (Matthew 11:28–30). *With me.*

Jesus, I want you to show me how to live. I'm so done with trying to prop that church up and help it along. My efforts have proven most unfruitful. If this church declines and falls off the map, so be it. It's your church. Whatever you want to do ... you don't need my efforts. They don't produce anything anyway. Help me Lord, as I think about the church and staff and my shifting role in it.

Lord, help me with this test today. I place it in your hands. Lord, again I pray this cancer hasn't spread. I pray for Bill and Irene and JP and Sharon and Kari and Karen. I place all these folks in your hands. Just today, Lord.

August 11. First meeting with fear

For the first time since hearing I have cancer, I woke in the night in fear. But Psalm 23 addresses that. "Even though the way goes through Death Valley, I'm not afraid when you walk at my side. Your trusty shepherd's crook makes me feel secure" (Psalm 23:4). Oh Lord, my Shepherd, I need you now more than ever. I'm worried about money and insurance. Yesterday I arrived at the clinic for my PET scan and the receptionist told me it was canceled because they're still waiting for insurance approval. Everything depends on that, and I'm worried about where things are headed—not only now, but also down the road. Does your treatment just get cut off if the insurance company decides not to pay? I can't change insurance companies now because I have cancer. What does the future hold? It's very scary. I'm not afraid of dying. I'm afraid of running out of money to pay for my treatments, whatever they may be.

Lord, what a ridiculous fear. Have you ever put us in a spot where we have no money? When Daddy died, you took care of us in so many ways. But I've been so flip, so arrogant when it comes to money. Now I'm in a lot of debt that must be paid off. I have to be aggressive about that and not incur any more. It stops now. With all that's going on, I must work to reduce my stress, and stressing over money is one huge issue.

Last night Mother and Marilyn and I talked for a long time about going to MD Anderson in Houston for my treatments. I so appreciate them saying they would help me if I wanted to do it. But ultimately we decided to start here. I need to be near my home during this time. I need a support group. I don't need to be isolated in some hotel in Houston for weeks going through chemo. I honestly don't think I could do it or ask Marilyn to do it and leave Mother here alone. But Lord, I pray for guidance to the best oncologist. Help me with that.

Marilyn gave me this from Kaye Dunn:

I AM your SHEPHERD

"You'll never have need of anything that I want for you. If you'll trust me and really allow me to be the Shepherd of your life, I will give to you such great peace of mind that it will be like lying in the cool green grass of a Springtime meadow. And as you learn to deepen your love and trust, a quietness will come over your soul like a serene, calm lake. It will be a time of great refreshment to your inner man thus preparing you to do whatever task that I give you to do as it is for my honor and glory not yours.

"There will be times because of my great love for you it will be necessary for me to lead you into great darkness—darkness that will be so great that you will feel as though you are standing at the very edge of life with death awaiting you below. But, always remember I am still your Shepherd. In the darkness you may not be able to see me but you have my eternal promise that I will never leave you or forsake you. If you will continue to trust me even after you have been through a time of darkness, I will again flood your heart with such peace that you could even sit down among your enemies. Your joy will be so great that it will spill over into the lives of others. And as your reward, I will give to you all the really important things of life. When you have completed all that I have planned for you to do on earth, I want you to come up and live with me forever and ever and ever."

Chapter Three: What Is This Path?

August 17. Bone marrow biopsy

Today I had a bone marrow biopsy. Whew. Not a lot of fun. But the oncologists tell me this is necessary to make sure the cancer hasn't spread to my bone marrow. I pray it hasn't. When I get the results of this test, the doctors can determine the stage of the cancer. Then I need to pick an oncologist. Then we have to make decisions about treatment strategy. This is a very crucial time. Lord, help me!

August 19. The waiting game

Still waiting for the results of another biopsy. There sure is a lot of waiting involved with cancer, and I'm a very poor patient. But I'm thankful for what God shows me daily in His Word.

Today I read Psalm 31, and the Spirit stopped me at verse 5: "I've put my life in your hands. You won't drop me; you'll never let me down." I can certainly affirm that. My New Testament reading was from Matthew 14. As the day grew long, the disciples tried to help Jesus out, saying: "Send everyone away so they can buy food in the nearby villages." But Jesus said, "No need to do that. You feed them." Jesus, thank you for your ability to meet needs and multiply your provision. I trust you today.

August 21. "You have no idea how God works"

Boy is that ever true. Jesus said this to Peter in Matthew 16:23.

The whole chapter of Matthew 16 is about who Jesus really is, what the church really is, and God's way of making it all come together. When Jesus told Peter about the suffering He was going to endure, Peter didn't understand and didn't want it to happen.

I've always been critical of Peter for saying what he said, but now I understand. *No one,* including and especially me, wants to suffer. Jesus knew exactly what was ahead of him and still went through with it. I have a little idea of what might be ahead of me in the coming days, and I'm balking.

Still no word on the bone marrow biopsy. I thought I might hear yesterday, but nothing—and that leaves another couple days to wait. But somehow it feels okay to have another couple days of reprieve. Sometimes it's better not to know.

Yesterday I told Marilyn I know God has the power to touch me and I'd be healed of cancer instantly. (Believe me, I'm praying every day He'll do that, and so are many others.) But if that doesn't happen today, I have to believe this is the course He's laid out for me *for now,* for today. But beyond that, I have no clue what's going on—and no one does.

If I could understand what I think is God's plan for me, it would certainly *not* be God's plan, as Isaiah 55 affirms. His ways and thoughts are higher than mine. Peter made a god out of his own understanding and Jesus saw through that idolatry (Satan, get behind me!).

Oh Lord, I'm thankful you know your plan and are working it out today in my life.

August 23. Part one (early in the day): the tank

"God met me more than halfway, he freed me from my anxious fears" (Psalm 34:4). This is what I need today, right now.

Lord, I fear the unknown in this. Last Monday night I was sitting there with no idea I was getting ready for the biopsy from hell. It was one of the most difficult and painful experiences I've ever been through in my life. I felt like I was blind-sided by that test. It's just one thing, but I'm afraid it's a harbinger of things to come. I fear what's ahead will be much more difficult to deal with than I can even imagine. I'm afraid of that, Lord. I'm afraid of pain. I'm afraid of being sick for months. I'm afraid of side effects from these drugs.

I'm angry about this stinking disease. I don't want to have to go through this. So, since you're the one who allowed this, I'm running to you as hard and fast as I can. Thank you for the circle of protection you provide. No one who runs to Him loses out. I'm banking on that statement and on your promises.

Matthew 16:24 says anyone who intends to come with me has to let me lead. Lord, sometimes I feel like I'm standing outside my body, watching myself do this, and I'm just thinking *wow*. I want to control things, slow them down, step out of this life and this body and do something else.

Jesus told Peter, "You're not in the driver's seat; I am." Oh Lord, I acknowledge this to you.

The Son of God went on to tell Peter, "Don't run from suffering; embrace it." Now, this is the hard part. I can't do this apart from the presence and power of your Holy Spirit. *Help!*

"Follow me and I will show you how," Jesus added. Okay Lord, I desperately need that today. I didn't ask for any of this. It just happened; now I need you to step in and deliver me.

I pray for Mother and Marilyn today. Strengthen and encourage both of them. I pray I can either see or make an appointment with Dr Meyer. I pray for wisdom as we meet with Dr Jotte. I pray the bone marrow biopsy will come back negative. I pray for clear direction.

Take care of the church. I turn it over to you.

August 23. Part two (later that day): thank you Jesus!

My heart is so full of gratitude to God. I'm encouraged.

First, according to the results of the bone marrow biopsy, this cancer is *not* in my bones.

Second, Mother and Marilyn and I visited with one of the oncologists I met last week. I'm really impressed with him and his assistants. He's very knowledgeable and very encouraging. So I think I'm pretty settled in that decision.

Dr Jotte told us that as a result of the good report on the bone marrow biopsy, I'm considered a stage 3A. They categorize me as a 3 because the PET scan revealed some extracellular activity in my chest and neck. But the nurse told us this is fairly typical for blood cancers like lymphoma. She didn't seem to be very concerned about it. The staging of lymphoma is not as critical and crucial as it is for other types of cancers.

I'm a 3A because I have no real symptoms. Typically, people with aggressive forms of non-Hodgkin's lymphoma have significant weight loss, night sweats, and/or extreme itching. I don't have any of those symptoms, so according to the oncologist I don't have an aggressive form of lymphoma. This doesn't mean I can goof off and do nothing, but neither do I have to make rushed decisions to get the ball rolling. I'm really thankful for that. I was worried I was going to be pressured into making treatment decisions, and I wasn't ready for that.

So the next step is to decide on the chemo treatment. There's either the standard treatment called *RCVP*, or participation in a clinical trial Dr Jotte has access to. I don't understand all there is to know about clinical trials, but if I choose to participate, I might get to take a new drug they're trying out for mantle cell lymphoma. There are some benefits to being involved in this trial.

Here's what's on the horizon. I'm going to make an appointment with a nutritionist to find out what I should be eating. On Thursday I have to have a port surgically implanted in my chest. That sounds awful, but the doctor explained that having this port makes chemo treatments a lot easier because the nurses don't have to set up a new IV every time I have a treatment.

Once I make the decision about treatment, the ball will start rolling. I have to have an EKG and some other minor tests (and I believe every test they could *ever* think of is minor compared to a bone marrow biopsy). One way or another, I hope to start treatments soon.

I won't make it through all this without the love and prayers of God's people. Here's the verse for today: "God met me more than halfway, he freed me from my anxious fears" (Psalm 34:4). Amen and amen.

August 24. Another brief note

Lord, I've already learned that I can't get too euphoric during this process, but thank you for a good day yesterday. Thank you for all the encouraging news. When we got home from seeing Dr Jotte, we took time as a family to thank you. You get all the credit for the lump in my abdomen. Thank you for showing me what's going on so I can address it.

Father, it looks like it's going to be a cloudy and rainy day. Beautiful. I don't know why, but the days when it clouds up and rains give me so much peace. It was raining yesterday afternoon on the way home from Dr Jotte's office.

You have to have clouds to have rain.

August 25. Everything works together for the good

"But those who want the best for me, let them have the last word—a glad shout!—and say, over and over and over, 'God is great—everything works together for good for his servant'" (Psalm 35:27).

This whole psalm is about a believer who's continually taunted and challenged for his faith in the Lord. His enemies cast aspersions on his faith in the Lord and make fun of him. But he prays that in and through it all, the Lord and those who love Him will rejoice in the end.

Yesterday a pastor friend sent me Philippians 4:4: "Rejoice in the Lord always, and again I say, rejoice." It was a very timely word.

Living every day with cancer is mostly a mental challenge. After all the good news of Monday—and I'm still thankful and grateful—I dropped like a rock yesterday.

I can relate to Psalm 35 today, not because I know of any *person* who wants to see me fall, but because in a strange way the cancer itself is like a voice inside my head, and Satan uses it. Cancer is taunting me, saying: "You still have me." I'm finding it harder and harder to keep those taunts out of my head.

I know I'm looking at a long road of chemo and further tests and uncertainty ahead. But I do believe the Lord has graciously allowed this illness in my life and today, if He chooses not to heal me instantly, He has a plan and purpose for it. I may not ever understand all the reasons why, and I don't need to. But I keep coming back to Romans 8:28, which says: "And we know that in all things God works for the good of those who love him, who have been called according to his purpose" (NIV).

Lord, I thank you today that everything, including cancer, falls in line with your purpose. Today I refuse to listen to cancer's taunts, and I choose to rejoice in you. I thank you for cancer. And I thank you because everyone who's reading these words right now and praying for me and wanting the best will eventually see you win, and we'll all rejoice together! Amen.

August 26. The straw that broke the camel's back

Everyone I've talked to about the port in my chest says I'll appreciate it down the road because it makes chemo treatments much easier. Dr Jotte said there's an added benefit. If there were any kind of accident with the use of an IV (which they'd have use for every treatment if I didn't have the port), these drugs they're giving me would cause a big problem. And I don't want any more of those in my life, for sure!

It's incredible how when you're going through something like this, other things tend to happen. Some say tragedies come in threes. I'm not sure about that, although it does seem to be true at times. Anyway, yesterday as my mother was leaving a doctor's office she tripped over something and fell on the sidewalk.

I wasn't with her when it happened, but when my sister called to tell me, the gravity of everything hit me again. I think when you're going through something like cancer, any added trouble quickly feels overwhelming, like the proverbial straw on the camel's back. Normally it wouldn't be that big a deal, but when a family is dealing with cancer, everything is magnified for the whole family.

I'm so thankful this incident didn't seem to affect Mother and Marilyn as much as it did me. But Lord, I pray for them because they're carrying a heavy load in caring for me.

I know none of this—not one thing—escapes your notice. I love the way Eugene Peterson captures the poetic elements of the Psalms, reflecting a very relevant truth for me in all of this: "God's love is meteoric, his loyalty is astronomic, His purpose titanic, his verdicts oceanic. Yet in his largeness nothing gets lost; Not a man, not a mouse [not a fall, not a moment of discouragement, not a cancer cell, not a surgery] slips through the cracks" (Psalm 36:5–6).

I'm so thankful our *great big God* pays attention to and cares about very tiny details in my life. So, onward and upward, always!

August 27. PowerPort

The port surgery was a little more involved than I expected. The device they implanted in my chest is actually an amazing piece of technology. It's called a *PowerPort*. Here's what the brochure says: "It is a cylinder with a hollow space inside that is sealed by a soft top. The PowerPort device connects to a small, flexible tube called a catheter that is inserted inside of one of the large central veins that deliver blood to your heart. When a special needle is put into the soft top of the PowerPort device, it creates access to your bloodstream, meaning that medications and fluids can be given and blood samples withdrawn.

"Your PowerPort implanted Port allows clinicians to easily deliver medications or fluids or withdraw blood samples with having to repeatedly stick your peripheral veins directly with a needle. ... Because the PowerPort device places medications into the large central veins instead of the small peripheral veins, the medications mix more thoroughly in the blood, diluting them so they are less harmful to your vascular system."

Sorry to include all this information, but the more I read about this thing I now carry in my body, the more I'm amazed at the mercy of the Lord.

So before I go further, I thank you Lord for the advancement in technology that makes this possible. I know my dad didn't have this gadget thirty-seven years ago when he had cancer. One of the major headaches he had was getting poked and prodded whenever he went in for chemo. So thank you for allowing this little bit of relief to my treatments in the future.

Going back to yesterday, they had to make two incisions—one in my chest and one in my neck—to implant the port in my chest. It was pretty involved, and while the operation itself only took about thirty minutes, getting ready for it and recovering from it in the hospital took well over four hours. And it will take several more days for me to get completely back on my feet.

Anyway, here's what stood out to me yesterday. I was lying on the operating table with a huge light about two feet above me. The nurses were prepping me for surgery, and one of them moved a metal bar extended about six inches over my face. Then they draped a sheet over the bar to cover my face but not my chest.

They told me to turn my head to the left. I could see from under the sheet where a nurse was seated. She was the gal who wheeled me into the operating room, and we had a conversation as we rolled along. She told me she had worked in an inner city hospital in Los Angeles, and on her first evening shift ever, she felt afraid as she left the parking garage to get on the elevator. So she prayed, "Lord, please protect me." Then she pushed the button on the elevator, and when the door opened a nun was standing there in full garb! She said, "That was the Lord's answer to my prayer and I was never afraid ever again in all the years I worked at that hospital."

Lord, thank you so much for taking care of me and for speaking truth in my life when I need it, even from unlikely sources.

Back to my story ... all I could see was the nurse sitting on a chair beside the operating table. She said, "John, I'm here. I'm going to start to put you to sleep sort of. You won't be completely out, but you'll be so sleepy you won't care and won't remember anything. But if you hurt in any way, please let me know and I'll adjust the medicine, or [and this is something I'll never forget], if you just need to hold my hand, I'll be glad to do that."

This is the verse for today from Psalm 37:24, "If he stumbles, he's not down for long; *God has a grip on his hand*" [emphasis mine]. Oh

Father, I'm thankful you're *always* closer than that nurse. You are in me and I am in you. And you already and always hold my hand. I cannot begin to express how much that means to me *today*.

August 28. Clinical trial versus standard treatment

Yesterday was a tough day. My chest is still very sore and a lot of times it feels like a giant mosquito bite. It itches like crazy but I can't scratch it. The only thing that gives me relief is an ice pack.

I decided against the clinical trial in favor of the standard chemo treatment for three reasons. First, if you submit to one, then they flip a coin and either put you in a group that gets the new medicine or else you go into a group that gets the standard medicine. You have no choice in the matter.

Second, they give you a lot of extra tests (for research purposes, I suppose). And right now, after my third surgery in three weeks, I'm not really up for doing anything extra.

Third, when you submit to a clinical trial, the trial calls the shots. You can opt out, but I get the idea that doing so wouldn't go over very well with the doctors, and I can understand why. When they're testing a new medicine for future cancer patients, they have to follow the correct procedures.

Those were the factors in my decision. But to be honest, I still wonder if I made the right decision. I wonder if the new medicine (*if* I got it, and that's a big *if*) will be better. Lord, I turn this decision over to you and trust you with it. I'm relying on you, not chemo, even though I know you can and do use medicine to accomplish your purposes.

Once I made the decision, I called the oncologist's assistant who immediately scheduled me for my first chemo treatment. Wham, bam! Here's the date: *Friday, September 10 at 8:30 A.M.* She then made this comment: "Come prepared to be at the clinic most of the day." I said, "Huh?" She said, "This first treatment will take at least *six hours.* We have to see how you tolerate the main drug we're giving you. That will take four hours alone. Then we give you the other drugs, and then we have you wait for an hour to see." Gulp.

All that hit me like a ton of bricks. *Six hours.* I guess I had the expectation that chemo was like taking a pill, except it was liquid they put in you through the port—fifteen to twenty minutes and done. I guess not.

I'm almost embarrassed to admit I thought that now. But still, apart from talking with folks who've been through this, how do you know? I wish someone would publish a cancer handbook that tells about what all these tests are and what will happen and how long and hard everything is, every step of the way!?! Probably won't happen ... but this just hit me: why do I need a cancer *handbook* when I have the Bible *footbook?*

Yes, the Bible is a *footbook*. Psalm 119:105 says, "Your word is a lamp to my feet and a light for my path." I really don't think it would help to know the future in detail. I really don't. I just need the grace and the light for my next step *today*. God keeps bringing me back to today.

The gravity of all that took me down a notch yesterday, and I had another one of those moments like I had facedown on the table when they were doing the bone marrow biopsy: "Lord, I can't do this."

Here's the verse for today: in Matthew 19, after the rich young man walked away from Jesus, the disciples said, "If this prime candidate didn't make it and it is very difficult for the rich to enter the Kingdom, who has a chance?" Jesus responds by saying, "No chance at all if you think you can pull it off yourself. Every chance in the world if you trust God to do it" (Matthew 19:26). I'll take my chances with God.

By the way, I want to thank everyone who wades through all this verbiage I'm writing. Somehow, continuing to journal as I have throughout most of my Christian life is helping me through all the steps with cancer.

August 29. Sunday morning but not in church—what to do?

Here I sit on Sunday morning at a time when I'd normally be arriving at the church to get things moving for the day. Kind of weird I'm not doing it, but I'm glad because I'm still not up to it physically. I know that.

But still, I have mixed emotions. On the one hand, I'm bummed out I can't be there today. I always miss preaching, even when I'm on vacation. Preaching has always been the eye of the hurricane for me. Plus I just miss the fellowship. Invariably, the Lord uses one or more people to tell me something I really need to hear. So I do miss that part as well, *big time.*

But on the other hand, I've been utterly amazed at the church's response to this illness of mine. And Lord, you know how redemptive this is for me. Besides preaching the past couple Sundays, I've only been in the office a few hours. And I've felt no pressure and nothing but affirmation. Betty and Mary Ann are taking care of office and financial stuff. Jim and Patti B and Jim M have stepped up to visit folks. JJ, our children's minister, is preaching for me today. Al and some other guys have stepped forward to say they're available to preach also. There are guys at North Metro available to preach, plus our state executive director, Mark. Knowing these men are willing and ready gives me great comfort. I name these names in thanksgiving to the Lord Jesus Christ.

In addition to these dear brothers and sisters, countless others in the congregation email me and pray for me. I thank you Lord for each one. Many have told me, "John, whatever you need, let me know." I think waiting is frustrating to some of these servants who want to do something for me right now. And down the road, I know I'll need something, but right now, just the fact they're available and praying is off the charts. There's no way to measure how valuable all this is.

It's great to see people step up to serve already. And I'm praying the Lord will bring revival to FSBCN by way of my cancer, as people are freed up to serve. I honestly think pastors like me sometimes inhibit people from serving just because they go ahead and do things others in the church can and should do. The Lord is convicting me of this.

So today, even though I'm bummed I will not be at church, I'm so thankful for the fact that my church family allows me to be away. From the bottom of my heart I'm grateful, eternally grateful, and I want to confess this gratitude to you today Lord. And I want everyone who reads this to give glory to you because of the way your people in the congregation of FSBCN have responded. Praise God!

One of the huge benefits of being away is I've had time to talk with Jesus and let him talk with me. I'm earnestly asking God to show me what He wants me to learn from this. I exchanged email with a dear sister in the Lord about this subject yesterday. Cancer has a way of reprioritizing your life. Some things that were important to me five weeks ago are not as urgent as they used to be. And God has moved some things up on the list by way of this illness. This process is not fun. It's spiritually painful when the Lord cuts things out of your life.

The psalmist expresses this pain as he thinks about his transitory life and troubles: "I'll say no more, I'll shut my mouth, since you, Lord, are behind all this. But I can't take it much longer. When you put us through the fire to purge us from our sin, our dearest idols go up in smoke. Are we also nothing but smoke?" (Psalm 39:9–11).

So Lord, I'll accept my surgeries, both physical and spiritual. Thanks again for my church family. Speak through the teachers and JJ. Bless your people. Amen.

September 1. A walk down memory lane

Yesterday started out so well. The nutritionist told me it's vital for me to walk every day for several reasons, so I drove down the street from my mother's house to an area near Kent Denver, my high school. There's a beautiful trail that follows the Highline Canal. It circles along the east side of the school's extensive property, around to University Boulevard, and south through Littleton.

I decided to divert off the main trail along a path that took me to a vantage point where I could see the back of the school and the gym on the east side of the property. Both places bring back great memories for me. I remember watching Marilyn play basketball in that gym. In one game she stole the ball from the opposing team's point guard several times in a row. She just out-hustled everyone on the other team. Soon I was looking for anyone I could find to tell, "Yeah, that's my sister. Taught her everything she knows."

Adjacent to the gym at the back of the school is a grassy area that forms a natural amphitheater that backs up to a lake. It's a student hangout during the school year, and also where graduation ceremonies are held. I remember my graduation in May 1977 (the dark ages); I invited my pastor Andy to come and lead the prayer. One of my classmates made a snide remark when Andy finished his prayer, and I remember thinking the ridicule was really a compliment to Jesus. It was so good to have Andy there.

I thought about all these things as I continued on the trail that cut through the school's property and wound back up to the main path. When I arrived at the trail, I turned right to begin the trek back toward my truck. I continued on the trail for half a mile or so, then diverted again and headed up Dahlia to Blackmer Road. My friend Gary used to live in a house near that corner. So I turned down that road and stood in front of his house.

On the spot, I pulled out my cell phone and called him. We reminisced about all the times we played basketball in the driveway at the back of his house, and all the cast of characters who joined in the fray: Gary's older brother Dave, his buddy Dave, Craig, Steve, and some other guys. I hadn't thought about those guys in years, but all the memories came back. Thank you Lord.

One of the blessings of this cancer (I don't know why this is happening per se, and I guess it doesn't matter why) is the memories. Maybe it happens to every believer with cancer. I hope so. This whole experience with illness has put my life in perspective—perspective with God on a vertical level for sure, but also on a horizontal level with memories and people.

I'm sad to say so much of my life has been like the lives of most of the folks I saw on that trail yesterday—running with my head down, preoccupied with my business and getting to the next thing *fast*. Yesterday I walked with my head up, talking to Jesus and trying to drink in the day and everything he brought to mind. By his grace, I want to live that way from now on.

So I had that great walk with all those wonderful memories and everything was peachy throughout the whole day, right? Wrong. Later in the day when I was at the church office, I came across a statement about mantle cell lymphoma in some material the nutritionist gave me. I don't know why I read it then, but I did, and I started going down. Thank goodness Betty and Mary Ann were there to encourage me on the spot, but this is the nature of this battle. It demands constant vigilance.

That's why I'm so glad I came across Psalm 41 in my devotional time today. I don't think I've ever noticed this before, but a sick person wrote this psalm! There are several clear indicators of this, like: "Whenever we're sick and in bed, God becomes our nurse, nurses us back to health" (verse 3). Verse 5 says, "The rumor goes out, 'He's got some dirty, deadly disease. The doctors have given up on him.'" So his sick situation is similar to mine—not that any *person* has attacked me, but the devil continues to bother me.

This is why I've determined to spend more time in the Word reading about God than I spend online or in literature reading about mantle cell lymphoma. In fact, I'm probably done reading about it altogether.

Psalm 41 ends on a high note for the sick person. *I love this*: "God, give grace, get me up on my feet. I'll show them a thing or two. Meanwhile, I'm sure you're on my side—no victory shouts yet from the enemy camp! You know me inside and out, you hold me together, you never fail to stand me tall in your presence so I can look you in the eye. Blessed is God, Israel's God, always, always, always. Yes. Yes. Yes" (verses 10–13).

So today Lord, I choose to trust you to beat cancer. I refuse to let it truncate this expansive and large life of Christ in whom I live and *walk,* and today I thank you for grace. I thank you for victory. And I thank you for allowing me to stand and look you in the eye, only because of grace and the victory you won on the cross on my behalf. Oh Dr Jesus and closer-than-a-brother Jesus, thank you for loving me. Amen.

September 2. Spiritual buoyancy

Today I read Psalms 42 and 43. I love the way the psalms show how prayer works across the gamut of human emotion—all the ups and downs of life. These two psalms are tied together and reflect someone who's struggling with depression.

I'm no professional counselor, so I'm not up on technical definitions, but I can honestly say I haven't experienced depression over the past several weeks. Now I want to be clear: I've been down *at times.* I've been angry. I've been frustrated. I've cried out to God, "I just can't do this." But depression? I don't think so.

Why? It's certainly nothing I can take credit for, because I'm a prime candidate for it. I've struggled with depression in various forms throughout my life, but not now. Here's the reason why: the power of God is at work through the prayers of God's people.

And I've felt—literally and actually felt—the prayers of God's people in the midst of all of this. It started in earnest before my first biopsy. I remember thinking, "This is scary. I could have cancer. My doctor and the surgeon are telling me I probably do. What if I do? Oh no …" And I remember feeling like I was headed down a fast track to the dumps, but *someone* stopped me.

Here's the analogy that comes to mind: it feels as if I'm floating on an inflatable air mattress on the top of water in a swimming pool. When you lie on one of those mattresses and someone tries to push you down under the water, they can do it, but only for a little while. Why? I believe it's called *buoyancy.*

A definition of buoyancy I found on the Internet is "the power of a fluid to exert an upward force on a body placed in it; also: the upward force exerted" (http://www.merriam-Internetster.com). So it's an upward-acting force that opposes an object's weight. Another source indicated the reason this occurs is the object is less dense than the liquid (physics.about.com). And I would think shape has something to do with buoyancy as well. That's why boats are built the way they are.

Okay, so there you go. Prayer is God's *upward acting force!* Because God's people were praying for me, I simply did not, cannot, and will not go under for good. He doesn't allow it to happen.

When you add in the fact that as believers, we're less dense (Jesus lives in us) and we're shaped appropriately (we are in Christ) you can't be in a better position! Right? Add those two huge factors together and you get spiritual buoyancy.

Again, all of us are human. This doesn't mean you don't go under. It just means with prayer and Jesus, you don't stay there.

And in fact, the lower you go, the faster you shoot up because of the upward-acting force. Try to push a beach ball under water and you'll see what I mean. It shoots up out of the water with great force.

I'm learning this upward-acting force is always more powerful than any weight—including cancer and all the scary unknowns that go with it—that tries to push me down. This is reflected in the refrain of Psalms 42 and 43. It's repeated three times, so it must be significant: "Why are you down in the dumps, dear soul? Why are you crying the blues? Fix my eyes on God—soon I'll be praising again. He puts a smile on my face. He's my God" (Psalm 42:5, 11 and 43:5).

September 3. Scars for the Lord

"Scars for the Lord" is the title of a sermon by W.A. Criswell I received on cassette tape decades ago. I listened to it over and over, and even shared it with my friend Andy. We loved to mimic Criswell saying, *"taw stigmataw"* (the Greek word for marks or scars is *stigmata*). It was a great message based on Paul's statement in Galatians 6:17: "Finally, let no one cause me trouble, for I bear on my body the marks of Jesus" (NIV).

Criswell said the Greek word *stigmata* actually means brand mark, and it was Paul's final defense in Galatians against those who questioned his authenticity as a true apostle.

It's a good bet those brand marks were quite extensive. Five times Paul received the infamous "forty lashes minus one" from the Jews. Three times they beat him with rods (we would call that caning). And on top of all that, he was stoned with rocks.

All these experiences left a mark on Paul. We would call them scars; Paul calls them brand marks.

I wonder what I'd do if someone said, "John, you know what, I think you're faking this cancer business. I don't think you have cancer at all. I think you made it up." If someone accused me of faking, what would I do?

Well, I'd show them my incisions and stitches from the procedures I've had. And I'd say, "These marks prove that I am genuinely sick."

Last night, for the first time, I looked at the scars from the port surgery. There are two. And I thought, "Lord, I hate this. I hate these scars."

And immediately, Criswell's sermon from years ago came to mind. "These aren't scars. They are brand marks. You are mine." My little procedures are miniscule compared to the beatings and canings and whippings Paul faced and God's servants across the world face even today.

Marilyn told me yesterday about a young woman named Bethany from Vancouver, Washington who was getting into a car when a total stranger came by and threw acid in her face. Her statements in the aftermath of this totally random act of violence indicate she's a believer. I've seen her picture on the Internet, and her face has burn marks on it. If she hadn't been wearing sunglasses, she would have been blinded also. What about that?

Lord, I sure wish I didn't have to go through this cancer business. But above and beyond everything, I know it's your *business.* You've allowed this trial in my life just like you allowed trials in Paul's life and Bethany's life. I don't like them, *but* I embrace them as coming from you. I know these experiences will mark me and become a part of me as long as I live in this human body. And I want them to be the final authoritative word for anyone who might have doubts: John Talbert and all of his experiences, including cancer, belong to God.

This puts me in good company, even though I don't deserve to be anywhere near the saints of old who suffered and even died because they belonged to God. This is the very issue the psalmist grapples with in Psalm 44: "No, you decided to make us martyrs, lambs assigned for sacrifice each day. ... And here we are—flat on our faces in the dirt, held down with a boot on our necks. Get up and come to our rescue. If you love us so much, help us!" (verses 22, 25, and 26). Again today I affirm that I belong to God *and,* if I genuinely believe that, I also affirm that He belongs to me. Praise His name today. Amen.

September 4. Tests ...

Yesterday I was talking to a friend on the phone. Bob said, "Well John, you need to look at these upcoming chemo treatments as the next exam the Lord's giving you." Test. And oh am I familiar with those.

When my parents took me out of Pitts Elementary (what a name for a school, huh? *Pitts*—it was, too) and wanted to put me in a private school, I had to take some tests in order to be admitted. I remember sitting in a room with Mr Larabee. He asked me, "John, where does ice cream come from?" I replied, "The drug store." I'll remember the look on his face as long as I live. (Oh and by the way, the drug store at Happy Canyon Shopping Center *did* have a freezer of ice cream, but I don't think he was asking where you could buy ice cream). But in spite of my very poor answer to Mr Larabee's question, I passed the test and the powers that be allowed me into the school.

At the new school I had a French teacher named Madame Guiberteau. I had her for French every year (except one) from fourth grade to ninth. She scared me to death. She gave a weekly test, and I studied hours and hours for each one. I don't know how she found this out, but when she did, she said to me, "Jean, this is not life and death." Was she kidding?

I remember the SAT test in a big room with hundreds of other high school students. I recall my first final in college. I was so nervous, my hands were shaking.

I took a test that lasted sixteen hours—eight hours a day over two days—to get into the Ph.D. program at Southwestern Seminary. Right in the middle of those two days I got a letter from a gal I liked, telling me she was getting engaged to someone else.

In one of the biggest miracles of all, I passed a two-year proficiency test in German after studying on my own and with a tutor for six months. I honestly believe the Lord gave me the gift of tongues (or more precisely, *tongue)* to pass that one. Right now I couldn't speak or read German if my life depended on it.

Then I had to take a day-long oral exam before starting the dissertation phase of my doctoral program. I remember leaving Scarborough Hall after the exam and turning the corner toward the parking lot next to the recreation center. There I saw a group of friends from seminary and church who had been praying for me, holding a banner that read, "You made it." We celebrated right there at the recreation center.

Tests. Even as I write this, I realize the tests didn't stop when I graduated from school. They just became different, like the first deacons' meeting at FSBCN when some members of the congregation weren't totally enamored of my new outreach idea. And it goes on from there.

Everything that comes into our lives, including good health, is a test. But God knows what grade we're in and always gives a test He knows we can—by His grace and strength—pass, *or* He wouldn't give it. This is what 1 Corinthians 10:13 says: "No temptation has seized you except what is common to man. And God is faithful; he will not let you be tempted beyond what you can bear. But when you are tempted, he will also provide a way out so you can stand up under it" (NIV).

So with less than a week to go before I start chemo, I realize He's getting me ready for the toughest test of my life—a six-month exam in which I have no idea what will come down the pike. But Rabbi Jesus is teaching me that everything in my life has prepared me for this test and now it's time to take it. And pass it.

Jesus is always teaching, and everything he allows and everything he says is a test. But he gives the tests and grades each one. The Sadducees found that out when they tried to play teacher, and gave Jesus a test with their silly question about seven brothers who died after marrying the same widow. Jesus turned the tables on them, saying, "You're off base on two counts: you don't know your Bibles, and you don't know how God works" [my paraphrase of Matthew 22:29]. Grade for the Sadducees: *F.*

God, as you're leading me to take out my number two pencil and get ready to take this long test, give me the grace and strength to stand up under it. Amen.

September 6. Apprehensive about chemo

Nancy, a dear sister in the church, is a prayer warrior who's seen the Lord do a miraculous work of healing in her life (on more than one occasion, I might add). She often sends me notes of encouragement, and included in those notes are verses of Scripture—not just a few, but a bunch of verses. Nancy seeks them out, writes them out, and lives them out. Not a bad progression, huh?

Nancy and her husband Jack weren't at church yesterday because she wasn't feeling well, but someone handed me a note from her. The card contained this verse: "Fear thou not; for I am with thee: be not dismayed; for I am thy God: I will strengthen thee; yea, I will help thee; yea, I will uphold thee with the right hand of my righteousness" (Isaiah 41:10, KJV). Other Scripture references from Nancy were handwritten on the card. I'm going to take the next couple days to look them up and read them.

Isaiah 41:10 is one of my favorite verses. I'm familiar with the NASB version, but not the KJV. I like the repetition of *yea*—an older word we've modernized for use in football stadiums and at other sporting events to cheer players on a field or affirm them when they make a great play.

As I get closer to the time when chemo will start for me, I'm getting apprehensive (there's my fancy word for afraid). I'm not fearful of death. I'm just afraid of being really sick. And I've been okay with trusting the Lord, but more and more, including last night, I'm becoming increasingly antsy and nervous and apprehensive and scared.

But once again, the Lord is amazing in the way He's ministering to me by way of this process. One FSBCN member, Sharon, has started chemo treatments herself and is doing great. A church sister God healed of cancer (Kay) told me yesterday she didn't get sick and lose her hair during chemo treatments, but things happened gradually afterwards. These two women, plus Juanita (healed of non-Hodgkin's lymphoma) and Linda (healed of cancer) are very visible and vocal reminders of God's power. God is using them to say, "Yea! Go, John, go."

When Mary Ann asked me if I was ready for chemo, my answer was less than enthusiastic. But she said, "You're healthy and ready to take on this cancer. I believe this chemo will knock out the cancer and you'll be done with it." She's not alone among folks in the church who are cheering me on. It's fantastic and it's a fear-buster.

Today I read Psalm 49, a very frank testimony. It says, "So why should I fear in bad times?" (verse 5). The psalmist takes a look at the healthy and wealthy in the world and recognizes that even the best among us end up in a new home called "The Coffin" (verse 11). Those who trust themselves and live for the moment end up with their lives wasting away to nothing. "But me? God snatches me from the clutch of death, he reaches down and grabs me" (verse 15).

This very vivid image reminds me of an incident that occurred when I was six or so, maybe younger. We were at a swimming pool and my mother had told me expressly and in no uncertain terms to stay away from the deep end. But somehow I wandered over to that part of the pool, and when I leaned over to try to see the bottom, guess what? I fell in! I remember sinking and struggling and looking up to the top of the water. And I saw a hand reach down and grab me and pull me up. It was my mother! She asked me how I was doing and then she spanked me.

Lord, I'm thankful for your loving and yes, disciplining, hand. Thank you for all the times you've rescued me and for Nancy, Sharon, Kay, Juanita, and Linda. Thank you for the cheerleader-encouragers you've brought into my life. Thank you for delivering me from fear today. I say, "Yea, God!" Amen.

September 7. Ready to get going

I continue to be amazed at how the Lord works by way of praying people. As each day passes, I feel more and more ready to get this show on the road. It isn't an anxious or nervous readiness. It's a *peace-deep-down-inside* readiness. It's amazing.

And it's the result of an influx of timely words and the Word. Going back to Nancy's list of *do not fear* verses, here's the one for today: Genesis 15:1. "Don't be afraid, Abram. I'm your shield, your very great reward" (NIV).

As I think and pray about these *do not fear* passages, one thing they have in common is they're a challenge to get ready for a great work of God. Think about Abraham's situation as he was waiting on God and had been in that mode for *years*. His task seemed more and more impossible as each day passed, and in the face of it, he was afraid.

I can relate to this very much, though on a smaller scale. This whole cancer thing has been a long and gradual revelation, and more of that will occur today, I'm sure, as I'm going to the oncologist's office for a pre-chemo seminar. I'm not exactly sure what this will be about. I think they'll show me a video, and they'll answer questions about the treatments (I hope). But it will be more information about what I'm facing. Information is good, but not always. I'm learning that sometimes not knowing every little gory detail isn't all bad.

As each day passed for Abraham, he had more and more time to think about how impossible it was for him to be a dad as he entered his eighties and nineties, but God said, "Don't be afraid." And it wasn't just a negative (don't smoke, don't chew, don't go with girls who do). Living a life focused on *don'ts* makes one very small and hesitant. A fencepost doesn't smoke either!

This command wasn't just a negative. It was a huge, huge positive. Abraham was not to fear because the Lord was about to perform a huge miracle in his life that would affect many people. I believe this cancer business will be the same for me. I really do.

I don't know how the Lord is going to do it, but I believe He already is.

Sunday I found a little book in my mailbox at church. The title is *Made for the Mountains* and the author is Bo Baker. I found a note inside the book from Patti, the wife of Jim, one of our deacons. Bo was Patti's previous pastor.

The note in the book said, "On Friday, a light went on with me. I have a book for you to read." I'm a fool if I don't take something like this very seriously. God has another fear-buster message for me! This is the amazing thing that happens when people pray diligently and are obedient when the Lord speaks to them. So I picked up the book today and opened it to the first chapter, a sermon about Moses' burning bush experience. The narrative in the first few pages jumped off the page at me, and I could read no further.

> The thing that happened to Moses can happen today. Indeed, it does happen today! God is still in the burning bush business and needs only those who are ignitable as reason for a holy happening. ... Although Moses wasn't aware of it, he was God's choice as the instrument for a nation's deliverance. All God needs to accomplish a mission or a work is one man or woman whose life is completely available to him. ... Greatly used men and women are often those who have come to the limit of their own strength and ingenuity.[1]

Wow is all I can say. I can hardly wait to read further. Thanks so much Lord for putting this message on Patti's heart.

The reason we shouldn't be afraid is because it douses our ignitability as an instrument of a holy happening. It's a bucket of cold water on the first sparks of a Holy Spirit revival forest fire.

That's why the Lord says this in Psalm 50 (the psalm for the day): "If I get hungry, do you think I'd tell you? All creation and its bounty are mine. Do you think I feast on venison? or drink draughts of goats' blood? Spread for me a banquet of praise, serve High God a feast of kept promises, and call for help when you're in trouble—I'll help you, and you'll honor me. ... It's the praising life that honors me. As soon as you set your foot on the Way, I'll show you my salvation" (Psalm 50:12–15, 23).

Help, Lord. I do cry out to you today. Thank you for Nancy and Patti and the countless others you're using to speak truth in my life at this critical time for me—just when I need it. I confess fear, but

I turn from it today. I will not fear no matter what I learn about chemo today. Make me as ignitable as that bush Moses saw in the wilderness. May the fire of who you are and what you're doing engulf cancer and everything else so you're on display. As the hymn says, "Set my soul afire, Lord." Amen.

September 8. The chemo orientation

Like everything else the Lord allows in our lives, cancer has unearthed some stuff in me that the Lord is bringing to the surface, so I have to deal with it—no choice.

Yesterday's chemo orientation pulled me down into the tank. My family and I watched a video. Then Dr Jotte's head nurse Terri came in and told us in detail about the drugs I'll be taking. They call my treatment for lymphoma *RCVP*. So, I learned about *R* and *C* and *V* and *P*—all four drugs. Each one has a benefit in helping me fight cancer, but they all have several possible side effects. I thought I was ready, but I guess I wasn't ready to hear about all of them.

Terri was careful to say not everyone has these side effects (and several folks I shared this with yesterday reminded me of the same thing), but still it was a cold reality slap in the face.

One of the things that's a challenge with treatment is the monitoring of my white and red blood cell counts. Both must stay at good levels. The nurse told me if my white blood cell count isn't high enough, I'm very susceptible to getting sick and must avoid crowds.

Avoid crowds? A pastor? Are you kidding me? That's going to be hard for me because I want to be with my church family and to preach as often as I can. If this problem develops, I guess I'll just have to arrive after greeting time is over and leave before the end of the service without shaking hands or having real close contact with anyone.

All these reflections rushed into my head, and I thought, "You might as well cut my arm off." I love greeting people on Sundays. I love looking them in the eye—my church family. I love the one-on-one contact and—I'll be honest, it's selfish—it encourages me!

But whatever—this is another part of all this that's in the Lord's hands.

So after an extensive conversation with Terri (who really did a good job of trying to prepare us for everything we'll face), she said, "Now let me take you on a tour." We left the seminar room and made our way across the lobby, and she opened a rather inconspicuous door. I hadn't noticed it before.

On the left as you enter is a rather expansive nurses' station with an open view of a large room. There were clusters of easy chairs and other types of chairs in spaces separated by walls just a couple feet high. Every chair could be seen from the nurse's station.

As we stood there listening to the nurse explain things in the room, it hit me. This is the room where I'll receive chemo treatments for the next four and a half months.

Do you ever enter a place and wonder, "How on earth did I ever end up here?"

But I'd seen this room before. A few weeks ago while we were waiting for an appointment with Dr Jotte, we were sitting in some chairs in a hallway. I got antsy, so I started walking around and peeked through a glass window in a door. I saw this room with all its easy chairs and cancer patients receiving treatments, and I thought, "I'm not going in there!" I told my family it reminded me of a nursing home.

But this time I actually looked at the people. In one corner a woman laughed as she talked with a man in a chair and he laughed too. A younger woman looked like she was struggling a bit as her husband held her hand. I noticed a young man with no hair, all by himself with his chair fully reclined, asleep.

That got me. How do you do this alone?

It didn't feel like a morgue. The nurses were busy visiting with folks and maneuvering catheters. We saw the snack counter and I perked up a bit. "You mean I can bring food in here?" "Absolutely," said our guide.

As we left, I said to Marilyn, "Whoa, why can't they put you in a private room? Why do I have to sit in that open space when I may be feeling like I want to vomit?"

Marilyn said, "Well, I guess that's just the way they do it, and maybe the Lord can use you to encourage some of the folks in there." *Gulp.*

Yesterday afternoon I met with some of my pastor friends—Rob, Bart, James, Allen, Mike, Ilamarques, his wife Edgy, Dan, Dan, and Steve. They anointed my head with a lot of oil. It dripped down my head onto my shirt (reminding me of what Psalm 133 says about fellowship and unity in the truest and deepest sense of the word). They laid their hands on me and prayed with me and we cried together. I love these folks. They're family in the truest sense of the word. I so appreciate the fellowship of pastors the Lord has allowed me to be a part of.

I remember what each of them prayed for me. One said, "Lord, I pray that the fruit of the Spirit will be evident through John's life as he goes through this."

Even when I'm nauseated in a room full of strangers? Even then? Can't I just be selfish when I'm sick?

No.

As I've already said, this illness is rolling the rock over and exposing some bugs. This is what happened to David in the conviction of his sin in Psalm 51. "Going through the motions doesn't please you, a flawless performance is nothing to you. I learned God-worship when my pride was shattered. Heart-shattered lives ready for love don't for a moment escape God's notice" (Psalm 51:16–17).

Likewise, in Matthew 23 Jesus condemns the religion scholars and Pharisees. "They talk a good line, but they don't live it. They don't take it into their hearts and live it out in their behavior. It's all spit-and-polish veneer" (Matthew 23:3).

Lord, as hard as it is to go through cancer, it's even harder to have the real me exposed. I confess selfishness. I confess pride. I acknowledge you've allowed me to have cancer not only to speak to people who are well, but also to share with other cancer patients in a hospital site. I'm now one of the folks who sit in that special room that reminds me of a nursing home. I know people in nursing homes who are there for your glory, and view it as a mission field.

This room and the people in it are now my mission field. I pray for that young man who was receiving treatment with no one there to hold his hand. I pray for that young woman and the other folks in there who didn't want to be in there any more than I did. I thank you Holy Spirit that you live in me. May the fruit of your character show through me all the time everywhere, especially when I'm throwing up. Amen.

September 9. The day before chemo

The roller coaster ride continues … I was so encouraged yesterday morning when I was able to pray with Jon and Lynda over the phone. Good friends from our days at college, they've been through a cancer experience themselves. While Jon had cancer, Lynda sent out email updates and prayer requests and testimonies about what the Lord was doing. It's really the inspiration for my own writing.

Not long ago they sent out an email entitled "Why Are the Hardins Smiling?" They shared the good news that the doctor recently told them he found no cancer in Jon. Praise God! My family and I continue to pray for them, but this was such a shot in the arm for me.

Anyway, Jon and Lynda prayed for me over the phone yesterday. One thing Lynda prayed was, "Lord, as the three of them go for chemo, go with them as you went with the three in the furnace." When Ilamarques mentioned this Old Testament story to me the other day, he said, "John, the furnace was God's plan. They had to go there, but He was with them." The chemo room is God's furnace. Right on! My family and I can handle the heat as long as He's there with us.

So the morning was great, but the afternoon wasn't so great. I had a long talk with someone in the medical profession that really pulled me down. When I finished, I realized I shouldn't have had that conversation, even though I learned some things. It cost me (but then my learning experiences always do).

As a result, the weight of the upcoming chemo started to press down on me. Fear, anxiety, the what-ifs … all those ball-and-chain encumbrances from the enemy. My port surgery even started hurting again.

But then once again, the fear-busters arrived. I wish I had a trumpet! My friend Gary (the one with the great basketball court) called and said, "Well, I'm excited for you." "Huh?" I muttered. "You get to start becoming well on Friday!" What a great perspective! Yes, right. It won't be fun, but it will be the first step to recovery. Right. Amen.

Then I got an email from Nancy. She told me about an eighteen-year-old young man named Alexander, the son of a co-worker who was recently diagnosed with cancer. Eighteen years old! Nancy told me about his treatments, and the way she and other folks at work are trying to minister to him. Then she added, "So, I'm praying that one day you'll have the opportunity to connect with Alexander in that room full of people God loves and has a plan for." Wow, me too. Fear-buster number two.

Fear-buster number three. Shortly after reading the story about Alexander, I got a call from a friend named Dee. Dee is a brother in Jesus who helps me with my golf game. He attends Calvary Chapel in Aurora and has shared my situation with his pastor, Ed Taylor, who's praying for me. Dee said, "John, tonight Pastor Ed's continuing a series of messages on manifestations of the Holy Spirit, and tonight the subject is healing. I'm in the service right now and I was wondering if it would be okay for my pastor to pray for you right now." Then Dee carried his phone up to the front of the auditorium. I could hear music and the sounds of folks praying. The service was going on!

He gave his phone to Pastor Ed, who said, "John, I'm going to anoint Dee's head on your behalf. And I want to pray for you." So right then and there he prayed for the Lord to heal me, finished, and handed the phone back to Dee.

Is God *awesome* or what????

God's box score in the life of John Talbert for September 9 … let's see. Oh, here it is: 4–1. Four hugely encouraging messages beat one discouraging message! God wins again. He's still undefeated.

This is the message of Psalm 52: "And I'm an olive tree, growing green in God's house. I trusted in the generous mercy of God then and now. I thank you always that you went into action. And I'll stay right here, your good name my hope, in company with your faithful friends" (verses 8–9). I'm one of God's hothouse plants, pampered and protected in his greenhouse with other well-tended flowers: Jon, Lynda, Gary, Nancy, Dee, Ed, and a whole congregation of folks in Aurora! Is there any better place to be in the universe?

In addition to the passage in Psalm 52, I read Matthew 24 with this challenge from Jesus in verse 13: "Staying with it—that's what God requires. Stay with it to the end. You won't be sorry, and you'll be saved."

Lord, thank you so much for the amazing ways you tend your garden, of which I'm privileged, honored, and overwhelmed to be a part. Thank you for using your beautiful people to pray for and encourage me, many of whom I've never met. Please bless Calvary Chapel of Aurora and Dee and Pastor Ed. Thank you for Christians from all denominations who value your Word and believe you're still in the healing business. For today, and twenty-four hours from right now when I'll be getting ready for chemo, I know you're going to win two more in my life. I'm sticking with you. I'm hanging my hat in your closet forever. I'm home. I'm thankful I'm well cared for. Care well for everyone reading these words, for Alexander, and for all the other cancer patients you'll allow me to meet tomorrow and in the future. I love you, Gardener God and Vine Jesus. Amen.

Chapter Four: The First Turn in the Path

September 10. The preseason is over; the regular season is here

It's kind of weird and bizarre to me (but not to the Lord) that the beginning of chemo treatments and the length of time from the first to the last correspond to the NFL season and playoffs. Lord willing, I'll conclude this "season" of my life at or near the time of the Super Bowl. Rob reminded me of this the other day at the pastors' prayer meeting. Mary Ann said we would celebrate then. Yes!

So this is the first game of the ECL—Eradicate Cancer League— powered by God. My eighteen-week season has six "games" lasting three weeks. I'm confident the God (big *G*) Team is better than the cancer (little *c*) team.

I've got great teammates. Yesterday I got an email from Bobby and Barbara, former members of FSBCN who've moved to Florida. Bobby's dad just passed away and they have a lot on their plate, but they continue to encourage me. And Bobby is a rare breed (in a lot of ways—a real servant). He's a Nuggets fan!

In the email Barbara said she and Bob are cheering me on from the balcony. She said there are two kinds of people—*balcony* people who lift you up and *basement* people who pull you down. The two of them are in the balcony, and God is on His throne above it all. What a beautiful picture to take into chemo today.

I put all of you who read this and pray for me in that balcony category. I've met a few basement folks in the course of this experience, but the vast majority are in the balcony.

This metaphor calls to mind what the author of Hebrews said: "Therefore, since we are surrounded by such a great cloud of witnesses, let us throw off everything that hinders and the sin that so easily entangles, and let us run with perseverance the race marked out for us. Let us fix our eyes on Jesus, the author and finisher of our faith, who for the joy set before him, endured the cross, scorning its shame, and sat down at the right hand of the throne of God" (Hebrews 12:1–2, NIV; one of my favorite passages).

The question I have this morning is whether this cloud of witnesses consists only of faithful people who've died and are with the Lord. I would've said yes before, but now I don't think so.

I think all of us have dual roles in each of the "leagues" the Lord places us in: cheering on other believers in other leagues *and* running the race in our own league. This is impossible from a human perspective—I can't be in the stands *and* on the field—but in the Christian life it's not only possible, it's God's calling. I was convicted early on in this cancer thing that the Lord has allowed this circumstance in my life for the purpose of testimony.

But it gives me a whole lot of comfort—I feel very buoyant this morning—to take into chemo the reality of a bunch of folks praying for me and cheering me on.

So here we go. I'm nervous. I will say that, but I'm glad the season of eradication has begun.

Kay, herself a fan and part of ECL and a real sister, told me Sunday she expected to get sick during treatments, but instead it happened the next day. So we'll see.

But again, the *G* Team has a good bench and plenty of reserves.

Here's the verse in the locker room for today from Psalm 54: "Oh, look! God's right here helping! God's on my side, evil is looping back on enemies. Don't let up! Finish them off!" (verses 4–5). My prediction for game one? It's going to be tough, but it's going to be a blowout.

Lord, thank you from the bottom of my heart for all the strength you provide for this huge thing, *and* I thank you so much for all my brothers and sisters who are there with me and for me throughout this. Give each of us grace and strength for each of our races. Today we fix our eyes on you. Amen.

September 11. One treatment down, five more to go, and God is still on His throne!

First of all, I didn't have to throw up in front of anyone (this time), although I was ready to do that. I made it through, by the power and grace of our wonderful Lord!

As the day progressed yesterday, I felt worse. One of the drugs they gave me really knocked me out. I was drowsy all day.

I developed a headache that seems worse today, plus I'm feeling a little nauseated and my mouth is bothering me and some other things … but that's enough about that. I promise this account won't include the gory details about all the symptoms I'm dealing with. Promise!

Today I've got to get a shot. Dr Jotte told me yesterday the concern is for my white blood cell count. They don't want it to get too low, so I have to get a shot to keep it propped up. Marilyn's going to take me downtown to get it this morning.

But back to yesterday … the Lord pulled me through and surprised me.

Usually when I'm facing a difficult situation (and this has been true my whole life) my stomach gets upset and I get very antsy. This has multiple effects for me physically and mentally, of course, but yesterday was *totally*—I mean *totally*—different. I was completely calm and at peace. The buoyancy principle—God's upward-acting force—was at work, *big time.*

Thank you all for praying for me. Once again, I could feel—literally feel, actually feel— your prayers and the power of God through them, one of the most powerful experiences of my entire life. It was very significant for me, and here's why.

Are you ready for another interesting feature of buoyancy? Here it is: "when you place a block of wood in a pail of water, the block displaces some of the water, and the water level goes up. If you could weigh the water that the wood displaces, you would find that its weight equals the weight of the wood." Makes sense, huh?

So here's a very heavy John (literally) with a heavy load on his back. This is maybe the heaviest load *ever* for me personally. Ever since my dad died of cancer thirty-seven years ago, I vowed to myself that if I ever got cancer, I was never doing chemo—*ever*. I've built this chemo thing up to be the monster of the midway. And the thing I vowed I'd never do is the thing I'm now doing (you know, never say never).

So it was huge for me, and I felt that yesterday. God said, "John, do you believe I can beat cancer and take you through the very thing you said you would never do? Do you believe I can do that?" Have you ever had the experience of your back against the wall with God in your face? That was yesterday and that was chemo for me.

That was me yesterday, but I knew this same God was on my side and I was confident there were so many folks in the balcony, cheering and praying—the buoyancy principle—that it will offset the weight of me and my huge, thirty-seven-year-old, mile-high chemo phobia. (You can build a pretty high mountain of fear over the course of thirty-seven years.)

Going back to Barbara's balcony metaphor, it felt like an experience I had several years ago. I went with some men from the church to one of the first Promise Keepers conferences at Folsom Field in Boulder.

I still remember Chuck Swindoll riding his Harley up on the stage to preach his sermon. Bill McCartney got up to speak next, and at the conclusion of his message he said, "Now I want all the pastors here to come down on the field." And so I ambled down the stairs and leaped over a small wall at the edge of the grandstand. Suddenly I was on the field! I huddled with the small crowd of pastors on the field in front of a much larger crowd of men.

Bill said, "Let these guys know how much you love them!" And this huge raucous and thunderous cheer flowed like a waterfall from the stadium. The cheers reverberated, and Bill was the cheerleader.

We pastors who were on that field were moved to tears, and I'll never forget how it moved me—up.

That's the way I felt yesterday, and I was the only one on the field, but the prayers of God's people through the buoyancy principle moved me *up*.

And I'll tell you the significance of yesterday for me. I felt like I grew up. That sounds strange, doesn't it? But until yesterday, I was a little kid with my adolescent fear of chemo. Up until yesterday I was fifteen, watching my dad suffer through chemo and die of cancer and selfishly saying I'd never go through what he went through. But fear does that. It stops us dead in our tracks. It halts growth and progress and maturity.

But by the grace of God and the power of God through the prayers of God's people, He enabled me to look my greatest fear in the eye and allow Him to conquer it.

I know preachers tend toward the overly dramatic (no, really??), but honestly, I'm not exaggerating. I'm just bragging on what God did yesterday. Praise His holy name!

This leads me to the psalm for today, Psalm 55:17–18 and 22. "At dusk, dawn, and noon I sigh deep sighs—he hears, he rescues. My life is well and whole, secure in the middle of danger even while thousands are lined up against me. … Pile your troubles on God's shoulders—he'll carry your load, he'll help you out. He'll never let good people topple into ruin." Amen and amen.

For everyone reading this, thanks again for raising the water level.

September 12. Expect a miracle

After a toss-and-turn night, my headache and nausea are noticeably worse today. Even though I'll miss being at my church today, I know I can't do it. I'm glad Doug is preaching for me today. He's on staff at the Colorado Baptist General Convention office; a golf buddy and a real brother.

So many people are helping me in so many ways. I'm grateful for them and for my extended Christian family, Lord. Thank you so much.

I want to go back to Friday … As much of a pain as the port surgery was (in more ways than one), I'm already seeing the benefit of having it. A couple hours before I went to the cancer center, I had to put ointment on my chest over the port to deaden the skin. And it was a good thing, too.

Jennifer, the nurse who helped me, stuck a hose in the port and drew a lot of blood from it, but it was a lot easier than all the IVs I've had so far. After the blood draw, we spoke with one of Dr Jotte's physician assistants.

Then the doctor came in. He shook my hand and greeted all of us warmly. He asked me if I was ready to get started and told me the chemo would be a piece of cake for me. We talked about the shot I had yesterday and he said, "Beyond that, if you need anything, call me. I'm on call this weekend, and I promise I'll remember you if you call me." He put his hand on my shoulder as he left.

Lord, I so appreciate this doctor and all the nurses at the Rocky Mountain Cancer Center. They don't have to be congenial and encouraging, but my family and I are grateful they are. I also thank you that they're very competent.

So after a brief stop at the appointment desk to make my second chemo appointment for October 1 at 8:30, I went into *the room*. I met my nurse Kayla and we found a chair in a corner.

As I was taking my place, I noticed a woman who was sitting next to a man I presumed was her husband in the area next to ours. She smiled and nodded as we sat down. Kayla hooked me up to a catheter and explained each drug she was giving me, saying, "For each one, I want to show you the label and make sure we're correct." I appreciate the fact that they're trying to be careful, but I hope this isn't something they have to do to prevent lawsuits. It seems that way to me. I mean, if I'm worried that these doctors and nurses aren't competent enough to give me the right medicine, I'm in the wrong place. But we do live in a litigation-dominated world.

The second drug Kayla gave me was to help me tolerate Rituxan, the first drug. And I tell you, it knocked me for a loop. I felt sleepy immediately and for the rest of the day. I wanted to doze off all the time, but it was difficult. Kayla told me she had to monitor my blood pressure continually, and I had to get up to go to the bathroom. Mother and Marilyn held my arms every time I did, as I was very wobbly.

This sets the stage for the main thing that happened. A few days ago, I wrote in this blog the Lord had dealt with me in the issue of being in the room with other cancer patients and vomiting in front of others. I needed that correction and discipline, but like everything, I think I carried it too far. I had it in mind that the Lord was going to use me (even though I might be nauseated myself) as Superman, ministering to everyone in the room in a single bound!

I know that sounds totally ludicrous, but that was my vision. Well, I can tell you, I could barely hold my head up. I didn't feel like throwing up (thank the Lord), but I didn't feel like doing anything period. My pastor friend Bart came in for a brief visit, and I was so out of it I could barely talk.

About midway through the day, the lady who'd smiled at us when we came in stopped by and said hi to us. She said her name was Betty and that she and her husband Roger were there from Colorado Springs for Roger's last chemo treatment. We all introduced ourselves and she said, "John, you're in good hands here. This is a good place."

Now, wait a minute! This isn't what I expected. I wasn't vomiting or ministering; I was receiving.

A little later in the day Roger stopped by with his rolling catheter, smiling. We congratulated him on his last chemo treatment. His big smile seemed even bigger to me because he had no hair on the top of his head.

Once again I, the Joan of Arc of the chemo room, did not initiate this contact. Roger came to me.

I was still very sleepy and out of it, and getting more fatigued with each new drug. The first drug took four hours, the second was just an injection, and the third took two hours.

Toward the end of my session (and I think Roger was nearing the end of his treatments), he stopped by again and said, "I just want to give you this." It was a little card that simply said, "Expect a miracle."

Marilyn was standing near me when he handed me that card, and said, "Oh yes, Roger, we do. We're Christians. We believe in miracles." That seemed to startle Roger a bit and he shuffled away from us. I don't know why. Maybe he wasn't a believer, or maybe he was just a positive thinker who didn't want to talk about the Lord. Who knows?

But here's what I learned: the Lord took me into that room to minister to me! And He used another cancer patient to do it. And whatever motivated him, I was given a message: "Expect a miracle."

Okay Lord, I will.

Like so many other times in my life, when I went out to minister, it ended up instead that Jesus ministered to me, just when I needed it.

"You've kept track of my every toss and turn through the sleepless night, each tear entered in your ledger, each ache written in your book" (Psalm 56:8). Amen.

September 13. Words of encouragement

Yesterday was one of the toughest days yet. I felt pretty lousy from the beginning of the day until the evening, when I started to get some relief. With the amount of medicine they give you in chemotherapy, it's no wonder, and I'm not surprised it takes a couple days to take effect.

Just a point of clarification: my chemo regimen is RCVP, but technically, *C* and *V* are the only chemo drugs. *R* (Rituxan—I hope I spelled it correctly; I can't even pronounce the names of the others), the one that took four hours, is the drug intended to help my body fight off this cancer. The *P* is a steroid that helps me deal with the side effects of the other drugs.

Anyway, with all that medicine going into my system, I now understand why it takes a couple days before everything hits. And it sure did.

But I'm amazed at the power of God through prayer from all over the world. Just yesterday, I know of at least five churches that raised the water level for me. Helen (a dear sister at FSBCN whose husband Bill has endured many ailments over the past few years and still retained a great sense of humor) shared with me that my church family prayed for me. (Bill and Helen have taught me how to keep laughing through tough illness—how valuable is that?) I *never* take that for granted and love my brothers and sisters there.

Lucinda is a wonderful praying sister and Missions Director at North Metro Church, our sister church in the area with whom we've shared ministry in the neighboring community of Federal Heights. She told me her church prayed for FSBCN and me yesterday. So many folks from this wonderful church often call or email me. I'm reaping the benefits of this beautiful ministry partnership, and it reminds me of what Paul says in 2 Corinthians 9:12: "This service that you perform is not only supplying the needs of God's people but is also overflowing in many expressions of thanks to God." Truly, in God's economy, what goes around comes around. North Metro Church is a primo example of this.

Phil is a member of North Metro Church with a ministry called IMD International that equips believers in all parts of the world. He's out of the country himself, and just this morning he forwarded me a message from two of his friends, a young couple in South Asia. Moses and Sharon are encouraging folks in their church and ministry to pray. They told Phil a group of folks prayed for me on Friday, and more people prayed at another setting this weekend. Then yesterday at a service (again, clear across the world—incredible!) they prayed for me again. At the conclusion of this forwarded email, Moses wrote, "Please tell Pastor John that about 100 people who are under my care are praying for him."

I tell you, this kind of thing brings me to my knees. Only God can motivate this kind of love and concern to pray for a total stranger clear across the world, and it makes me want to be fervent to do the same and encourage the church I serve to continue to do it. *Who cares if* you *know who* you *are praying for? God knows them.*

It gets better.

A dear couple in our church told a church in Atlanta about me. And the pastor of this church, Charles Stanley, wrote me a letter. In it he cited Hebrews 6:10-15 and the final promise, "I will surely bless you, and I will surely multiply you." Amen, but wow, huh?

Then yesterday Barbara told me about a prayer quilt ministry at her church in Jacksonville, Florida—she's going to have the ladies in that ministry make me a quilt. I was so glad to accept this gracious offer, and when I did, I thought about a quilt I received earlier this year from Ione, Vera Belle, Leota, Cookie, Stella, Linda, Cheryl Lynn, Pat, Patty, Mary, Robin, and Gus—a wonderful group of sisters at the Free Will Baptist Church in Bowie, Texas. They made me a quilt that I consider a prayer quilt before I *needed* prayer. I'll tell you, I needed prayer just as much then as I do now, but there's something about cancer that awakens us to that need.

I wonder why we don't pray for one another when we're healthy with just as much fervor as we do for cancer people? Hmm.

Anyway, I'm humbled and deeply grateful for all these *churches* who are praying for me. Little *c* has no chance!

And I'm thankful that in the course of this experience, the Lord is doing in my life what happened to the psalmist at the end of Psalm 56: "God, you did everything you promised, and I'm thanking you with all my heart. You pulled me from the brink of death, my feet from the cliff-edge of doom. Now I stroll at leisure with God in the sunlit fields of life" (verses 12–13).

Lord, I thank you for the leisure cancer has provided (defined by merriam-webster.com as "freedom provided by the cessation of activities; especially: time free from work or duties"). I know *leisure* as it's stated in this verse isn't a vacation, but you've provided this illness to take me off the regular path and point me in a new direction.

Lord, allow all who read this to know what *strolling at leisure in the sunlit fields of life* means.

May your grace abound in the lives of all the folks in all the churches who are praying for me, as it has in mine through answered prayer. You're amazing, Lord. Thank you for Jesus and His church. Amen.

September 14. More about leisure

Sometimes phrases or words I run across during my devotional time arrest me. That's the only way I can say it. They capture my attention. That happened yesterday with a word in the final verse of Psalm 56 in the Message version.

The 56th Psalm is about a man who suffers harassment from his enemies and he takes it to bed with him at night. But then he comes around to the praise of God and fearlessness in light of the attacks of men. He learns about God's faithfulness and salvation and then he learns how to "stroll at leisure in the sunlit fields of life" (verse 13). I took the time to look at other translations of this verse—for example, "walk before God in the light of life" (NIV). Rather mundane, huh?

Well, I was just so curious about this phrase that I did some study on it. I honestly don't do this with quiet time stuff except when a phrase arrests me. Usually, when I do look up a verse Peterson translates differently in the Message from other versions, I find he has a point.

This verse is no exception. The Hebrew word translated *walk* in the NIV—*halak*—is the basic word for this action in the Old Testament, but here the particular form of this verb could be translated *travel* or *walk about*. In other words, ambling or *strolling at leisure*.

The word that captured me was *leisure*. This word has a kind of negative connotation in our culture. "Life of leisure" could refer to someone in retirement, but it's not always positive, is it? At least it hasn't been for me. Sitting around doing nothing was something I just did not tolerate. I didn't and don't do well with leisure.

Leisure means goofing off and doing nothing, right? It means sitting around and watching soap operas like all retirees do, right? (Even as I write this, I'm laughing. I don't know *one* retired person who does this. They're all much busier than many of us, but it's a perception some have.)

Well, since I was in the looking-up mood, I looked up *leisure*. It comes from a French verb *leisir* that means "to permit." To repeat Webster's definition I cited a couple days ago, leisure is "freedom provided by the cessation of activities, especially time free from work or duties" (www.merriam-webster.com).

Hmm. That's a little different, isn't it?

Leisure isn't inherently a negative thing, necessarily, but it's permission to be free from activity, especially work and duty. So this psalm ends with a man who's free to be at leisure.

I know the Bible lauds work. God put Adam and Eve in the Garden of Eden to work. Work is a calling from God and is noble, but all the time?? I know I'm famous for turning a day off into work—working at golf, working at getting things done, goals, duties, and so on. Have I ever really experienced leisure? I'm not sure.

Until now.

My church family has blessed me in so many ways. I love them deeply, but one of the main ways they've blessed me since my cancer diagnosis is they've handed me the opportunity to stroll at leisure with God. I'm not totally incapacitated. I exercise and run errands (and that's my choice), but I haven't been in the office much, and my church family has given me permission to *not* be there.

It's been hard, not because anyone in the congregation has made me feel bad—quite the opposite. I want to go there and work, not sit around, but this cancer has forced me to take a good hard look at leisure.

Honestly, I'm convicted that living life in denial of leisure, even on my days off, is a narrow and selfish and small life. It confines life to activity—doing, doing, and doing—the compulsive drive to do something every minute to prove something. What?

Cancer (with the time and space the church has allowed me) has caused me to think and act differently.

I take walks every day. I take my phone. Because it has a camera, I take pictures of trees and flowers and anything that strikes my fancy. I'm walking and listening and talking with Jesus; long, good talks—strolls at leisure with God.

When I'm not walking, I'm sitting. I pray. I think about people and what they mean to me. I study for my next sermon, but I'm not in a big hurry. Then I pick up books and read.

Sometimes I just sit on the back porch of my family's house. It was very hard at first—Mr Type A that I am—but now it's not so hard. I sit and enjoy the fact that I have another day on this earth.

To be honest, all of this is hard to admit, but I guarantee you it's more difficult to put into action (or *inaction,* to be more precise).

Today, what I've just mentioned is literally all I feel like doing. I have some more symptoms I'm dealing with, but last night I didn't sleep a wink. I'm totally exhausted, but I'm going to stroll; I'm going to think and pray; I'm going to study; but mainly I'm going to enjoy the freedom of cessation from activity. This is what the Lord wants me to learn right now.

Actually, leisure is very daring, if you think about it. It's the recognition that God is doing things even when I'm not. It trusts Him to do the big things I can never do anyway. It's living large with Him in his large beautiful world and not being in a hurry. It's being confident in his loving character and letting life fly.

Oh and by the way, I'm very confident the Lord can run His church without me pulling the strings. In fact, it may run even better. I'm so excited to see people step forward and take responsibility and learn. I had a great talk yesterday with my associate JJ, the director of our children's ministries. He said he's learning the difference between being a worker and a leader. And I'm seeing this played out in his life. He's a great brother.

But I didn't bring that about. In fact, maybe the Lord had more freedom to do that in JJ's life because I'm not around as much. Who knows? God's teaching JJ and He's teaching me. I'm now in this marvelous adventure of learning leisure. It's a huge risk—it really is, but I'm never going back to the way I was before, even when God heals me of cancer and I'm back in the saddle.

It almost sounds contradictory, but honestly, it's like the first two guys the rich investor commended in Matthew 25. They were willing to take a risk, but the "one-talent man" wasn't. When Mr Narrow handed the talent and his excuses back, "The master was furious. 'That's a terrible way to live! It is criminal to live cautiously like that! If you knew I was after the best, why did you do less than the least? . . . Take the thousand and give it to the one who risked the most. And get rid of this "play-it-safe" who won't go out on a limb'" (verses 26–29).

So Lord, today I dare to risk another leisurely stroll with you. Thanks again, from the bottom of my heart, for cancer and all you're teaching me by way of it. Thank you for my church family and the way you're using them not only to help me but also to teach me. I always learn more from them than they ever learn from me. Lord, I thank you that you're doing big things all the time, even when I'm strolling or sitting. My cessation from activity, especially normal work schedules and duties today, is my way of acknowledging you have it all under control. What's new? Amen and amen.

September 15. Irene and Thurman are ill

My heart is heavy today because a dear friend is critically ill. Her name is Irene. Lord, I lift her up to you today.

Irene and her family joined the church I serve several years ago. Her husband Al cracks me up. For a couple years in a row on Christmas, he gave me a *laugh box*. What's that? He collected comic strips and other funny snippets from various places and put them all in a small box. Then he handed it to me and said, "Pull one of these out any time you need a laugh." What a gift, huh?

I have to avoid talking to him right before the service each Sunday because he'll give me something or tell me a story that cracks me up to the point where I can't concentrate on my sermon. Al is a character.

Like father, like sons. One of Al and Irene's sons is Joe, a golf buddy and fellow theologian who lives in Houston with his wife Nancy. Their other son Jim and his wife Judy and their two kids Michael and Danielle are still at FSBCN. Jim and Judy and I took Spanish lessons together. They serve faithfully in our church and teach Sunday school for the Hispanic congregation.

So you get the idea about this family. I've spent a lot of time with them and with Irene. Over the past few years, her health hasn't been good. She's been in and out of hospitals and has recently been in a nursing home. I made a point of visiting her often (though I'll admit most of my motivation for visiting was selfish).

Irene is a surrogate mother to me. It's hard even to write this. Every time she sees me, she always asks, "John, how is your heart today?"

And I know I have to answer honestly. I can't lie because she can see right through me. She asks it and it just opens me up to tell her—straight. Here she is, confined to a bed in a nursing home with a plethora of physical issues and ailments of her own to deal with, and she asks me how I'm doing. Are you kidding me?

Now don't get the wrong idea. Irene calls them as she sees them. Make no mistake about it—she's the real thing, and genuinely cares not only for me but also for others while she's lying in that bed.

For many years she sent out birthday cards to everyone in our church. (When she had to stop recently, it broke her heart.) She wrote them from her bed and mailed them out.

Her example is the one of the huge motivations for this book. If she can do it, why can't I?

I'll tell you, a sickbed is a powerful platform. It is, as Marilyn said yesterday, a proving ground of sorts. It demonstrates whether or not I believe all the stuff I've preached. Gulp. Is that ever true!

This is the gift cancer is to me. It has opened up the Word for sure, but also valuable relationships with Irene and others with some type of illness.

I have another good friend in Florida, Thurman. I always enjoy visiting with him and his wife Mollie (who gave me her recipe for key lime pie—one of the few things I can actually bake) when I go to Florida. My secretary Betty's brother Dean and his wife Willene are also friends I enjoy seeing every year. This is my yearly retreat, and it's beyond-words wonderful.

Anyway, Thurman has been ill himself the past couple years and has suffered through a lot of difficult symptoms and treatments, but he's done it with dignity and grace as a man of God. He talks about his illness if you ask him, and he and Mollie send out periodic updates, but it's not their focus. It's not a preoccupation. He still likes to ask about my church and me, or to talk about what's going on in his church. The congregation has asked him to be the lay leader of several building programs.

They've had me in their home, along with Dean and Willene. We've laughed. I've been so warmly welcomed and received on my trips to Florida.

Is there a theme here?

Thurman is such an example to me, but yesterday he wrote me and said, "I'm not rejoicing over what I'm dealing with, but I *know* this is *nothing* compared to what you're experiencing." That statement causes me to weep. Oh brother Thurman, it's exactly the opposite! Thank you brother for demonstrating how to suffer for the glory of God. I look up to Thurman so much. Lord, encourage and strengthen Thurman for the battle today.

My experience with cancer has raised my level of perception and appreciation and respect for anyone who's dealing with an illness of any kind. It's all difficult, whatever the situation.

But Irene and Thurman have taught me not to lose focus, not to divert my attention from the Lord and others *ever*, no matter what happens to me. And that's hard to do. My symptoms and side effects from chemo seem to be diminishing, but I had another difficult time trying to sleep last night. I'm even more exhausted, but I'm glad God isn't!

"I'm thanking you, God, out loud in the streets, singing your praises in town and country. The deeper your love, the higher it goes; every cloud is a flag to your faithfulness" (Psalm 56:9–10). Even the cancer cloud? You bet! I raise my flag of testimony to the faithfulness of God alongside the flags of Irene and Thurman.

And in so doing, I want to be part of the group of sheep on Judgment Day to whom Jesus proclaims, "I'm telling you the solemn truth: whenever you did one of these things to someone overlooked or ignored [even a visiting Baptist preacher], that was me—you did it to me" (Matthew 25:41). Amen.

September 17. "Cancer brain"

I discovered this term in a list of side effects from chemo in the *Guide to Chemotherapy* magazine at a doctor's office. Here's the definition given: "a vague term that refers to an all-too-real condition that has been associated with chemo. Patients describe it as mental fog or cloudiness; it affects memory, concentration and the ability to process thoughts quickly. Although these symptoms can be distressing, they're usually temporary."

I think this is one of my major challenges right now—the mental aspect of this disease.

Yesterday I went in to the office and had a really good visit with my secretary Betty. We'll be celebrating her fortieth year of ministry in our church next month. She's a wonderful sister in Jesus who's always been so supportive of me, but especially these last few weeks. She's done a great job taking care of things and coordinating ministry since I've been out of commission. Lord, thank you for Betty.

After we visited I set about getting some things done. One of my weekly duties is to record a message to the whole congregation and send it out. We use a gadget called a *phone tree*. I record a brief message and this gadget calls everyone in the church. It actually works quite well.

Every week I put announcements and prayer requests on the phone tree, and yesterday I had several prayer concerns to share, but for some reason I couldn't get them straight. I struggled with even remembering what to say, and had to stop and start over several times. It was weird.

It did seem like I was in a fog yesterday, and what's really disturbing is I can't figure out why. I've finished taking all the medicine they ask me to take after chemotherapy. I'm done with all that, but I'm still having symptoms. And my frustration level is mounting.

Another very disturbing symptom that raised its head yesterday was a weak voice. Again, that sounds strange, doesn't it? But for the past couple days it's seemed like someone had their fist in my throat, and my language has been muffled. This has caused me a lot of anxiety. I'm concerned about preaching. Will I be able to preach Sunday as I've planned? What does this mean?

In describing the past week and its challenges in an email to a friend last night I said, "This past week has been sneaky tough." I described it that way because I went into the week expecting severe side effects like nausea and vomiting and the shakes. I've had a little bit of nausea, but mainly the aftermath has been a series of lesser irritations that basically knock me off my perch. It's been one after another—bang, bang, bang.

I bet the psalmist can relate. One commentator classifies Psalm 60 as a *soldier psalm*. At first it seems to him God has forsaken him—"walked off and left us" (verse 1), but he rallies and asks God to answer quickly. And of course, the Lord does. I thank you for answering prayer, Lord, *always*.

Beginning in verse 6, the Lord lists places and nations and enemies: Shechem, Succoth Valley, Gilead, Manasseh, Ephraim, Judah, Moab, Edom, Philistia. And as I read this list and think about it, I can't help making a list of my own.

I can't believe I've got cancer—*argh!*

Fear of chemo, hospitals, needles, pain, nausea, stomach problems, lack of sleep, cancer brain, muffled speech ... but this list, like the psalmist's, is all in God's "pocket," hanging on his belt. Not as an obstacle but as a *tool* in the hand of a skilled worker. Even the nations are a pair of pliers to the Lord! Everything and everyone is under His sovereign control.

This image reminds me of a brother in our church named Bill. His wife Jerri, a wonderful woman who encouraged us all, passed away recently. It was a big loss not only for Bill but for the whole church. But Bill continues to serve Jesus and work with wood. He has a shop in his garage where he makes all sorts of things.

Bill made me a cedar chest for my twentieth anniversary as pastor and the church gave it to me as a gift—off-the-charts fantastic! I've always liked cedar chests, and this is the best one ever. I love it!

The point is, Bill has all the tools. He knows how to use each one to craft toys and chests and Bronco emblems and whatever else he wants to make out of wood.

God, I thank you for being a skilled craftsman in my life, using cancer and all its side effects to make me into someone who pleases you. I confess my impatience with your work. I want it to speed up. I want this cancer and all its impacts on me to be gone forever *now*. But I thank you that you're in charge of this work. I thank you that if you leave this enemy called cancer and all its "buddies" in my life, you know what you're doing. I don't, but I thank you that you do. I'm going to step out of the way and let you do your job. Carve and cut away!

I affirm today: "You aren't giving up on us, are you, God? Refusing to go out with the troops? Give us help for the hard task; human help is worthless. In God we'll do our very best; he'll flatten the opposition for good" (Psalm 60:10–12). God, I praise you that you're so powerful you can not only defeat the Philistines and the symptoms of cancer brain in me, but also turn them around and use them for your glory. So bring on the next *--ine* today! Amen.

September 18. My friend Irene passed away yesterday

Lord, I thank you so much for Irene and what she meant not only to me but also to the church and to the Kingdom of God. I lift up her family as they grieve. Selfishly, I'll miss having her around. But I thank you that you answered her son Jim's prayer for healing. Now she's well and whole in your presence!

Irene really suffered greatly the past several years. On more than one occasion she almost died, and in one of our conversations she said, "John, I don't want any artificial means of keeping me going. If it's my time, then I'm ready to go." And I'm glad on this occasion she didn't have to suffer more.

But she sure went through a lot of pain and suffering the past few years, and a lot of setbacks where she thought she was going to get better and things turned. A lesser person would have given up. Irene didn't, but many times as I watched her struggle, in my mind and heart I asked, "Why are you allowing this, Lord? Please heal her or just take her home."

As I was dealing with all this, I received a note on Facebook from Pam. Pam and her husband Lou and two kids Keith and Brittany were members of the church a few years back and a huge encouragement to me. I used to hang out at their house on occasion and eat junk food after Sunday night service. We had a lot of laughs. The Lord moved them to Oklahoma a few years ago, but we still stay in touch. They're great buds.

Pam's brother Mike recently experienced a recurrence of cancer, and as a result the doctors thought it best to amputate his leg. The surgery was last week. Mike's had a lot of pain, but he's doing well. Thank you Jesus for taking him through. Give comfort and peace to the family.

In Pam's message she chronicles the family's struggles with all the questions, but mainly the question *why?* This is natural in the midst of tough stuff like this, and Pam gave some great answers to her family.

All this has sparked the question in my mind: why? Why does a good and gracious God allow good people to suffer?

I know some of the intellectual answers I've given before, but now that I have cancer, I have a different perspective on all of it. Two things emerge in my mind (sounds like a sermon brewing).

Somehow I just can't dwell on the *why* question, and here's the reason. I've lived fifty-two years in the remarkably good health the Lord has allowed me to have. I've been reminded of that over and over.

For each surgery I've had—the first biopsy, the bone marrow biopsy, and the port surgery—a nurse has gone through a long list of questions about my health. Stroke? No. Diabetes? No. Heart issues? No. Surgeries? Well, I had my tonsils taken out when I was four.

And it was as if the Lord was speaking to me each time, "John, I am in charge of you, always have been. I've allowed you to be healthy. Now I'm allowing you to have cancer (and still be healthy, by the way). Still the same."

So who am I to question God? How can I receive all the blessings He's given me (health is only one of many) and then turn and question Him when I get cancer? I won't do it.

Here's another question. Why is it no one cries out in desperation, "Oh Lord, why, why, why have you blessed me?"

Our questions, if you think about it, are pretty arrogant. Job found that out. He had a bunch of questions for God and when he finally shut up, God had more questions for him—questions neither he nor any human on the face of the earth can answer. God answered Job's questions with more questions. Deal with it.

So why do I have cancer? I have no idea!

Why not? Who am I to expect to be exempt from illnesses others like Irene and Mike have? Do I expect to live my life on a feather bed without ever having to suffer physical malady? That's my first answer to the *why* question.

Lord, I'm thankful that you've given grace to me so far in this process, but I know I've only begun to suffer. And as the chemo treatments progress, I trust you to help me down the road as you've helped me to this point.

My second answer to the *why* question involves the value of suffering. There are some things the Lord wants us to learn, and we can only learn them through pain.

I can't begin to list the good things the Lord has done in my life, in my church, and in the Kingdom because of this cancer. I don't even know where to start. But here's the one big thing: cancer is forcing me to get my life back together.

I can honestly say that before mid-July 2010 my life was disjointed. It's amazing how that happens over time. Thank you Jesus for bringing my relationship with you back into focus. Thank you for bringing my previously frantic daily life back under your control. Thank you for all you're doing in the church through people who are more engaged in serving you. Thank you for showing us your work doesn't depend on one person. (I think I needed this lesson more than the folks at church did.)

Therefore, here's the reality for me: I think I'm more "well" now than I've been in years, and I have cancer! I know that sounds strange, but it's so true.

Thank you Jesus for cancer. I want to thank you for cancer every day for the rest of my life because it's a wonderful gift. Lord, it's hard and I have questions—many questions—but I'll bring each one to you and leave it there.

I still marvel at the way God speaks through a consecutive reading of the Word. He never fails! Amazingly enough, today I came to Jesus' prayer in Gethsemane that sums up all of this: "Going a little ahead, he fell on his face, praying, 'My Father, if there is any way, get me out of this. But please, not what I want. You, what do you want?'" (Matthew 26:39).

"You've always taken me seriously, God, made me welcome among those who know and love you" (Psalm 61:5). Thank you for allowing me to join Irene (in heaven now), Mike, and all those who are suffering for you. Thank you for questions, yours and mine. Thank you today that you're bigger than any question. I embrace the road of suffering you've put me on and I trust you to lead me today. Amen and amen.

September 19. Scary good, today

Yesterday was a good day. I felt better than I had in weeks actually. When my mother asked me how I was doing, I replied, "So good it's scary."

And here's why I said that. One of the things I've discovered is because of the chemotherapy, both the physical and emotional ups and downs are much more severe. And this played out yesterday. About 2:00 p.m., all my energy was gone—poof.

Dee told me the rhythm of my life now should be work, rest, work, rest, work, and rest. Very good counsel.

This roller coaster makes me especially vulnerable to attacks from the enemy. For some reason he likes to swoop in when we're exposed. And yesterday he sure did. I felt him shooting at me from both barrels, and he always attacks me in the very area of my preaching.

Today I'm excited to be able to go to church and to preach. I'm preaching from the Sermon on the Mount. My focus is the fourth, fifth, and sixth Beatitudes, especially the sixth: "Blessed are the pure in heart, for they shall see God" (Matthew 5:8, NIV). This declaration from Jesus hit home for me for several reasons.

More than anything else in my life, cancer has exposed my heart to me, and it hasn't been pretty. During those times when I'm at leisure (which is most of the time), the Holy Spirit has been bringing issues and sins to mind, and I've been confessing—*a lot*. I feel He's been doing "spiritual chemo" on me, and it's very painful.

In addition, my relative inactivity has forced me to evaluate myself by another criterion. Up until the last few weeks, I always defined a good day by how much I got done; in other words, activity. A lot of activity meant a good day; less activity meant a bad day. Wow, just writing that convicts me again. That's certainly *not* God's standard.

So this Beatitude reminds me I can be blessed if I do absolutely nothing but my heart is pure before the Lord. And I'll go a step further—if my heart isn't pure, then nothing I do matters.

I'm learning to be guarded even when I have a good day (which again, I defined at first in terms of how I'm feeling—not a good barometer either, really). The two passages I read today hit home in this regard, *big time.*

The narrator of Psalm 62 is under attack from multiple enemies. He learns the only solid place of safety is waiting on God in complete trust. Once this issue is settled, all things human take their proper place: "Man as such is smoke, woman as such, a mirage. Put them together, they're nothing; two times nothing is nothing." And here's the verse that literally jumped off the page at me this morning: "And a windfall, if it comes—don't make too much of it." The psalmist concludes with the affirmation: "God said this once and for all: how many times have I heard it repeated? 'Strength comes straight from God'" (Psalm 62:9–11).

And in the garden, as Jesus is praying, struggling, and preparing for Calvary, he comes back to find his disciples snoozing away and makes this proclamation (and I love the picture here—so descriptive). "Stay alert; be in prayer so you don't wander into temptation without even knowing you're in danger. There's a part of you that is eager, ready for anything in God. But there's another part of you that's as lazy as an old dog sleeping by the fire" (Matthew 26:41). Only the Holy Spirit can teach old dogs new tricks!

Lord, I pray my voice will work today and my heart will be pure before you, today and always. Amen.

September 20. The elbow bump

I value corporate worship more than ever, now that I have cancer. Yesterday went so well, especially the voice part of my sermon. I felt stronger and stronger as the message progressed. For some reason, this has been the most troubling of the side effects from chemo. I was worried I wouldn't be able to continue to preach.

Yesterday I introduced my new hug/handshake alternative. One of my oncologist's nurses told me once I start chemo, I shouldn't be around crowds because of my low white blood cell count and susceptibility to infections. Well, of course that wasn't going to happen, and I think she could tell right off the bat from my initial response to her directive that I wasn't going to stay away from church.

So she followed up by saying, "Well, limit your contact with folks." I certainly understand that, but this is also difficult for me. I *love* to shake hands. I *love* hugs now. Yesterday several people swooped in on me like hawks for a hug, and I had to push them away.

My substitute now is the elbow bump, a new greeting method I shared with the church. Everyone responded very well, although some exhorted me to also wear a mask in the future. Okay. I agree. I just want to make it through chemo without any further complications, but I'm glad I can do something to continue having contact with my church family.

Contact is so vital, especially because of the isolation cancer causes. For example, I'll be isolated most of today, I'm sure; not because I want to, but because I'm totally—I mean totally—exhausted. Yesterday after preaching and visiting with folks and going home to eat a small lunch, the bottom fell out of my energy. I was a limp rag the rest of the day—physically (but not emotionally).

Let me explain. Emotionally, I was up, *big time*. Why? It has to do with just being with fellow believers and sharing fellowship. A couple who recently joined our church, Tom and Lorna, approached me yesterday and said they had had occasion to attend some special revival services at their former church. And Tom added, "All the time we were there, all we could think about was our church and praying for you. And we just wanted you to know that. This is now our home and our family."

After the service, Diane approached me. She and her husband and son William and the boys she brings to worship live in Federal Heights, the community near FSBCN the Lord has asked us to reach (our Judea, so to speak, in Acts 1:8 terms). Acts 1:8 says, "What you'll get is the Holy Spirit. And when the Holy Spirit comes on you, you will be able to be my witnesses in Jerusalem, all over Judea and Samaria, even to the ends of the world." They've recently come to know Jesus, and it stirs me deeply to see how they're growing, each one of them, in their faith and walk with Jesus. I love them.

Diane told me about her neighbors, Art and Rachel, who live across the street. Diane has recently begun taking care of our children's minister's baby girl, Elizabeth. When Rachel heard about this she brought some baby things to the Stevensons' house. Diane thanked her and said, "Blessings on you." Well, the Lord did indeed bless Art and Rachel in some amazing ways. Later Rachel came back and inquired, "Diane, what did you do?" Diane replied, "I did nothing, but it is apparent to me that the Lord is at work in your life."

This past summer through some mission outreach activities and through the consistent witness of Diane's family, the Lord has been reaching out to Art and Rachel. It was so wonderful to hear about how that's continuing and more than that, how the Lord is using Diane and her family. When I heard that story, something stirred within me.

Now, both of these encounters with folks in the church had nothing to do with cancer per se (except Tom's assertion that they were praying for me while they were worshipping at another church). I don't want or need people talking specifically about my cancer all the time. In fact, that would be depressing. That's not what I need!

What I do need is to be in contact with fellow believers and share in the work of God. That's what I need.

During a family conversation the other night, the subject of cancer support groups came up. Some people have suggested it might be helpful to find one and join it. But my immediate response is always a quick "nope."

Now, before I go further, I'm not putting down support groups. I think they serve an important purpose, and indeed I might be going to one down the road. Who knows? But to be honest, I think they offer a surrogate church experience for people who may not be believers and may not have a church. (Again, I'm not intimating that if someone goes to a support group they're not saved! To each his or her own to some degree with cancer, for sure!)

All of this to say, I don't need a support group because I already have one—my church family!

The church provides me with plenty of encouragers who are going through or have gone through cancer, like Sharon, Juanita, Linda, and Kay. All these sisters were in church yesterday and encouraged me. Others like Gloria (who's going through her own physical trials) were there also. Just the fact she was there was a huge boost for me.

The majority of others have never had cancer, but the Lord still uses them in the corporate experience as huge encouragers. That's the way the body of Christ works, by means of the interconnectedness we enjoy through the Holy Spirit who indwells us.

This is what the psalmist is talking about in Psalm 62: "God—you're my God! I can't get enough of you! I've worked up such hunger and thirst for God, traveling across dry and weary deserts. So here I am in the place of worship, eyes open, drinking in your strength and glory. In your generous love I am really living at last! … I hold on to you for dear life, and you hold me steady as a post" (Psalm 62:1–3, 8).

Lord, thank you for the place of worship, because it includes your people. Thank you for the genius of the church. Thank you for creating us to be in community. Thank you for the *broadening* that occurs during fellowship. I thank you for your work not only in my tiny life, but also in the world as a whole. As I'm exposed to it through my brothers and sisters, it enlarges my capacity to trust you in all things. Thank you for being a *big* God, bigger than cancer for sure, but also bigger than anything that will come down the road. I choose to hold on to you for dear life today. Amen.

September 21. Cutting and running, the challenge for endurance, part one

One of the most ominous verses in all of the New Testament is Matthew 26:56b: "Then all the disciples cut and ran." I read it today. Here's Jesus under arrest in the Garden of Gethsemane. Peter took a swing with a sword to "help" Jesus out. Jesus responds, "I could call twelve or more fighting companies of angels if I wanted to, but I don't because this arrest and everything that comes after it is part of the plan." And it was *at that point* the disciples, those eleven guys who had walked so closely with him and had shared with Jesus at an intimate level and knew him better than anyone—cut and ran.

I struggle with understanding that (but I don't struggle for long, especially these days). Yesterday was a case in point—a very long day.

One of the many difficulties of dealing with cancer is handling what comes down the pike each day. To be honest, I'm becoming increasingly frustrated with the physical roller coaster. After the high of Sunday when I felt good and preached my sermon with a strong voice (the Lord gets all the credit there, in answer to prayer), I've now been down physically. I just don't have the sustained strength to be up for even two days in a row.

I know the medical reasons for it—what's going on with my white and red blood cells (something I have to get checked out tomorrow with the oncologist). I know all that, but it doesn't seem to help. I've never really had to deal with anything like this for a long period of time—months—*ever* in my life.

I'm tired of being tired, and I'm tempted to cut and run.

The issue, as a couple friends from North Metro Church reminded me in email messages yesterday, is *endurance*. David, a good brother from our sister church who's gifted in sharing the gospel with kids, sent me a message yesterday entitled *endurance*. His pastor has begun a new series of messages from the book of James, and David's teaching the children from the same book. Here's what he said: "One example seemed to catch the kids' attention more than others. I have a friend who makes knives. He takes some steel, heats it, beats it, grinds it, shapes it, cools it, adds a handle, and out comes a beautiful knife that sells for more than two hundred dollars. He looks at a piece of steel and sees the knife inside. A beautiful, balanced, useful, and sharp tool."

Using that analogy, he went on to exhort me. It was a very powerful word and one I needed yesterday and all days, *big time.*

Alluding to the same sermon series, Lucinda sent this verse to me: "Blessed is a man who perseveres under trial; for once he has been approved, he will receive the crown of life which the Lord has promised to those who love Him" (James 1:12).

Okay, so isn't it incredible that through the loving concern of a brother and sister who go to another church, I get to hear *exactly* the message I need to hear through the preaching ministry of another church?? Is God incredible or what? These messages from David and Lucinda came to me in the morning before I faced the temptation to cut and run later in the day.

Cut and run? Yes. I know that sounds crazy. How can anyone cut and run from cancer? Well obviously I can't just say, "You know what? I'm tired of cancer. I don't want it anymore. I'm done with it." Ha, I wish.

No, it's subtler and more profound than just not wanting cancer. And yesterday I learned what endurance means in three ways.

First, I got an email from Barbara, my buddy in Florida, reminding me about the quilt ministry her church wanted to do for me. When I emailed Karen, the leader of this ministry, her immediate response was: "John, please tell us what to pray for and our church will lift you up." Well my first thought was: "What to pray for? Are you kidding?"

But then the Holy Spirit stopped me, dead in my tracks: "Yes, John, what's your main prayer request?" With my cut-and-run attitude, I wanted to tell Karen, "Pray for my total healing and soon, by the way." I do pray that and I know many others do, and there's nothing wrong with that prayer request. Believe me.

But somehow there was a check in my spirit. I couldn't ask Karen and her church to pray that for me. After wrestling with the wording of several different requests, here's what I wrote: "Karen, have your church pray I can honor the Lord Jesus Christ through this cancer as long as He chooses to allow me to have it. Thanks a lot, John."

Honestly, this is my number one prayer request *now* that the Lord beat it out of me—ha!

Second, I can cut and run simply by giving in to despair. Just sitting around yesterday, too tired to do anything else, all those nagging thoughts came rushing in: "Are you kidding? You're not ever going to get over this. You'll never feel better. This is it for the rest of your life ..." In all of Satan's taunts, cutting and running means listening to Satan and his lies.

Can't and won't for several reasons.

God helped me through this in a very specific way. I also learned cutting and running means clamming up about God. Yesterday I was in a store and met a salesman I'd seen before who asked me how I was doing. Well, I've learned to be very careful who I tell about my having cancer when it comes to strangers. So I was just going to give the stock answer and go on, but the Lord nudged me to tell him.

So I told the salesman I have cancer, and of course he freaked out. (People do that perhaps because they're afraid of getting it themselves.) When he asked how I was dealing with it, the door was then wide open door for me to tell him I trust the Lord and His power to see me through, whatever the outcome.

So in spite of my natural inclinations, once again the Lord helped me in some very specific ways. As Psalm 64 says, "The God of the Arrow shoots! They double up in pain ... Be glad, good people! Fly to God! Good-hearted people, make praise your habit" (Psalm 64:7, 10).

Lord, today I choose to keep on praying the right thing, thinking the right thing, and saying the right thing. I thank you for your refining processes at work during this cancer experience. May the daily product—me—perfectly reflect your purposes and plans to everyone I see in public or to only you who sees in solitude today. Amen.

September 22. The challenge for endurance, part two

Hey, I may have cancer, but I'm still a preacher who can't resist the pull to have a two-part message every now and again. This whole issue of endurance is heavy on my heart these days because it's so difficult for all of us, whether we have cancer or not.

As I continue to read the narratives in Matthew about Jesus on the way to Calvary, I'm continually amazed at how his disciples let him down. Yesterday I cited the verse that said all of them cut and ran. Today I read the story of Peter's denials; after all his vows and promises and prideful comparisons ("even though everyone may deny you, I won't") he went down in flames in ignominious defeat, and Matthew 26 ends with Peter remembering what Jesus said: "Before the rooster crows, you will deny me three times." And then "he went out and cried and cried and cried" (Matthew 26:75).

In spite of Peter's best intentions, he failed to stick with Jesus. It would be terribly tragic, if we didn't know the rest of the story of Peter. The Holy Spirit turned him around and made him a bold preacher, but a huge building block in that process was brokenness.

The Lord has amazing ways of breaking us so He can fill us with His spirit and power and then use us.

This cancer thing and the fatigue I feel is just such an experience for me. With my human strength diminished in many ways, I now have to trust His strength, and a huge part of that involves prayer.

My good friend and mentor Kenny has taught me a lot about this. One of his very memorable comments is we usually pray for a while and then default to activity. I can see this in the church from my perspective as a pastor. It's much easier to come up with programs in the flesh to address issues than to just wait on God and pray. It's hard because God is always concerned with character before He jumps through all the hoops I put in front of Him.

So, He'll allow me to keep praying for something and let me wait it out because He wants to teach me something. This is another process of brokenness, because things always end up differently than I'd planned *and* when He pulls something together, He gets the glory, not me.

A case in point is our Wednesday night program at FSBCN. God raised up a young couple in our church, Ron and Hope, to take the lead. They gather folks together for prayer and then lead a discipleship study. Last week we had more adults present than we've had in years—I mean *years*. The Lord is using them in great ways. I've had nothing to do with it and haven't even been there.

Honestly, for years I've been frustrated with Wednesday nights and have tried everything I can think of to boost attendance—all human efforts and programs. But to get things going, God took me out of the way and then He was free to work! This is one example of how the Lord is working without his *primary helper*—me. How can He do that?

All of this adds to my lesson regarding endurance. Yesterday I said one of the huge challenges of endurance is thinking the right thing. When I'm sitting there, my physical body drained of energy, what do I think about?

The cut-and-run, Peter-denial answer is to feel sorry for myself, focus on myself, and creep into unbelief. But the endurance answer is very different and it hit me like a Mack truck two days ago.

I received an email from Bobby, a good brother who always encourages and challenges me. He said: "Hunter is a boy who attends Creekside Community Church in Elizabeth. He's ahead of you on the path." Bobby included a link to a YouTube video showing ten-year-old Hunter sitting in a hospital bed with his dad asking him questions.

Hunter has cancer in his leg and is receiving aggressive treatments. So you might think the video would be rather maudlin and depressing, but *far from it*. One of the questions Hunter's dad asks him is what he does while he's in the hospital. Hunter talks about playing video games and watching movies, and then he says, "And I pray."

When his dad asks him what he prays about, Hunter replies, "I pray my friends here could beat cancer and I could. And I pray for my family because this is hard on them." I'm telling you, when I heard that ten-year old boy say that, it broke me.

Instead of the cut-and-run, woe-is-me, poor-John approach, I need to take this wonderful opportunity to *pray*. Hunter prays for his family, and besides everything else, I need to pray more concertedly for my family who have to put up with me—at least do that.

If Hunter can do it, so can I.

I tell you, God is using the testimony of this young man to challenge me.

When I told Bobby to tell Hunter's dad Alan that I wanted to meet Hunter in person, Alan replied by saying, "Hunter is in this week for an intense five-day treatment and then after tests, they'll be looking to do surgery on his femur in three weeks or so followed up by a year of more intensive treatments." Please, please pray for this boy.

My heart goes out to him. I love him and I haven't even met him yet.

"Blessed are the chosen! Blessed the guest at home in your place! We expect our fill of good things in your house, your heavenly manse" (Psalm 65:4). Oh Lord, thank you that because of your son and what he did for me, I'm a part of the chosen, a guest in your home with your people. Thank you for the challenge and encouragement of others who are following you and persevering. I pray for Hunter as he goes through treatment this week, and in the hard road ahead of him. Heal him Lord. Help him to be able to play football again very soon. Thank you for using him in my life at a significant point to call me back to prayer. By your grace and by the power of the Holy Spirit, I determine to use these days of inactivity to focus my thoughts on you and others, just like Hunter does. Amen.

September 23. Checkup

Yesterday I had to go to the oncologist for a mid-term checkup. They said I was doing fine. Thank you for this good report, Jesus.

I still have to be cautious about exposure to viruses. In fact, the nurse who spoke with us urged my mother and sister to get their flu shots and said they were going to give me mine as a part of my next chemo treatment.

We talked about all the side effects I'd experienced during the past ten days or so, and then the nurse said, "Well, as Dr Jotte likes to say, this chemo thing is like running a race on a track. Each lap is pretty much the same, except you'll experience more fatigue as this process goes on."

The main thing I learned yesterday is fatigue is a huge part of chemotherapy, and these drops in energy I experience just about every day are a major part of the deal. Okay. So I'm learning more and more what to expect. That's huge.

Dealing with it is another.

Psalm 66 starts out with praise to God for what He performs in creation and redemption. Verse 6 is a reference to the Exodus: "He converted sea to dry land; travelers crossed the river on foot. Now isn't that cause for a song?"

But then the psalm moves to describe the experience of God's people in the wilderness. "Didn't he set us on the road to life? Didn't he keep us out of the ditch? He trained us first, passed us like silver through refining fires, brought us into hardscrabble country, pushed us to our very limit, road-tested us inside and out, took us to hell and back; finally he brought us to this well-watered place" (Psalm 66:9–12).

Two phrases hit me between the eyes this morning. "Passed like silver through refining fires" is the first. It reminds me of 1 Peter 1:7: "Pure gold put in the fire comes out of it proved pure; genuine faith put through this suffering comes out proved genuine. When Jesus wraps this all up, it's your faith, not your gold, that God will have on display as evidence of his victory."

So cancer is a refining process that shows several things. It shows me where I am with the Lord. I tell you, all through my life, fatigue has been a challenge for me. When I'm tired, the real John comes out. Everyone in my family knows this and so, the more I think about it, cancer and chemo are introducing me to a huge fiery furnace called *fatigue*. And it's painful. It really is, but it's the real John with all his warts and weaknesses.

These passages teach us that the fires of trial show God where we really are. They're a test from Him. Will John's faith prove genuine when you make him do prolonged laps around a track—the same thing spoon-fed to him day after day after day in the same cauldron? The fires prove the reality of pure faith.

I think going through refining fires is also a demonstration to the world. Several days ago I mentioned Shadrach, Meshach, and Abednego. When they were standing in the furnace alive with *someone else* in there with them, it caused Nebuchadnezzar and everyone else to worship the true God. So this refining process has a lot of angles and purposes.

The other phrase in Psalm 66 that caught my attention is "pushed us to our very limit." The language in this psalm reminds me of the car ads on TV where the sports car is going a hundred miles an hour on a test track and there's a message at the bottom of the screen: "This is a professional driver on a closed track. Do not imitate." Auto companies push cars to the limit to see how they will perform. (I wish I could find a closed track to see how my truck would really perform. But right now I can't afford the repair bill when I get confirmation I'm nowhere near to being a professional driver.)

"Pushed us to our very limit" also reminds me of my seventh grade soccer coach, Tuck Ganzenmueller. (How can I ever forget a name like that? I can't, for many reasons.) Mr G (as I'll refer to him from now on since I don't have the energy to write out his name every time!) was really the first coach I ever had. He was tall and muscular and soft-spoken, but he got his messages across. I think he was way ahead of his time back in the early 1970s because of his focus. I'll never forget the first day of practice when he looked at a group of rag-tag junior high boys and said, "Guys, one of the main things we're going to work on is your physical conditioning. You will be in shape for this season."

He ran us into the ground, literally. I remember lying on the grass at Cheesman Park (our practice field across the street from the school) after we'd run so many sprints I couldn't count them, and looking up at the sky and thinking, "I'm going to die right here."

One day Mr G saw our anguish and said, "Guys, if it doesn't hurt, you're not getting in shape." He taught us the reason he was pushing us was so we would be strong all the way through the game and especially at the end. When our opponent was tired, we'd be strong. The psalmist's phrase is "road tested." Mr G pushed the pedal to the metal; he took us to hell and back so when we played games, we'd be ready.

And we did win the Front Range League Championship that year! Hey, it doesn't measure up to the Broncos winning the Super Bowl, but I got the point.

Mr G pushed me to my limit, but in doing so he expanded my limit.

Psalm 66:9–12 describes the wilderness wanderings of the people of Israel. God made them run sprints in the wilderness, not so they would fail (which they did), but to challenge them to grow in the exercise of their faith. His purpose was to make them into a group that could handle the coming challenges of the Promised Land. Only two individuals—Joshua and Caleb—passed the test. And so they were able to lead the next generation into "a well-watered place."

I wonder if I'll pass.

You know what? I think I will, not because of any inherent strength or ability on my part (believe me), but because God in his sovereignty allowed this furnace, this sprint, in my life. He's placed me in this situation, so I have to conclude that as the *best coach ever,* He already knows I can handle it through Him. But He wants me to learn this lesson by way of this effort called cancer.

Lord, today I thank you for the refining fires. I pray everything in my life that doesn't look like Jesus will be burned away so you'll enable me to pass the test and the world will know that you and you alone are God. And thank you for the *workout* cancer is in my life. In the midst of my fatigue, may your strength and grace and stamina and endurance take over my tired self and be stronger through me than ever before. May your strength be evident and may you win another championship for the cause of Jesus. Amen.

John D. Talbert

September 24. Irene's funeral is today

The verse she picked to be read at her service is Psalm 118:24: "This is the day the Lord has made; let us rejoice and be glad in it." This is a very appropriate description of Irene, but also an amazing passage. Once I read it, I decided to use it as the text for the message.

This happens to me so often. Somehow, someone shares a verse with me and when I study it in context, it opens up vistas of truth. The Word of God is amazing! Lord, thank you that your Word is "living and active and sharper than any two-edged sword," as you always use it to get to the heart of the matter (Hebrews 4:12–13).

Psalm 118 is actually a "gate" psalm (like 15 and 24). It depicts the procession of a triumphant king into Jerusalem through the gate of the temple (verse 20) and ultimately to the altar (verse 27). It's an antiphonal psalm in that one person speaks (in this instance the victorious king) and then beginning in verse 22, the congregation responds.

I love all the king's affirmations about the Lord's help. They appear in triplicate. Here they are: "his love never quits" (verses 1–3); "far better to take refuge in the Lord than anything else" (verses 8–9); "hemmed in, the Lord intervened" (verses 10–12); and "the Lord is my strength, my song, and my salvation" (verse 14).

After the king's affirmations, the people respond. Here's where it gets interesting. I concur with those who contend that verse 22 is actually originally a proverb about an unlikely stone that becomes the most important stone in the building—the capstone or cornerstone. This proverb is followed by a declaration that only "the Lord has done this, and it is marvelous in our eyes" (verse 23). Then Irene's verse, "This is the day … ." The psalm concludes with a plea to the Lord for future success and more praises to the Lord as the congregation gathers around the altar to thank the Lord whose love endures forever (Psalm 118:25–29).

The study of this psalm has impacted me profoundly. I can add my own triplet to the poem:

When I found out I had cancer, the Lord was there;

When I faced biopsies and diagnoses, the Lord took me through;

80

When I feared the side effects of cancer treatment, the Lord triumphed over my anxious fears!

Like the king in Psalm 118, the Lord has helped me, but that's not all.

In one commentary on this psalm, Artur Weiser makes this amazing statement: "The Psalm is a powerful testimony to the strength of faith that flows from the direct experience of the help of God and in gratitude and joyful surrender to him is able to overcome all human afflictions and fears."[2]

Wow! That's all I can say to that statement. Once you see the Lord work in one battle (cancer), you learn that the scope of His help transcends one narrow issue and is applicable to others. What this means is I'm learning to trust Him with other challenges. But it doesn't stop even there.

Weiser goes on, "With such a character, it is well able to be a help to others in adversity, comforting them by the uplifting power of the strength of its faith, when depressing thoughts weigh heavily upon them, and leading them to trust for help in the living force of God's loving kindness."[3]

Weiser's statement reflects how Irene lived and it challenges me to do the same, wherever I am.

When I was getting my hair cut yesterday (it still hasn't fallen out, by the way) I met a man who told me about his cancer experience and said he credits wheat grass as the reason he recovered from cancer. (I'm not kidding. I guess some folks actually put it in juice!?!) His comment gave me an opportunity to tell him I'm trusting in the Lord. My response set him back a bit, but I'm going to proclaim to others the Lord is helping me. Amen!

Psalm 118 is quoted in several New Testament passages in reference to what happened to Jesus: "the stone rejected by the builders became the cornerstone" (Matthew 21:42, Acts 4:11, and 1 Peter 2:7). God accepted Jesus, even though men rejected him. "This is the day the Lord has made ...." This verse was actually adopted by the early church as a passage read on Easter. Sunday, this is the day the Lord has made.

This is all about the triumph of the help of the Lord. Through difficulties, battles, and yes, even through rejection and crucifixion, the Lord's life is triumphant!

You're seeing how this thing has worked for me since 1978 when God called me to preach. God preaches a sermon to me and calls me to live it out (most of the time I fail in this regard and honestly, I could have said more to that guy yesterday) *before* I have the privilege of preaching this passage at Irene's victory celebration funeral service today. I love it, and even though it's often painful, it always fulfills me deeply.

God is amazing and deserves all the praise that today's psalm (Psalm 67) gives Him: "God, let people thank and enjoy you. Let all people thank and enjoy you. Let all far-flung people become happy and shout their happiness because you judge them fair and square, you tend the far-flung peoples. God! Let people thank and enjoy you. Let all people thank and enjoy you" (verses 4–5).

Father, I thank you and I definitely enjoy you! Thank you for all the ways you've helped me through my life, but especially now with cancer. Thank you for Irene's example. Thank you for the way she shared with others *about how* you helped her. Thank you that I now have the same opportunity to share from the platform of cancer. Thank you for Jesus who enables all this because, even though he was rejected, he triumphed over death and the grave. Lord, because every day is resurrection day (not just Sunday), I affirm today, "*This is the day the Lord has made, I will rejoice [even at Irene's funeral and especially there] and be glad in it." Amen.

September 25. Irene's funeral service

Irene's funeral went great yesterday. It was indeed a victory celebration, just as Irene requested, in more ways than one.

I asked permission from the family before I did this, but we allowed people opportunity for testimony. After preaching from Psalm 118, a passage that's all about the help of God, I encouraged people to stand up and give a one-sentence testimony with the following structure, "When I was [blank], God helped me by [blank]." I instructed the congregation to respond to each person's testimony by saying, "This is the day the Lord has made. Let us rejoice and be glad in it" (Psalm 118:24, Irene's verse).

It was indeed unorthodox, but very powerful. Irene's youngest son Joe raised his hand during the service to say, "When I had cancer, the Lord healed me." I talked with him on the phone later that day and he said , "When I found out I had cancer, I learned very quickly I had to believe God was in charge of everything, including my cancer, or He was in charge of nothing." Great concept!

Cancer does force the issue of faith. That's for sure.

But something else happened to me yesterday that was a huge lesson. One of the main things I'll miss about Irene is her asking me, "How is your heart?" She asked me this question just about every time I saw her, and she meant it. It always elicited a totally honest response from me, and I needed and still need folks in my life with whom I can be brutally honest. All of us do.

I was already missing that and thinking about that when the funeral procession pulled up to the graveside at Fort Logan National Cemetery. I got out of my car along with the others and made my way up the sidewalk to the hearse. As I was heading that way, I saw Pam, her sister Melissa, and Melissa's son Cameron. Pam and Melissa and their families are huge encouragers for me and everyone else in our church, even during tough times. Right now, neither Pam nor her husband Josh nor Melissa have jobs, and they've been looking for a while.

Lord, right now I continue to pray you'll provide for Pam, Josh, and Melissa according to your riches in glory.

Pam approached me and said, "Hi John, how's your heart?" Her question and the fact that she thought of it then and there touched me deeply. God is awesome! I know I keep saying this but it's true, so I'm going to keep saying it!

Right then and there, God prompted me to remember what I've told others who are grieving: He's able to fill up the empty spaces in our lives! I've told others this, but yesterday I experienced it myself through Pam.

All of this demonstrates the power of God, and Psalm 68 talks about it. (I can see I'm going to be spending some time in this psalm today.) Here's the verse that arrested me: "Father of orphans, champion of widows, is God in his holy house" (Psalm 68:5). That's who God has proven Himself to be for my family since my dad died of cancer in 1973. I qualify as an orphan from a biblical standpoint, because since the age of fifteen I haven't had an earthly dad and neither has Marilyn, and of course my mother has been a widow for thirty-seven years.

Father, thank you for filling up the empty spaces for me as my Heavenly Father and for fulfilling that role even when my earthly dad was still alive! Thank you for showing me yesterday you're still meeting needs. Thank you for using Pam, Joe, and all the others who affirmed you are the God of help for everyone. Amen.

September 26. Never the same

Yesterday I felt so good I was actually scared. I was able to be outside for some of the day. And I was thankful because it seems like I'm coming out of most of the side effects of chemo. I still tire very easily in the afternoon, but I've learned to just rest when I do.

I was talking with a couple from church yesterday and sharing with them some of the things I'm learning about ministry by way of this cancer. I told them I'm learning to wait on God and let Him call folks to serve. I'm learning I'm not vital to the work of God at the church. He can do it without me! Thank you very much, Lord! And I told them this cancer experience has confirmed I can never be the same kind of pastor I was before. It's radically altered my perspective on ministry forever.

After listening to all that, the man said, "Wow, great. Glad to hear it. It's a shame though, that for all of us [he wasn't just talking about me] it takes a crisis to bring us to where we need to be. Why can't good times do that?"

Great question.

I can honestly say the Lord has spoken to me in many ways during these past few weeks, but I haven't heard a lot of new information. He's *reminded* me of many things He told me before, things I brushed by because I was too active, too busy, and too preoccupied (but not now). Not by my choice but of necessity.

I have the same amount of time I've always had, but now I have more time for Him—to listen. I know that sounds contradictory—I have the same amount of time and I have more time—but it's true.

For example, yesterday I got up very early to write and so I had more time to spend with the Lord. I crave that now. I've always needed it , but now I recognize the fact that I need it.

This is one of those areas from which I'll never go back to my old ways. I just can't.

But back to feeling good … I want to learn by way of cancer to seek the Lord with the same intensity I had before my first chemo treatment. I want to learn to follow Him when things are good.

Psalm 68 has given me some great help with that. In addition to its affirmation that He is God of orphans and widows, this psalm declares two huge truths about the Lord. First, God is on the move. The psalm describes how God moved with His people out of Egypt and into the wilderness. "God, when you took the lead with your people, when you marched out into the wild …" (verse 7). The psalmist goes on to describe earthquakes, rain, camp provisions, and the other ways the Lord provided for His people while they were on the move.

And the thought occurred to me that God's people were always nomads. Beginning with nomad number one, old Abraham, the Lord never let His people settle for very long—the wilderness wanderings, the conquest of Canaan, and the development of the land of Israel. They were in their land for a few hundred years but then, because of His judgment on Israel and Judah, He took them to Babylon and then brought them back. They were on the move.

I'm reminded of Jesus' statement in Luke 9:58: "Foxes have holes and birds of the air have nests, but the Son of Man has no place to lay his head" (NIV). How about that?

God's people and God's Son were always on the move. That's the nature of the life of faith, *but* God moves with us in every twist and turn in the road, in all the ups and downs, before chemo, during chemo, one day after chemo, one week after chemo, and two weeks after chemo. The Lord moves and is there at every juncture.

But the Lord is also very stationary! Psalm 68:16 says, "All you mountains not chosen, sulk now, and feel sorry for yourselves, for this is the mountain God has chosen to live on; he'll rule from this mountain forever." Wow, incredible. This is impossible from a human standpoint, but the One who is everywhere at all times has a stable and consistent and solid residence—the mountain of the Lord!

Father, I'm thankful again today for your enduring and abiding presence with me in all the twists and turns of the cancer road. Thank you for being there in the ups and downs. Help me to be there with you. I'm grateful today that your throne is firmly established and it will not be moved. Thank you for letting me preach again today. Thank you for another day of letting me follow you, the *moving but immovable* God. Amen.

September 27. What does it matter?

Twenty-five years ago I had the opportunity to take a trip to England. One of the places I wanted to go was Westminster Chapel, a famous church in downtown London. It was made famous because of the men who served as its pastors. Perhaps the most famous of these preachers was G. Campbell Morgan. I'd just written a paper about him for a preaching seminar in my first year of Ph.D. work at Southwestern Seminary. I learned a lot about preaching by studying his life and ministry.

The pastor who succeeded Morgan was D. Martyn Lloyd-Jones. Lloyd-Jones was also a skilled expositor and very detailed. I heard he took seventeen years to preach through the book of Romans! I have the series of books of his sermons on Romans to prove it. That's pretty detailed!

The man who succeeded these two giants of the pulpit was R. T. Kendall, an American and former Southern Baptist. I'd heard a lot about his ministry as well.

All of that to say, that's why I visited Westminster Chapel on a Sunday morning in June 1985. Kendall was preaching from the first chapter of Philippians, and I'll never forget his sermon on Philippians 1:18. "But what does it matter? The important thing is that in every way, whether from false motives or true, Christ is preached. And because of this I rejoice. Yes, and I will continue to rejoice." Kendall reminded me Paul was so committed to preach Christ that he continued preaching even when he was in a Roman prison. He preached to the guards who were chained to him on both sides twenty-four hours a day (at least six a day in eight-hour shifts) *and* he preached by means of his writings. Most of the New Testament letters we have are a result of Paul's commitment to get the Word out any way he could.

And Kendall added, "Paul was so concerned that Jesus be proclaimed that he didn't even care what the motives of his enemies were. He was just glad that the gospel was proclaimed." Amen.

Actually, the first chapter of Philippians is one of my favorite chapters in the Bible. Another statement Paul makes in this chapter resonates with me: "Now I want you to know, brothers, that what has happened to me has really served to advance the gospel" (verse 12). Nothing stopped Paul from preaching Jesus.

All of that to say that Kendall's sermon and the other truths from Philippians 1 have come to mind the past few days because of a couple things that happened.

Last Sunday Fran, a dear sister and huge encourager in the church was talking with me after the service. She told me she read my blog as often as she could, but was having computer issues lately and couldn't access it. Fran said something like, "You need to be careful coming to preach here in the church. You don't need to be exposed to viruses. [She's right about that.] You don't need to feel compelled to come to church and preach if you don't feel like it. After all, you're preaching every day on Caring Bridge, so we get to hear you that way."

Lucinda made a similar comment a few days earlier. Half joking she said, "I've always wanted to hear you preach. Now I get to through your blog." She laughed when she said it.

Those two comments hit home. I hadn't really realized it. I'm preaching every day now through the written word, and it's all because of the platform of cancer. Thank you Lord for this avenue and platform.

But here's another thing. I'm amazed at who's reading my blog. Honestly, when I started writing at Marilyn's suggestion, I thought I'd just write some things for my own therapy and a few people would wade through all my verbiage late at night to help them sleep. Honestly, I thought that.

But I'm amazed to see how the Lord is at work. I was talking with someone after the service yesterday who reminded me that even people who don't go to church and don't know the Lord may be reading my blog. And the truth of that dawned on me.

Recently folks have asked me if they can give out the name of the website or share printouts of blog entries with others. Here's my blanket response to any and all: *Yes*. Please share this with anyone and everyone.

Why? Because this whole thing is the Lord's doing. He's allowed cancer into my life, and by the grace of God through the power of the Holy Spirit, I want Him to enable me to emulate Paul in making this "prison a pulpit for his power."

Cancer is His divinely allowed pulpit to put His power on parade. That's the end of Psalm 68—God on parade! "See God on parade to the sanctuary, my God, my King on the march!" (verse 24). Can you imagine this God parade? The singers are out front. The least and smallest of the tribes of Israel takes the lead. His power squashes enemies like "the old crocodile, Egypt" [just squashed in the wake of the parade]. All enemy kings end up singing his praises. He rides through the sky with thunder as a companion. "Call out 'Bravo' to God, the High God of Israel. His splendor and strength rise huge as thunderheads. A terrible beauty, O God, streams from your sanctuary. It's Israel's strong God! He gives power and might to his people! O you, his people—bless God!" (verses 34–35).

Oh Lord, you are *big, big, big*. I thank you for the privilege of allowing what you've brought into my life to be caught up in your *big* victory parade. May my smallness never hinder your bigness but only join in, only march along in step and in cadence with the display of your power as you march to victory as King of Kings and Lord of Lords! *Amen*.

September 28. Under attack

That would be my description of yesterday. And it came as anxiety and worry. I'm learning it's safe to say the *opposite* of Philippians 4:6–7 is also true. Here's that famous verse in the Amplified Version (it's long but good):

"Do not fret or have any anxiety about anything, but in every circumstance and in everything, by prayer and petition (definite requests), with thanksgiving, continue to make your wants known to God. And God's peace shall be yours, that tranquil state of a soul assured of its salvation through Christ, and so fearing nothing from God and being content with its earthly lot of whatever sort that is, that peace which transcends all understanding shall garrison and mount guard over your hearts and minds in Christ Jesus."

As I said, there are a lot of words there, but they're all good.

But, having read that, I'm learning that if I do the opposite, which is "fret and have anxiety about everything" (John's quote), I've learned from painful experience the garrison is down and the mounted guard takes a coffee break *with the inevitable result* that you're vulnerable to attack from the enemy.

That's my story for yesterday, and looking back on it, I'm embarrassed. But I started to worry about money again, and it got worse as the day progressed.

I have health insurance, but the bills keep coming in and it's not pretty. The Lord has taken care of me so far, and when I'm thinking right (like right now, not yesterday), I believe He'll continue to take care of me.

Yesterday I spoke with Barbara in the billing office at the Rocky Mountain Cancer Center. I said, "Barbara, I think it would help me to get an idea of what I'm looking at from a financial standpoint for these chemo treatments. The bills are coming in and I just need to know how to plan."

She was very cordial and accommodating, but I could tell she was hesitant at first. "Well, John, this chemo thing isn't cheap. That's for sure. Let me see if I can pull up your records and give you an idea of what your costs are."

Then she told me what each chemo treatment costs.

Can you guess?

Each of my treatments (this isn't the total for all of them, this is *each one*—can you hear the drum roll?) costs:

$22,688.00

When she said that I nearly fainted. Are you kidding me? I know she could hear the nauseated silence on the other end of the line. She added, "Yeah, it's very expensive. The shot they gave you the day after chemo—you know, the one to help with your white blood cell count—that shot alone costs $8,000.00." Huh?

Then she got out her calculator. I could hear her punching keys over the phone. "How many treatments are you going to have?"

I could barely get the three-letter word out of my mouth, "Ssssiiiixxxxx." Multiply 22,688 times six equals *gulp.*

This experience reminded me of the way my parents disciplined me as a child when I got into one of my whiny, pouting moods (which was way too often until their lesson sank in). My dad's words still ring in my ears: "If you don't stop right now, I'll give you something to cry about." And he usually did, and then my mood lifted rather quickly.

So here I was worried about money, and when she started quoting all those huge numbers, the top of my head blew off!

But the Holy Spirit is so gentle and persistent. If you keep worrying when He's told you not to, He disciplines you. As Barbara was speaking and my head was spinning, I felt as if the Spirit said, "If you don't stop worrying, I'll give you something to worry about."

I know God doesn't usually do that. I know that, but that's how He dealt with me yesterday. He used Barbara to remind me this whole thing is way too big for me, not just a little large, but *way* too big. So my little worries are futile.

But back to the conversation—Barbara quickly went on (after quoting *astronomical times six)* to say, "But John, you have insurance and after your deductible and out-of-pocket expenses, your insurance should take care of a big part of this."

Oh, really? Okay.

The Lord lifted me up when once again I stopped and gave this whole cancer thing back to Him, all of it: chemo on Friday with another charge of $22,688 (cha-ching) and all the side effects I'll experience once again and everything that will happen after chemo is completed (a vast unknown at this point; cha-ching)—all of it in a lump at the feet of the Savior *again*.

The rest of the day was a battle (mostly a losing battle) as I struggled to keep turning this whole thing over to Jesus.

That's the way worry works. Give the enemy an inch and he'll take a mile.

Here's God's Word from Psalm 69 for the worrier and the one who fails to trust God: "Rescue me from the swamp, Don't let me go under for good, Pull me out of the clutch of the enemy; This whirlpool is sucking me down. ... Now answer me, God, because you love me; Let me see your great mercy full-face. ... I'm hurt and in pain; give me space for healing, and mountain air. ... For God listens to the poor, He doesn't walk out on the wretched. ... God is out to help Zion, Rebuilding the wrecked towns of Judah" (Psalm 69:14, 16, 29, 33).

This is a very honest prayer, a cry to God in the midst of many taunting enemies. But the Lord has the glorious last and final word.

The same thing happened to Jesus on the cross. In the passage I read today, Matthew 27:46, Jesus cried out the first verse of Psalm 22: "My God my God, why have you abandoned me?" The words and experience are similar to Psalm 69 in some ways.

In quoting the first verse, Jesus was really referring to the whole psalm. Psalm 22 ends with a shout of victory: "God does what he says" (Psalm 22:31).

So no matter what I think or feel, Jesus always has the last word! He will take care of me, whether it costs $22,688 or $22,688,000,000.

Lord, thank you for helping me again yesterday. I confess the sin of worry and all that went with it. Thank you for the provision of health insurance, but above and beyond that, thank you for being my *primary health provider*. Big numbers and lots of money from our perspective is chump change to you. You're able to turn things around while taking care of everything and everyone and me. I praise you for turning things around and winning the victory at Calvary and allowing me to be in on your victory. I love you and I come back today to the place of total dependence on you. Amen.

September 29. Fellowship with two brothers

Yesterday was a great day in several respects. But the best thing about it was the opportunity to share fellowship with two brothers.

Bob is Director of Missions for the Mile High Baptist Association and was a huge encourager of the first prayer meeting with all my pastor buds before the first chemo treatment. He himself was unable to attend because he was in New Mexico, but told me he was available to pray with me and would be glad to do so any time. Bob offers a unique perspective because he practiced medicine for ten years.

Because we couldn't find a time to meet face to face this week, we just talked and prayed on the phone yesterday. I said I was struggling with worry. I said I was apprehensive about the next chemo treatment. I said I was feeling anxious about finances. I said I was struggling with fear about what the future held after chemo.

I also said I believe God is going to heal me, but I want to be prepared if it doesn't happen in the way I think it will, or if it doesn't happen at all. I told Bob I'm vulnerable to attacks from the enemy. *And* I shared the fact that I'm struggling with the fact that I'm struggling!

When I finished my litany of issues, he asked, "What would you say to someone if the shoe were on the other foot?" Hmm. Interesting perspective. I replied, "Well, I'd tell them these are very normal emotions given the gravity of what you're going through. Don't be too hard on yourself. Just know the Lord loves you and cares for you always." To which he said, "There you go."

We went on to talk about the fact that in Christian circles we really don't allow and encourage people to be human. We really do see two extremes when it comes to all this. There are some who advocate that the ideal is an emotionless person who just ignores feelings and says with fake bravado, "I'm great. Praise the Lord anyhow!"

And then the other extreme is someone who allows their emotions to take over, to the extent that they crawl into bed and hide under the covers in the fetal position.

Somewhere between those two extremes is where we need to be. As I was preaching the message to myself on the phone with Bob, I realized that I've tended to lean toward the former. Many times I've suppressed my emotions.

The more I think about it, the more I realize that in a lot of ways I may just now be coming to grips with the fact that I have cancer. I know it sounds strange, but I honestly think after almost three months of dealing with this, since the bulge appeared, the shock is wearing off. I'm actually comprehending some of what it really means to have cancer. And it's a huge thing.

I think for most of my life, especially after my dad's death, I've wanted to minimize cancer just because I didn't want to think about it—really think about it—because it was just too painful. I just couldn't go there again.

So I guess I'm learning more about what it means to be human and learning it's okay to have feelings and emotions and struggles. And I think the important thing is not letting those feelings and emotions and struggles take over and have the final word.

There's so much involved in this when it comes to ministry. How many times have I told someone, either subtly or overtly, to deny their emotions because their expression of humanity made me uncomfortable?

No one during the course of any of this has made me feel uncomfortable, for sure. The last time I got together with my friend Andy, we were eating sandwiches in the food court at Park Meadows Mall. My emotions overwhelmed me and I bawled like a baby right in front of him and the whole world. That certainly didn't faze Andy (and I can't tell you how much that meant to me). He allowed me to be real.

Anyway, after my conversation with Bob I met with Ilamarques, the pastor of our Brazilian congregation. I cannot express in words how much encouragement this brother, his family, and New Generation Christian Community Church have given me. Thank you Jesus for bringing this congregation to FSBCN!

For the last few months, we've been working with Ilamarques to complete the process of securing green cards for him and his family. It's been a lot of work, but the process is finally coming to an end. We made sure we had all the paperwork for his family's visas in order, then we drove up to Boulder to have it checked by an attorney. All the way up and all the way back we talked and laughed and shared fellowship with one another. I'm so encouraged when I'm around Ilamarques and realize what the Lord has done in his life. He was serving a church in Brazil and the Lord called him to uproot his family and come to the United States. It hasn't been easy and there have been many challenges.

Ilamarques told me how the Lord ministered to him several days ago when he was struggling. The Lord lifted him up.

By sharing in the Lord's lifting up Ilamarques, the Lord lifted me up. And I realized a huge resource the Lord has provided to help us through our humanity is fellowship with brothers and sisters in the Lord. I value that now much more than I ever have in my life. Thank you Jesus for Ilamarques and the Brazilian congregation. Give him wisdom and direction as pastor. I pray you'll continue to use New Generation to advance your Kingdom. Thank you also for my friendship with this dear brother.

Thank you Lord for today's passages. Psalm 70 reflects the cries of a person who needs you desperately: "God, please hurry to my rescue! God, come quickly to my side … But I've lost it. I'm wasted. God—quickly, quickly! Quick to my side, quick to my rescue! God, don't lose a minute" (Psalm 70:1, 5). This is the Old Testament passage I read today.

The New Testament passage in Matthew 27 ends with this statement in verse 66: "So they went out and secured the tomb, sealing the stone and posting guards." Praise God! Jesus actually, physically died! And they tried to bottle him up in the grave. They remembered he had said he would come back from the dead, and they tried to keep that from happening!

Lord, thank you today for my humanity with all its emotions. Thank you that you and my Christian brothers and sisters can not only handle my emotions, but also walk with me through them. I praise you for the family of God and fellowship. But I also thank you that you always have the last and final and decisive word, and thank you today that through your bodily death and bodily burial you bodily came back from the grave! Yahoo! Amen.

September 30. Human emotions

Throughout the day yesterday I continued to think about human emotions. According to dictionary.com, the derivation of the word is "apparently < Middle French *esmotion,* derived on the model of *movoir: motion,* from *esmovoir* to set in motion, move the feelings." Interesting. Emotions move us.

Boy, is that ever true! They're a huge part, the biggest part of our daily motivation. Emotion shows me I'm alive!

So Lord, thank you for the wonderfully complex mixture of emotions that move us outward each and every day. They're an amazing gift from you.

Yesterday I realized the foundational step in dealing with emotion is praise. Instead of fighting what I consider to be *bad* emotions, I need to choose to thank God for each and every one. The psalms I've been reading remind me that in all of life's ups and downs I can pray those to the Lord, who knows better than anyone how I'm feeling (after all, He made me!).

As I approach chemo treatment number two tomorrow, I'm dealing with fear once again, but here's the strange thing about it. I'm now less apprehensive about the chemo treatment itself than about what's going to happen after I've completed all six of the chemo treatments!

This is typical for me. Fear always gravitates to the next unknown. I was afraid of what was going to happen before my first treatment, but now that I've had one, instead of fearing number two, my fear gravitates to something even further down the road.

So yesterday I just started thanking the Lord for all of this: for the fear, for the chemo treatments (each one), for helping me through the first cycle, for giving me the grace to get this far, and for everything I could think of about this process. And here's how the Lord worked with me.

First, He brought to mind something I heard from both Barbara in the finance office and Duane, a good friend and leader from church. It was the fact that occasionally patients don't need as many treatments because the chemo eliminates the cancer.

I saw Duane on Tuesday when he and his co-worker Eddie were doing some electrical work on my townhouse property. He waved when I drove up and we chatted for a moment. Then he asked how I was doing and asked whether they were going to check me during the chemo.

I told him the plan was to have a CAT scan after the first two treatments to see how the treatment was going, and hopefully see the cancer had diminished. And Duane finished my statement, "Or it's gone."

Yeah, right.

So I don't have to fear what happens after number six because the Lord may heal me before I even get there! Right!! Amen!

The Lord brought these comments to mind along with Cindy's. She's always been huge encourager for me just like her folks, Bill and Helen. Cindy reminded me of Jesus in the Garden of Gethsemane. He knew what was ahead of him and yet, because he was fully human in addition to being fully God, he struggled as he submitted to the will of God.

Jesus has been there, done that, just like me.

Taking the emotion of fear to the Lord in praise and thanksgiving has taught me a lot. Unchecked, the emotion of fear moves me out, for sure, but not to a good place. It truncates life, making me self-absorbed and causing me to miss what He's trying to show me.

But prayer with fear moves me out to God. Going to Him opens me up to the benefits of fellowship with brothers and sisters in Jesus.

Therefore, the process is: going to the Lord in praise and thanksgiving, sharing in fellowship with brothers and sisters in Jesus (this always lightens the load), and number three: turning it all over to Jesus in total dependence on him.

This is what Psalm 71 is all about. There's an amazing statement in verses 20 and 21: "You, who made me stare trouble in the face, turn me around; now let me look life in the face. I've been to the bottom; bring me up, streaming with honors; turn to me; be tender to me." The psalmist is under attack by numerous enemies who taunt him and challenge his trust in God, but he turns to God and thanks Him for His faithful help even from birth (verse 6). He goes on to affirm the Lord will care for him even when he's old (verses 9 and 18).

Turning things over to Jesus provides a powerful release of emotion and brings to mind that famous verse in 1 Peter, "Cast all your anxiety on him because he cares for you" (1 Peter 5:7). But it doesn't stop there, as Psalm 71 reminds me today.

The fourth step in this whole thing is the commitment to testify and tell others what the Lord has done. "All day long I'm chanting about you and your righteous ways, while those who tried to do me in slink off looking ashamed" (verse 24).

In other words, what I'm learning by way of cancer is the Lord wants to do more than just help me deal with trouble and the emotions that accompany it. He's teaching me how to live—how to look life in the face no matter what *and* proclaim the goodness of the Lord!

Lord, I praise you for your awesome work of creation. Thank you for making us with emotions that are divinely intended to move us out of ourselves and toward you. Thank you again for cancer and all you're teaching me through it. Lord, I gladly anticipate all you're doing in my life. If you choose to heal me before I have all six chemo treatments, great! If not, it will still be great because you've taken care of me from the moment of my birth and I have no reason to doubt that will continue for as long as you choose to keep me alive.

Thank you for fellowship. Thank you for the grace you're giving me when I turn things over to you, and I do that with chemo again today. I give it to you. And Lord, like the psalmist, I commit today to broadcast your faithfulness to the world and I will not shut up no matter what. You're awesome! Amen.

October 1. Chemo number two: cocoon

If the Lord wills, when I finish today, I'll be one third of the way through treatments. Hooray!

And again, I have to say I have a total peace that began yesterday. The flotation prayers are at work as the Lord's upward acting force is making me positively buoyant. Here's another term I came across in my study of buoyancy (now one of my favorite concepts): objects that float are positively buoyant; objects that sink are *negatively buoyant.*

Negative buoyancy is *not* Christian! And it has nothing to do with positive thinking. It's because the Lord has created us and *recreated* us by His grace to be recipients of His upward acting forces. I'm *in the loop* of answered prayer because I know the King of Kings and Lord of Lords.

Today I'm realizing the Lord's care is even broader than buoyancy. His sustenance and protection are on the "sides" of my life and over my head also. In my flotation life, I'm in a cocoon!

Cocoons have always fascinated me, ever since my sixth grade science class with Mr McKenna. I see them all the time when I walk the trail near the school (as I do walk in all seasons, not just since being diagnosed with cancer). I see cocoons in the foliage along the trail, and sometimes right on the path, having fallen off a tree. When you touch them, they're soft, but they're tough! They come in various forms for different kinds of critters, but they're a protected container where metamorphosis can occur. That larva has a place to grow. If you think about it, a cocoon is a public womb for a bug!

Let me see if I can put this together. Right now today, I'm in a floating cocoon! (When I woke up this morning, the verse we recited over and over at Irene's funeral came to mind: *"This* is the day the Lord has made; let us rejoice and be glad in it"—Psalm 118:24.)

Call me Bubble Boy!

I'm supported by the prayers of God's people, and today God is also surrounding me with His protection and shielding me with His love so I'm in a cozy (well, not always cozy, but definitely protected) place for metamorphosis to occur. God is right now today making radical changes in me.

This reminds me of what Paul says in Romans: "Therefore, I urge you, brothers, in view of God's mercy, to offer your bodies as living sacrifices, holy and pleasing to God—this is your spiritual act of worship. Do not conform any longer to the pattern of this world, but be transformed by the renewing of your mind [spiritual metamorphosis]. Then you will be able to test and approve what God's will is—his good, pleasing and perfect will" (Romans 12:1–2, NIV).

This is all because I know the King about whom Psalm 72:15 says, "And live! Oh, let him live! Deck him out in Sheba gold. Offer prayers unceasing to him, bless him from morning to night." Amen.

And of all days and times (coincidence? Not!), today I read the Easter passage in Matthew 28. Here's what Jesus said to the women at the grave in verse 5:"There is nothing to fear here." The guards were petrified when they saw the angels, but for the women, for God's people at the empty tomb, *nothing* to fear! And again I say, *amen.*

Lord, thank you for *this day,* this *Easter* day. *This* is the day you have made. I rejoice in it! Thank you for being a King to whom I can offer prayers unceasing, day and night. Thank you for answering the prayers of your people today and allowing me to feel them right now.

Thank you for allowing cancer into my life to expand greatly my intimate knowledge of your comprehensive care for me. Thank you for the cocoon you put me in that's as strong as Fort Knox. Thank you for an occasion and opportunity called *cancer* to be changed from the inside out. It's my cocoon and I embrace the bubble!

Change me today from the worm I know I am (and you know better than I do) into a butterfly that soars like you do.

I'm totally available to you today to live out your will, even in—especially in—the cancer room. To God be the glory! Amen.

October 2. Two down four to go!

I'm one third of the way finished. Now all those fractions Miss Canon taught us in fourth grade math have meaning! I've figured them out: one-sixth, one-third, one-half, two-thirds, five-sixths, *done.*

Or how about this? Dr Jotte talked with us briefly before the treatment yesterday. When I asked him when they were going to do a CAT scan, he said he planned to do it after the third treatment, to check my progress. So how about this progression: one-sixth, one-third, one-half, *done!* I'd take that—whatever the Lord wants; however He wants to handle it.

Yesterday went very well even though I was knocked for a loop again. I had a new nurse named Karen administering the treatments. I could tell she was really concerned watching Mother and Marilyn guide me to the bathroom with my movable catheter. I was very wobbly and my speech was slurred. One drug they give me in chemotherapy is benadryl; it always seems to hit me hard. I can barely stay awake.

Before I was totally out, I looked up and saw Roger and Betty again (Roger gave me the *Expect a Miracle* card). As I mentioned before, Roger has finished his chemo treatments but he and his wife just stopped by to say hi to the nurses.

They recognized us when they saw us, and chatted for a few minutes. I thanked Roger for the card and told him how much I appreciated it, then I asked him about his illness. He said he has cancer in his leg. He came in for four hours of chemo for four days in a row with a two-week break between treatments. I don't remember how many cycles he had, but he told me the next step for him is radiation.

We laughed when he said besides losing his hair, he experiences watery eyes. It looks like he's crying all the time. Betty laughed, "We feel like we have to tell people our dog just died or something!" It was great to see them both, and again, another indication of God's care of the *Floating Cocoon Man*—me.

It was very busy in the cancer room yesterday—many folks coming and going, some just getting a shot, some staying longer.

One woman had several visitors and I could see one of the nurses was visibly bothered. He eventually asked them to step out because they obstructed his access to the corner of the room to help his patient and another man in that area.

What I've described might make it sound like I was taking in a lot, but frankly I was out most of the time. My family woke me to tell me they were going to get some lunch. I roused myself when they returned, ate a little, and then dropped off again. Things went faster this time because I appear to be tolerating the medicine well. After Karen gave me a flu shot, they let us go.

I spent the rest of the day knocked for a loop, but all in all, it went well. I anticipate feeling a little worse after I get my $8,000 shot this morning to raise my white blood cell count. Remember when I said one chemo treatment costs $22,688? Well, $8,000 of it is the shot I'm going to take this morning. Yep.

But this whole experience of chemo number two confirms that Jesus has things well in hand.

I want to go back to what I said yesterday about the cocoon. The final verses of Matthew 27 tell the story of Jesus' burial. Joseph of Arimathea took the body of the Lord to a new tomb and they rolled a huge stone in front of the entrance. In addition, the high priests and Pharisees arranged to post guards so no one could steal the body and claim Jesus had come back from the dead.

They tried to keep him in the grave, but his tomb was a cocoon! Jesus experienced *metamorphosis* in that he came back to life bodily, but it was a different body. However he or the angels dealt with the stone—it was nothing to them—he walked out of the grave alive.

I was struck by these statements about the resurrection story in Matthew 28. The angels told the women who found the empty tomb and the petrified guards (in my imagination I've pictured them being so afraid they froze dead in their tracks and looked like stone men), "There is nothing to fear here." For the stone men it was very frightening, but not for the believers. There's nothing to fear about the work of God, even though our minds can't comprehend it. I'm sure the women were bewildered. "You mean, the stone is rolled away and these angels are here. What is going on?"

The next statement is even more glorious. The angel said, "He is not here. He was raised, just as he said. Come and look at the place where he was placed." *Wow.* Nothing to fear here because he's not here. Jesus was no longer in the grave. He was/is alive!

After this news, the women received one final instruction: "Now, get on your way quickly and tell his disciples, 'He is risen from the dead. He is going on ahead of you to Galilee. You will see him there.' That's the message."

Nothing to fear *here* because he's not *here* (in the grave). He's ahead of you in Galilee. Meet him *there.*

I love this. God broke Jesus out of the cocoon and moved him. As I've already said, Jesus had a new body that wasn't limited by time and space. And here's the key: he was ahead of the disciples. He always is.

This whole process is being replayed in my life by means of cancer. Paul describes it extremely well in 2 Corinthians 4: "We are hard pressed on every side, but not crushed; perplexed, but not in despair; persecuted, but not abandoned; struck down, but not destroyed [or as Charles B. Williams puts it in *The New Testament in the Language of the People*, and *I love this*—'always getting a knock down, but never a knock out'!]. We always carry around in our body the death of Jesus, so the life of Jesus may also be revealed in our body. For we who are alive are always being given over to death for Jesus' sake, so his life may be revealed in our mortal body" (verses 8–11).

In identification with Jesus, the whole cancer cocoon is God's workshop to bring me to the end of myself so His life is evident in me, whether I'm healed of cancer after three treatments or six or *not.* But Jesus is in charge of life and death, and he's also in charge of time and space—bet on it. Believe it. He's ahead of the game.

Matthew's gospel doesn't tell the story of the women actually seeing the resurrected Christ. It tells of the empty tomb and Jesus down the road.

This is the whole picture the psalmist comes to realize in Psalm 73. At the beginning of the psalm he's overwhelmed by the fact that the wicked seem to prosper at every turn. And for him: "I've been stupid to play by the rules; what has it gotten me? A long run of bad luck, that's what—a slap in the face every time I walk out the door" (verses 13–14). I've followed you and I have cancer. What's up with that?

But everything changes when the psalmist comes to the sanctuary and sees things from an eternal perspective. As far as the wicked are concerned: "There's nothing to them. And there never was" (verse 20). But as for me: "You wisely and tenderly lead me, and then you bless me. You're all I want in heaven! You're all I want on earth! ... But I'm in the very presence of God—oh, how refreshing it is! I've made the Lord God my home. God, I'm telling the world what you do" (verses 24–25, 28).

Thank you Jesus for helping me through yesterday. Thank you for the floating cocoon. Thank you for the process of continually handing me over to death so the metamorphosis, the life of Jesus, may be evident. I don't understand what this means or where it's headed, but I'm glad you do and I rejoice that I'll never go anywhere throughout this process where you haven't already gone.

Thank you for allowing me to see Roger and Betty again. Thank you for Karen and the other nurses. I pray for all the other folks in that room who were getting chemo yesterday.

Thank you for everyone who's praying for me. Your upward acting force below, your cocoon above and around—your very presence—is with me. I, Bubble Boy, love you and praise you and choose to follow you wherever you lead me. Amen.

October 5. Sometimes ignorance is bliss

After another tough day and a long sleepless night, I'm not sure how coherent this will be today, but I'm determined to write something. I was trying to get the right mix of medicine from everything the doctors gave me, and I guess I was off because it affected me negatively, especially last night and right now.

I've heard this from other folks going through chemo. It's a learning process as you try to figure out what you can do, what you can eat, and what you can take. Someone told me when you figure it all out, you're done. Great.

This is one of the main reasons why *now* I don't want to talk to any other people who are in the same boat as me with lymphoma. At first I really wanted to, just to get a feel for what I'd be dealing with. Now I don't. I'm learning the value of ignorance! There are some things I just don't want to know in advance. If I have to deal with them, so be it.

But the other major thing is everyone is different and responds to things very differently. The past couple days and last night are a case in point. One of the medicines the doctors gave me caused a weird reaction. I really didn't feel well.

In spite of this, I'm just thankful the Lord is equipping me daily in Christ for the hard task this is turning out to be; the *tough stuff,* as my friend Jon calls it. I certainly don't have the wherewithal to pull it off, but once again, Bo Baker's words are a great reminder and segue into the truths of God's Word.

Chapter three of *Made for the Mountains* has the same title. "Every genuine believer of Christ has his mountain to climb. A world of adventure awaits those who will dare to do the will of God and seek out his place on the Master's Matterhorn."[4] Boy is that ever true, and it brings two passages and a story to mind.

"The Sovereign Lord is my strength; he makes my feet like the feet of a deer, he enables me to go on the heights" (Habakkuk 3:19, NIV). Curiously enough, I discovered this statement also appears in Psalm 18:33 and 2 Samuel 22:34. Both of these passages elaborate on the verse from Habakkuk. They talk about God arming me with strength, enabling me to stand on the heights (not just go there), training my hands for battle, and giving me the shield for victory (Psalm 18:32–35). It's a very comprehensive equipping for the mountain He's called me to climb.

Sometimes Jesus just removes it. "I tell you the truth, if anyone says to this mountain, 'Go, throw yourself into the sea,' and does not doubt in his heart but believes that what he says will happen, it will be done for him" (Mark 11:23).

This actually happened to me in a sense. Thirty-two years ago I went on a backpacking trip in western Colorado with my pastor Andy and several other hearty souls, on a Royal Ambassador Adventure

Training trip. The purpose was to learn how to take boys on a long hike in the mountains.

Runoff from the snowmelt had been rather severe that spring, and about the fourth day we realized our trail was washed out. So the only solution was to climb up the mountain and look for another route on top. Our guide Steve picked Howard and me to be the scouts, but just as we were about to head out, the strap on my pack broke. So he chose Andy instead.

When Andy got back from the scouting trip, he walked over and looked me in the eye and said, "You'll never know what the Lord saved you from because of that broken strap. I thought I was going to die more than once on the scouting trip." I really didn't have any response for Andy, but I praised God under my breath. In a very real sense, He removed the mountain for me.

We still had to climb up the mountain to get out of there, but God had protected me.

But here's the point: no matter what the Lord asks you to do, He'll equip you to do it. He'll enable you to have feet like a deer or "a good hard rear end."

Excuse the expression, but that's what Dr Brooks told a group of Ph.D. students who were preparing for seminars. When someone in our research and teaching seminar asked, "What's the main thing you need to be a good Ph.D. student?" Dr Brooks' answer was: "a good hard rear end. It isn't about being smart. It's about sticking with it and working hard." Oh, okay.

So whether I need the feet of a deer or a good hard rear end, God is providing it. Over the course of my life and studies I have needed both, and this is one of those times. Lord, give my rear end strength to sit or lie on this couch as long as you want me to and give me the feet of deer to overcome the mountain of Satanic attack, so that today you will emerge victorious once again as the One who lives in me, because as I sit here most of the time alone, it's all about you. You're the "one who watches our every move. Nobody gets by with anything, no one plays fast and loose with him" (Psalm 75:11b–12).

Having finished Matthew in my New Testament reading, I go back and pick up where I left off in the Old Testament and coincidentally enough, it's the book of Ezra—another mountain story. "Who among you belongs to this people? God be with you! Go to Jerusalem which is in Judah and build the temple of God, the God of Israel, Jerusalem's God" (Ezra 1:3). God gave the word to the Babylonian captives to cross the mountains and finally to go back home—an exciting but scary prospect, I'm sure.

Every mountain adventure is. So is cancer. This fourteener He's calling me to climb is formidable.

But I rest today in the assurance that the climb is God-authorized, God-equipped, and God-whipped. Like Howard and Andy, Jesus has already scouted the way to show me the best course up and out.

Lord, thank you for infusing me with strength. Wow! I feel better right now. But for whatever challenge this day holds, whether it's a foot challenge or a rear end challenge, may the life of the One in me and in whom I live rise to the challenge again. Every mountain with you is a molehill—eventually, ultimately, finally. Win another one even through and especially through me today. I love you Jesus. Amen.

October 7. "The work of God on hold!"

What a headline, huh? What a tragedy also, but not for long!

First I say praise God for a good night's sleep last night. After not sleeping well for the past three nights and not *at all* the night before, it was beginning to wear on me psychologically. Yesterday I spent a lot of time worrying about some type of mental block—I've had them before—where I've literally gone days without sleeping. Insomnia can be that way.

But thanks be to God! I want to thank everyone who's praying for me. I received several email messages yesterday, all of which talked about my sleep issue and assured me of prayer.

It was a huge encouragement because I still felt lousy yesterday. Not only was I exhausted, but also I just didn't feel like eating much of anything. Marilyn cooked me a very basic dinner of rice and chicken with soup and a spinach salad. It was perfect, and it seemed to help me on my way yesterday.

I know I keep saying this, but these past few days have been really strange; it feels like I've been in prison. I don't want to be overly dramatic (preachers don't do that, do they?). I know my experience, especially the past few days, doesn't come anywhere near actually being in a jail. But again, I'm just being honest.

Maybe it felt that way because I wasn't up to doing anything. I hardly moved off the couch, and I was getting to the point where I wasn't sure I ever would. I guess you could say the gravity of the couch was pulling me down.

So because the day had a *prison* feel, I decided to watch one of my favorite movies ever, "Shawshank Redemption." Now before I talk about this movie, I want to be careful. As a believer, referring to movies these days is a dicey business. I'm not recommending it; the language is bad and it's not a movie for children. But the message is very powerful. In fact, I talked about a scene from the movie during a sermon a few years ago.

It's the story of a man named Andy Dufresne who was falsely accused of a crime and sent to prison, but refused to become an "institutional man." Andy's friend and fellow inmate Red explained his view of being institutionalized to a group of men in the prison yard this way: "These walls are funny. First you hate 'em. Then you get used to 'em. Enough time passes, you get so you depend on 'em. That's institutionalized."

All of this hit me yesterday. I'm now seeing how it's so easy to just give in to an illness or disease like cancer. At first you hate the sick couch. Then you get used to it. Then you depend on it. The walls of a prison. The gravity of the couch. Same song, different verse.

This is the battle.

But I'm just so grateful for the fact that the gates of hell cannot prevail against one of God's children. I'm thankful for the "upward [gravity-reversing] calling of God in Christ" (Philippians 3:14; I still love that KJV phrase).

Yesterday I received an email from a guy I haven't heard from in years. His name is Owen. He and his family were members at

Calvary of Englewood when my family and I belonged there in the late 1970s. They were very prominent and active encouragers in the church, and Marilyn and I hung around with their kids. We still see them on occasion here and there. Everyone in the family—from Owen and his wife Ruth Ann on down—has a great sense of humor.

Anyway, Owen emailed me yesterday. A few years ago he contracted non-Hodgkin's lymphoma, just like me. He received treatment for several months, went on maintenance for a couple years, and now is fine. He added, "My oncologist, Dr Jotte with Rocky Mountain Cancer Center, is great." How about that? Same type of cancer. Same doctor. Doing great! I praise God for that message yesterday.

It actually lifted me off the couch—hooray! Andy Dufresne lives! I refuse to become an institutional man, even if I have to go through days of not feeling well.

I refuse to let the work of God be put on hold. Ezra 4 is an interesting chapter. The refugees returning from Babylon began the work of rebuilding the temple in Jerusalem but "old enemies" tried to stop them, first by joining them. That didn't work. (If you can't join 'em, beat 'em through propaganda for fifteen years.) *That* didn't work, so they wrote the king of Persia, Artaxerxes, to ask *him* to tell them to stop, and he did.

I'm reading this story this morning and it dawned on me the enemy wants this—to put God's work on hold. That's what he wants to do in my life, even through cancer. He wants to get me down. He wants to *institutionalize* me. He wants to stop my testimony.

I say *no*.

And I'm grateful today for the power to continue. Psalm 78 reminds me of this power. This psalm chronicles the tragic history of Israel in the wilderness and beyond. Having seen the awesome miracle of the Exodus and the amazing provision of God in the wilderness, the people still rebelled and failed over and over and over. They tried God's patience and mercy for decades.

But the Lord didn't wipe them out. He forgave them and even fought on behalf of His people.

Toward the end of the psalm, the narrative takes a new turn. After describing this history of total failure, verse 67 reads, "He disqualified Joseph as leader, told Ephraim he didn't have what it takes, and chose the tribe of Judah instead ... Then he chose David, his servant, handpicked him from his work in the sheep pens. One day he was caring for the ewes and their lambs, the next day God had him shepherding Jacob, his people Israel, his prize possession. His good heart made him a good shepherd; he guided the people wisely and well" (Psalm 78:67–68, 70–72).

Plan *B* was really Plan *A* all along. I can't accomplish anything, especially reversing gravity, but He can. And He *did*.

Lord, my heart is so full of gratitude today. Thank you for answering the prayers of all who prayed I would have a good night's sleep. Thank you for allowing me to sleep. Thank you for all the ways you're encouraging me by means of this cancer experience. Thank you for healing Owen. Thank you for using people and movies and notes and email messages and books to jolt me out of institutionalism.

Thank you for the descendant of David, Jesus the Son of God, who came to free us from the downward cycle of sin and death and through the Resurrection, extend the upward calling of God in Christ. Hooray! I say *yes* to that call today. Amen.

October 8. Always on time

I continue to be amazed at the way the Lord speaks and the timing of His speaking through His Word, just when I need it, just when things are kind of getting me down. That's an indictment of my unbelief, for sure. Circumstances tend to influence my faith in God when I let them.

But the Word of God is incredibly pertinent and relevant, more so than the newspaper. Who would have guessed in the counsel of God in eternity, He would have designed a set of circumstances that one, called me to get cancer almost thirty-eight years to the day after my dad died of cancer; two, had technology advance to the point where blogs were possible; and, three, led me to the book of Ezra in my quiet time.

If someone had asked me a few months ago, "I know this guy that got lymphoma. What book of the Bible would you recommend he read to help him deal with his illness?" *Ezra.* Yeah, right! Are you kidding me?

I haven't spent enough time in this book over the years, but I guarantee you, I will now.

In yesterday's episode in chapter 4 of Ezra it says, "That put a stop to the work on the Temple of God in Jerusalem. Nothing more was done until the second year of the reign of Darius king of Persia" (Ezra 4:24). If the book ended there, it would really be discouraging, but we know God and we know it doesn't end there.

I was anxious to get to chapter 5 this morning to find out what happened next, and here's how it starts, "Meanwhile the prophets Haggai and Zechariah son of Iddo were preaching to the Jews in Judah and Jerusalem in the authority of the God of Israel who ruled them" (verse 1). So in essence, even though construction on the temple had ceased (temporarily), the work of God wasn't stopped!

How many tinhorn leaders throughout the centuries have tried to stop the work of God? I'm reminded of Jehoiakim in Jeremiah 36, who cut up the scroll and threw it into the fire on a cold winter's night after his assistant Jehudi read a few lines (Jeremiah 36:23). Did that stop God?

Here's Artaxerxes, king of Persia, telling the returning exiles, "Stop! I order all rebuilding work to stop" (Ezra 4:21). And they did, but Haggai and Zechariah didn't stop preaching. They were under a greater authority—God. And so they obeyed Him.

This reminds me of a statement Paul made in 2 Timothy 2:8–9: "This is my gospel, for which I am suffering even to the point of being chained like a criminal. But God's word is not chained" (NIV).

So Haggai and Zechariah continued to preach, and verse 2 says the leaders of the exiles began to work on rebuilding the temple again. Well, the Persian officials found out about it and challenged them. "Who authorized you to rebuild this temple and restore this structure?" (verse 3). It must have been rather intimidating.

"But the eye of their God was watching over the elders of the Jews, and they were not stopped until a report could go to Darius [the successor to Artaxerxes] and his written reply could be received" (verse 5). All God needs is a little opening!

They sent a letter of appeal to Darius, saying, "We are the servants of the God of heaven and earth, and we are rebuilding the temple that was built many years ago, one that a great king of Israel built and finished" (verse 11). In other words, they affirmed that the Lord was leading them to rebuild it. They went on to ask Darius to find the original decree of Cyrus who released the exiles and sent them back to the land of Israel and told them to rebuild the temple. That's how chapter 5 ends.

All of that to say, no matter what my situation is, even if I'm lying on my back dealing with the side effects of chemo, doing nothing but lying there, the work of God is *never* stopped. Jesus is building his church and it's on the move even to the gates of hell. Not even those gates can stop God's *tank* called the Church.

No circumstance, no decree, no cancer, and no weakness—nothing can stop God and His Word. And I'm not going to stop sharing what the Lord is teaching me. *Ever.*

I was so encouraged yesterday to receive an email from my seminary buddy Phil who's serving as a missionary overseas. He reminded me that he, his wife Nancy, and folks in South Asia are praying for me. He wrote to let me know he was thinking of me, and said, "Hang in there and again know you are being lifted up regularly."

The tank rolls on!

All this is reflected in the cries of vengeance and vindication in Psalm 79. Here are the last three verses: "Give groaning prisoners a hearing; pardon those on death row from their doom—you can do it! Give our jeering neighbors what they've got coming to them; let their God taunts boomerang and knock them flat. Then we, your people, the ones you love and care for, will thank you over and over and over. We'll tell everyone we meet how wonderful you are, how praiseworthy you are!" (Psalm 79:11–13).

Father, thank you today for allowing me to be part of your tank crew. Thank you that nothing can stop you and nothing can chain your Word.

Thank you for taking care of my mother when she fell today. Thank you for working even by means of cancer to spread your Word through me. Thank you for people all over—in Northglenn, Thornton, Denver, South Asia, and Istanbul, Turkey—who are praying for me.

Lord, I'm not an Alabama fan, but *roll, God, roll*. Amen.

October 9. I flunked second grade!

My parents switched me to a different school when I started my third grade year. They realized I was struggling—I could barely read—and they knew a change needed to be made.

They tested me at the new school and determined it would be best for me to repeat second grade. I realize now *repeat* is a genteel way of saying flunk. But it was merited. I knew it even back then. I certainly wasn't the brightest crayon in the box.

As a part of the testing process, Mrs Glasscock, who was the principal of the new elementary school told my mother I was going to be a scholar. Well, nobody in any school I'd ever attended had put the two words *John* and *scholar* in the same sentence.

But something happened to me from the very first day I walked into that new school to repeat second grade. I started to study and learn and wanted to learn more. I became what my parents and Mrs Glasscock said I would become.

Don't get me wrong! I didn't turn into Albert Einstein or anything, but the change of environment coupled with folks who actually believed in me made all the difference for me. In fact, as I progressed into junior high in that same school, I even moved into accelerated classes. My point is everything changed radically for me because I flunked second grade, and my life was never the same.

In a very real way, that's what cancer is for me. I've flunked my previous life and I'm in a brand new school in accelerated classes.

Stick with me in this comparison. I know I didn't fail a class to get cancer, but I'm using the word *flunk* to refer to two things. First, flunking makes you do something out of the ordinary—repeat a grade instead of going on to the next one like all the rest of the so-called normal kids. Second, in the realm of *feelings* and *thoughts*, it's hard to deal with a perception that somehow, if I'd done something different or responded in some other way, I wouldn't have cancer now. This is called *grief.*

So in those two senses, I feel like I've flunked and now I'm in a different environment in an accelerated learning setting. Boy, is that an understatement! *Accelerated*—in the parlance of the school I attended and on a practical level—meant more class work, speeded up, along with more homework, for sure. That's certainly how I feel these days, and it's part of the reason I'm writing in this journal every day. I'm trying to keep up with my class work and homework, and I have a ton of it!

I want to go into more detail about these two views of flunking as they relate to cancer. One of the weird things about this illness is it makes you feel more and more like an outsider to the human race. When I walk each day, I see the mad rush of automobiles as folks speed off to work. I see folks running or cycling feverishly, trying to get their workout in before they hurry off to the next activity, and honestly, I feel so distant from all that.

One of the main reasons is when you get cancer and start thinking about life and death, all that feverish activity seems so meaningless and pointless. I'm not talking about work being meaningless. I'm referring to the rush and frantic pace of human life in our culture. I'm outside of that now, and frankly, the leisure of my life now, though radically different, is putting me in a position to hear from God and to learn again. *And I like it.* More than that, I know I can never go back to that old school again. *Ever.*

Most days, for my walk, I just walk around my mother's neighborhood. It occurs to me that even though I've lived here (not continuously) for forty-eight years, I didn't really even know this neighborhood. Forty-eight years is a long time, but I'm just now in these weeks discovering streets and parks and houses and trees I never have seen before, as I stroll at leisure with God.

They've been there all along. Kenyon Street off Hillcrest Drive has been there all this time, but I never saw it as I speeded up and down Hillcrest.

Flunking has allowed me to *see* this *new* old street!

But not only that, flunking has also introduced me to the grieving process. A church member named Alisa (who's a huge encourager in my life due to her own experiences with a close friend who had cancer) mentioned this to me the other day in an email. I'm grieving. Cancer feels as if I've flunked another grade.

Alisa's comments reminded me of Elizabeth Kubler-Ross' stages of grief (she was a CU professor who outlined these stages in her 1969 book *Death and Dying;* I learned about the book in seminary). Here are the stages of grief: denial, anger, bargaining, depression, and acceptance. Kubler-Ross contends everyone who experiences the death of a friend or loved one goes through these stages of grief.

But Alisa's comment—and I agree with her wholeheartedly because I've seen this in my experience as a pastor—reminds me everyone who faces a big trauma like cancer goes through the grieving process as well. I'm experiencing all these stages to some degree, but right now I can honestly confess I'm dealing with a lot of anger.

I really need the Lord's help and grace because it's rather all-consuming. To be more specific, I'm looking back on things that happened to me—what people did or said and how it affected me and my family—and wondering how I could have responded or reacted differently. And this process makes me angry because I wonder whether I would have been in a better position to fight off cancer if I had just handled things differently (on an emotional or physical level).

Now again, I know intellectually nothing I did gave me cancer. It happened, really, because God purposefully allowed it in my life, *period.*

But I'm just being honest when I say these feelings of grief are very real, and because of all this, I feel like I'm starting over in a new school.

And for that reason, I have a lot of hope! None of this, though difficult and potentially damaging (if I don't deal with my anger in a biblical way) is negative! Anger in and of itself is not wrong. Jesus got angry. Paul said, "In your anger do not sin: do not let the sun go down while you are still angry, and do not give the devil a foothold" (Ephesians 4:26–27). In other words, it's okay to be angry as long as you don't sin against God in it. *Wow!*

All this goes back to what I'm learning about emotions and being human. I've learned as a pastor to encourage people to grieve. Watching someone weep is very uncomfortable for me. I've actually said to folks (oh Lord, forgive me), "Don't cry. Everything is going to be okay." The fact that everything is going to be okay is one thing. That's never in doubt with the Lord, but crying is okay!!!!! I learned *never* to try to stop someone from crying just because it's uncomfortable for me.

Seeing someone deal with anger makes me want to tell them to stop being angry. *No. No. No.* That's a part of the grieving process and it's *good*. Hard, yes. Gut-wrenching at times, definitely but *good*. And so I'm going to let myself get angry.

All this points me back to the Lord again, and His marvelous care of His children. Psalm 80 does the same thing. It picks up the very prominent Old Testament theme of Israel being God's vineyard (Isaiah 5 is one of the main passages in this regard). The psalmist looks at his present situation and wonders, "Remember how you brought a young vine from Egypt, cleared out the brambles and briers and planted your very own vineyard? ... So why do you no longer protect your vine? Trespassers pick its grapes at will ... God of the angel armies, turn our way! Take a good look at what's happened and attend to this vine" (Psalm 80:8, 12, 14).

God did answer this prayer. Out of the failure of Israel and the old covenant, Jesus came to set things right, and I'm reminded today that He said, "I am the Vine, you are the branches. When you're joined with me and I with you, the relation is intimate and organic, the harvest is sure to be abundant. Separated, you can't produce a thing" (John 15:5). *I love it!*

Jesus, thank you for coming to set things right. I acknowledge to you today my feelings of alienation and anger. Thank you again for cancer, from the bottom of my heart. Thank you that in it you're allowing me to live and see life in a new learning environment. Thank you for the elementary school of grief. Thank you for allowing me to grieve, and in fact putting me in a protected place where I can do so at leisure with you. Deliver me from the mad rush of our culture. I choose never to go back to that lifestyle, even if and after you heal me. I thank you for another flunk, and I'm looking forward to all you want to teach me. I just want to stay connected to you, precious Jesus. Amen.

October 10. George Karl said it

After the preseason game against the Trail Blazers, reporters asked George Karl how it felt to return to coaching a real game after his bout with cancer. The article indicated, and rightfully so, that some doubted whether he would be back on the court this year or ever. Karl said, "Cancer is a scary competitor. There are nights you think the worst. But I think I was pretty dominant in thinking I could get through this. I've had a lot of good help, a lot of good love, and now it's time to get back to competing and enjoying the court."

Okay, there's a good point he makes and some others I disagree with. On the negative side, first of all, he sounds like Lance Armstrong in some ways. When I first found out I had cancer, I looked for a shot in the arm from someone who had had cancer and now was well. Who came to mind? Well naturally, Lance Armstrong.

So I went out and bought a couple Armstrong biographies and started to read them, but realized very quickly they weren't going to be of any help to me. Why? Because getting through cancer for Lance Armstrong was all about him and his ability to beat it. For the biographers and for Lance the approach to cancer was the same as the way he won seven Tour de France bike races—by the sheer force of his will.

George Karl's comments remind me of Lance, and I know humans can accomplish a lot through effort; there are examples all over the place. I just read today that Tony Gwynn, the famous San Diego Padres baseball player has oral cancer (ostensibly caused by chewing tobacco), and he's out front talking about his disease and recent surgery—very brave.

But honestly, even though I'm inspired by the stories of Lance Armstrong, George Karl, and Tony Gwynn, their experiences don't encourage me much because I know the only way I'm going to get through cancer is *not* by the sheer force of my will. It will be only by the power of my *very strong God* and the force of His will.

That having been said, one thing George Karl said that I agree with is, "Cancer is a scary competitor." *That's* true. But I want to be careful to frame the competition correctly. It's not a contest between cancer and me, although as I said early on in this process, I want to be careful *never* to define myself in terms of this cancer. As my brother Donnie in Louisiana stated, "I may have cancer but cancer does not have me."

That's a crucial distinction, but I personally am not the chief competitor. Nope. This is a battle between God and cancer. And I believe it's similar to the conflict between God and Satan in this regard: they're not peers or equals.

God is in charge of everything and everyone and every situation and every conflict and every disease, but He allows temptation and cancer to demonstrate His glory.

So this is a battle between God and cancer, with the outcome already in the bag. I know who will win because He already has. It reminds me of a common experience I've had when football season started and we used to have Sunday evening services at church. I realized early on I'd never be fully prepared to teach or preach on Sunday night if I allowed myself to get embroiled in watching a Bronco game on Sunday afternoon (and believe me, I do get *into* Bronco games way too much).

So I decided I'd just record the games on my Tivo DVR and watch them when I got home on Sunday nights. Good plan, right? But here's what invariably occurred. Someone would stroll into church and say, "Wow, I'm glad the Broncos pulled that game out." So, they let the cat out of the bag and I knew the outcome before I watched the game!

And sure enough, even though most of the time it's suspenseful when it comes to my beloved Broncos, they did win the game! What do you know?

But this conflict between God and cancer is exactly the same! We have to play the tape out, but the outcome of the game is already in the bag! Hooray!

This changes everything, but from a human standpoint, when you're right in the middle of it, it doesn't relieve the suspense. The question isn't *if* the Lord is going to win; the issue is *how* is He going to do it?

That's why this story in Ezra is so incredibly encouraging to me. Remember where we left things a couple days ago? The exiles sent a request back to Persia asking the government to check the archives to find out if Cyrus authorized the rebuilding of the Temple when he issued his decree.

Well sure enough, they found it, and so Darius affirmed that decree, lifted his prohibition against construction, and told the exiles to go for it. But it's significant that he also said two other things. First, he said he would pay for it—all the construction costs. Second, he provided for the worship of God.

So the people started back to work and built the Temple. Then they celebrated *big time.* "With great joy they celebrated the Feast of Unraised Bread for seven days. God had plunged them into a sea of joy; he had changed the mind of the king of Assyria to back them in rebuilding the Temple of God, the God of Israel" (Ezra 6:22).

Who won that one? From the standpoint of time and eternity, God! And sure enough, God did change the mind of Darius to authorize rebuilding *and* pay for it *and* order God's people to worship Him.

That's the way God wins—56 to 0.

So the challenge is to trust Him and not my own efforts when I don't know *how* God's going to pull it off.

Okay, *I will.*

That's what the psalmist learned the hard way, just like all of us do. "But my people didn't listen, Israel paid no attention. So I let go of the reins and told them, 'Run! Do it your own way! Oh, dear people, will you listen to me now? Israel, will you follow my map?'" (Psalm 81: 11–13). Then he says, "I'll make short work of your enemies, give your foes the back of my hand" (verse 14).

God swats enemies away like flies!

Father, thank you that you've already beaten cancer. Thank you for this battle. Thank you for the adventure of seeing how you're going to do it in my life. I affirm and declare your victory over this even before the *tape* plays out. I'm determined to listen to you and follow your map, one step at a time. I'm excited to see how you're going to give cancer a swat through me. I love you, Lord. Thanks for letting me preach today. Gotta go. I love you. Amen.

October 11. More on George Karl's quote

Today I want to continue reflecting on George Karl's comment about cancer, that it's a fierce competitor. By the way, yesterday I found out about another famous athlete who now has cancer. (I say famous because pro basketball fans in Denver who have been around for thirty-five years know the name.) Bernard, one of our deacons and a very faithful early Sunday morning prayer warrior in our church (I love him and his family) works with a guy named Roland Taylor. In his basketball days, they called him Fatty. He was a guard for the Nuggets the last time they had a good team and played in the transition years from the ABA to the NBA.

Ten years ago Fatty was diagnosed with breast cancer, but after surgery and treatment he had been cancer-free until December last year, when they found cancer in his other breast. (You don't often hear about breast cancer in *men,* but it does happen.)

Fatty goes to Bernard's daughter's church—Macedonia Baptist Church in Aurora. I'm going to give Bernard one of my Fatty Taylor basketball cards and have him sign it, and hopefully get a chance to meet him someday.

Bernard, John, and I commented on this yesterday morning before our prayer time: if you stop and think about it, there are a lot of folks dealing with cancer, a lot more than you think. I guess I'm just more sensitized to the whole thing now because I have cancer.

But going back to my comments from yesterday, I do feel inspired when I hear about athletes who have cancer because for me it reinforces the whole idea that this battle between God and cancer is like an athletic contest. It's not only a struggle with the disease itself on a physical level, but there are so many other factors that come into play in this *game.*

One, as I've already said, is grief. And I continue to want to learn more about this. I'm asking God to help me, and He is in rather amazing ways. Yesterday evening my mother told me she wants to clear some books out of her closet. She wondered if I'd be interested in them. My mother is a voracious reader, always has been, but especially in the early years of her faith. She bought and read a ton of books. I really had no idea until last night.

She has a veritable library in her closet—a lot of good stuff I can paw through, especially on those days when I'm confined to the couch. But I started this process last night, and by coincidence (by the way, I don't believe in coincidences, but here's what I believe: the more I pray, the more *coincidences* occur!) I found one of the classic books written on grief. I heard about it in seminary. I'm sure it's out of print now. It's a little paperback entitled *Good Grief* by Granger Westberg.

Westberg elaborates on the stages of grief. In the chapter on depression, he says, "One way to describe depression is to say it is very much like a dark day when the clouds have so blacked out the sun that everyone says, 'The sun isn't shining today.' We know the sun is shining, but it appears as if it is not."[5] What a fantastic analogy! But the apparent darkness of the days is one of the defensive linemen on the opposing team, and he is imposing!

Another player on the enemy's side—and this was very apparent in church yesterday—is the enemy's attacks. We had special prayer for one another in the area of temptation and trial. Before we prayed, I said to the congregation: "We need to take seriously the fact that as believers we're organically connected to one another. If you have a bad day, instead of writing it off as an individual aberration, how about doing this? How about taking time to pray for some of your brothers and sisters in Christ? It's a good bet if you're having a bad day, they are too." Now, before I go further, I'm *not* saying the devil is under every rock. Bad things happen to good people sometimes for no apparent reason. Cancer fits into that category, *but* I think as believers we minimize the whole spiritual warfare aspect of our daily lives. That's what I was saying yesterday.

Before my exhortation in this regard, Lorraine did a wonderful job of singing the hymn that is the Lord's Prayer. Her solo brought to mind the teaching of Jesus to the disciples and us to pray: "lead us not into temptation, but deliver us from evil" (Matthew 6:13, NIV). I think we neglect that aspect of prayer for another to our peril. I also read Ephesians 6:18, "And pray in the Spirit on all occasions with all kinds of prayers and requests. With this in mind, be alert and always keep on praying for all the saints" (NIV). Praying for all the saints. This is the battlefield for warfare.

But that having been said, one of the linebackers for the opposition is temptation. I don't really have an explanation. Maybe it's because the enemy attacks us when we're most vulnerable and weak. Maybe it's because I spend so much time with this disease thinking, thinking, and thinking. Maybe it's because in my present circumstances, I'm not distracted with activity. Who knows?

But it's there, and I'm not ashamed to admit I need prayer in the areas of spiritual warfare, temptation, and Satanic attack. It's there, *big time.*

So grief and spiritual warfare are two opposing players in this game, but they're really marshmallows. Why? Well, I want to go back to my football and Tivo analogies from yesterday. I thought of two more things the Lord does in the battle against the enemy (or cancer, in my case) or anything else that fits in the category of opposition for one of his kids.

Here's how God would win a football game: God scores such a victory that all the *enemy* players end up on His team! Can you imagine what the score would be if a team lined up with twenty-two players and no opposition? They would score every time even on kickoffs. I really wonder what the final score would be in a game of sixty minutes with only one team of twenty-two players competing! No contest!

That's the reality of what the Lord does, and this is evident in Ezra. Not only does Darius authorize the exiles to rebuild the Temple (that's all they asked—permission), but also the king who once stood in their way came to be on the side of God's people and ultimately—get this—*paid* for the construction out of his own bank account (of course, every bank account including mine is actually God's bank account anyway) *and* provided all the animals for sacrifice so the Israelites could worship their God and pray for him!

I'm not making this up! Read it for yourself in Ezra 6! God has so much power He can make enemies—kings, grief, and even Satanic attack—into his friends. These are enemies and they're real, but they're not peers with God. He is still and always in control. Amen.

But here's the kicker: as humans viewing the game from a human perspective with all our feelings and emotions, it doesn't appear the way I've described it above. The enemy linemen are big and the other team's linebackers are breathing down my neck.

Another thing I realized about recorded games is when I watch a game and know the outcome before I watch it, I don't get worried no matter what happens! The Broncos can be way down (like yesterday), but if I know they eventually and ultimately win the game (unlike yesterday), then I don't worry!

So I'm right in the middle of things right now and it seems like the sun isn't shining. But I'm asking the Lord for the grace to keep running plays and trusting him.

This is what the psalmist did when he prayed against corrupt judges in Psalm 82. He asked the Lord to judge the judges and concluded by saying, "O God, give them their just deserts! You've got the whole world in your hands!" (verse 8).

Lord, thank you again today that there's no doubt who's going to win this game. I know because you've already won it! It is finished, as you said from the cross.

But Lord, I'm living the tape in the second quarter and it's very hard. I pray for everyone reading this today that you'll keep them from temptation and deliver them from evil. I pray that as people read these words today, you'll start an epidemic of prayer for the worldwide body of Christ to turn the tide on the enemy as you marshal more and more players from the *bad side* to the *good side.*

Thank you for lifting me up over and over and over. You're the *best quarterback ever.* Amen.

October 12. The season is changing!

As I write this today, I hear the sound of rain hitting the metal roof on the porch outside my room. It reminds me of the change of seasons. Normally I feel rather depressed as winter approaches because snow limits my walks in the morning. But this year I have a different perspective.

The changing seasons indicate time is moving on, and that's a good thing. It always has been, even before I recognized it as so. But it's a beneficial thing because it confirms to me that the chemo treatments and the medical process are moving forward and someday, if the Lord wills, I'll see the end of this phase.

Maybe sooner than later.

Yesterday I told my family that lately not a day goes by without someone alluding to the CAT scan I'll have after chemo number three and then saying something like, "and the doctors may find no cancer and you will be done right there." Yesterday, it was Betty and ER and Jackie who said it.

Okay, I'd take that. But in this regard, I feel like the man who was lowered through the roof to Jesus. The people praying for me believe in the Lord for my healing. I believe also, but sometimes I really do wrestle with unbelief. I just have to take it one day at a time.

So in the meantime I'm left with a lot of time—time for reflection, time in inactivity. I'd say today I'm discovering inactivity is also a player on the opposing team. Yes, that's right—*inactivity.* It's becoming increasingly difficult not to do something, especially with regard to the church I serve as pastor.

For the past twenty-one years, when I've seen what I perceive to be a problem or challenge the church was facing, *I did something.* You know the old expression, "Don't just stand there. Do something!" That was me—Mr. Do Something, Anything.

It's funny how the Lord is dealing with that incorrect attitude and posture in my life. He's putting me in a position where I can't do anything. (I'm not a total invalid, but I can't take the reins and do things *at church* like I used to.)

And here's how the Lord is working with me. The longer I deal with cancer, the less I *want* to approach life and ministry that way. It's weird. When I talk to pastor buddies and they share information about the three B's (buildings, budgets, and bodies; the traditional evaluators of *success* in ministry, and the reasons for my penchant for doing something, anything), I'm glad for them, but honestly, those things mean very little to me now.

Why? It isn't that I don't still want to see people saved and churches (including the one I serve) grow. It's more that I've lost energy to pursue those things. I guess what I'm saying is I think it's the wrong pursuit and leaves you (or at least me) empty and tired and discouraged.

My efforts in all areas of life but especially in church life don't produce much. Much of the time, unlike the glowing testimonies of other pastors who say things like, "well, we did this and thousands more people showed up," my experience has been, "I did this and thousands fewer people showed up!" I can't speak for other churches and their situations, God bless them, but for me it hasn't been a simple logic formula: I do this or that and success follows.

Not that way for me. Never has been. And I'm finally realizing God has been trying gently over the years (and now more firmly, as I have cancer and can't do all I used to do) to break me of this false perspective.

I'm in the same boat Jack Taylor was in years ago.

Here's another book I came across yesterday in my mother's library: Jack Taylor's book, *The Key to Triumphant Living.* In the early chapters, Taylor describes his experiences that led to a revelation. He writes, "I sought more success in *buildings, budgets, and baptisms,* too often our 'holy trinity' of success. Nothing seemed to lessen the miseries, depression, and pressures [I know this from personal experience as well; I've seen pastors who are successful as far as the three B's are concerned, but experience burnout or moral failure … now really, is that *successful* in God's eyes?] … But God was laying hold of me."[6]

I wholeheartedly affirm what Taylor said. This is part of the process that brought him to a central truth of God's Word: it isn't about me. It's about Christ in me. This changes everything.

And things they are a-changin' with me. God is breaking me. He's remolding my entire perspective and approach to life and leadership. Here's what I'm learning. Instead of "don't just stand there do something," it's "don't just stand there, get out of my way so I can *do* my thing." Gulp. Very hard lesson.

My well-intentioned activity not only doesn't produce anything (and of course results are up to Him and He sees everything), but often it gets in God's way, hindering what He wants to accomplish.

I think the greatest enemy God faces is religion, defined as man's efforts to please God.

So in that vein, here's another thought: maybe right now I'm doing the best pastoral work I've ever done because I'm out of God's way and letting Him do His thing. How about that?

Hey, I wonder how many people would buy a book on how to be a successful pastor (the caveat being successful in *God's* eyes) that only had two words on one page, "Get cancer." I wonder how many would sign up for that course. Not me!

So just how do I act if I want to stay out of God's way? There's my concern for today. I know it involves prayer. I know it involves waiting on God—certainly a polar opposite to the perspective of the Mr-Do-Anythings out there (like I was).

But here's another thing it involves. For me, it means abandoning forever the three-B model of success. I'm done with it. Now I'm prepared to accept God's perspective of success, which may be *less* of the three B's. I don't know how a church experiences less *buildings* (I'll have to ponder that one), but I certainly know how a church experiences less *budget* and *baptisms* (or *bodies*). And if that's what

God is doing as the Gardener who prunes branches in His vineyard (John 15), then it's successful!

So Lord, thank you for all you're teaching me in this accelerated-learning grade I flunked into!

This process of enemies emerging (and certainly false attitudes and perspectives fit into that category; are you kidding me?) and being defeated reflects the assertions of the psalmist in Psalm 83. He lists enemy nations. He cites examples of times and places in Old Testament history when God won. Then he concludes with a prayer for God's enemies. "Bring them to the end of their rope, and leave them there dangling, helpless. Then they'll learn your name: 'God,' the one and only High God on earth" (verses 17–18).

My reading in Ezra reinforces the same idea. In chapter 7 we finally meet Ezra, whom Artaxerxes sent to Israel. Verse 10 says, "Ezra had committed himself to studying the Revelation of God, to living it, and to teaching Israel to live its truths and ways" (Ezra 7:10). And the Lord used him.

How about that as an *activity* for someone who wants to stay out of God's way? Commit to studying the Word, living the Word, and teaching the Word. Hmmm. Pretty good, I'd say.

Lord, as the number of words in this blog *daily* reflects, thanks for everything you're teaching me. In spite of appearances, you're saying a lot and doing *a lot* right now. Thank you for what you're doing.

Keep me out of your way. Continue to show me what it means to wait on you.

Thank you for the change of seasons and how you're changing me. Amen.

October 13. I am a road!

Psalm 84 turns a rather familiar image on its head in a profound way. Let me explain. Jesus said, "I am the way, the truth, and the life. No one comes to the Father, except through me" (John 14:6). All Christians affirm Jesus is the only avenue to get to God. Another verse that affirms this is Acts 4:12: "Salvation is found in no one else, for there is no other name under heaven given to me by which we must be saved" (NIV). Amen.

We affirm that Jesus is the only road *we* can travel on to get to God.

But in Psalm 84 the psalmist makes another radical statement about roads (I'll get to it in a moment). The image hit me in the face this morning as I face another day with cancer (and by the way, feeling better and better, and I'm so grateful to the Lord for this). This is day ten after chemo, and it's definitely proving to be a turning point in the process. The oncologist told me it would, and he was so right!

I'm noticing how folks in our culture deal with having cancer. I'm referring primarily to folks who don't know the Lord, although believers fall into this trap as well. Rob commented to me on this just after I was diagnosed. Without the Lord, they make their bout with cancer all about them. They advocate for their kind of cancer (nothing wrong with this, per se). They become kind of a cult hero because they won their battle. They make their cancer experience all about them.

As Christians, if we're not careful we can fall into the same kind of trap. We can focus on ourselves and plead for the Lord to go *with us on our journey.* I'm learning this imagery and perspective are skewed, and Psalm 84 addresses it.

The psalm starts out talking about God's house and the psalmist's yearning to be there. "Always dreamed of a room in your house, where I could sing for joy to God-alive! . . . How blessed they are to live and sing there!" (verses 2 and 4).

But then the imagery makes a dramatic shift in verse 5, and here's the image that hit me today: "And how blessed all those in whom you live, whose lives become roads you travel." Huh?

God intends my life to be a road for Him!

Wow, this changes everything. First, if I know the God of the Angel Armies (as Psalm 84 calls Him), then He is to be the one who's prominent. Second, it's all about His journey in me, not my journey with Him as some invisible companion.

Whether we realize it or not, I think oftentimes when we ask God to be *with us,* we're really asking Him to go along with our plans and intentions, to bless us. I've learned the fallacy of that perspective. Who's in charge here? Who's the boss? Me?

He's not the servant. I am. It's my responsibility to go along with Him.

So back to Psalm 84; here's the truth: if I'm on the *Road to God equals Jesus,* I become a road for God.

What does this mean? Well, it's my responsibility to be a flat and smooth surface for God to travel on, even if I have cancer, no matter where He decides to go. Psalm 84 affirms this: "they [referring to God's people as roads] wind through lonesome valleys, come upon brooks, discover cool springs and pools brimming with rain. God-traveled, these roads curve up the mountain, and at the last turn—Zion! God in full view!" (verses 6–7). Again I say *wow!*

When we are God's roads, He travels on us through all kinds of terrain, but the destination is certain. For the believer, all roads lead to God! (I want to be clear here. This isn't universalism. Universalists believe all roads and all religions eventually lead to the one true God. I'm not saying that! I've heard that expression before. No, no, no. This isn't a statement about unbelievers, but an affirmation (reflected in Romans 8 also, by the way) that we as believers are going to make it. It's not universalism; it's God's sovereign plan and design to make us all look like Jesus and we'll make it. Why? Because He made it!) So I'm excited that my responsibility today is very simple.

Several years ago in our church I had the opportunity to share fellowship with a very dear brother by the name of Harvey White. I'd known Harvey and his wife Mollie from the very first days of my Christian walk at University Hills Baptist Church. The two of them went on from that church to serve a couple churches in Colorado, then when they retired, they joined the church I serve, FSBCN.

At first encounter with Harvey, you might think he was rather gruff, but the longer you know him the more you realize he had a tender heart and loved to serve Jesus. We spent a lot of time together. I remember in particular the drives we took to Glendale for a Bible study in an office building. Harvey was always there as a supporter and encourager. We spent time commiserating about issues at church on the way there and back to Northglenn.

Here's one of Harvey's main sayings: "John, it's our responsibility to be available and faithful. That's it." What great instruction for *roads*. If I understand Psalm 84 correctly, then today isn't about where I want to go and asking God to go with me. It's about me being a flat and smooth surface, with no potholes and not too many curves—to be a straight path for Jesus to travel on!

This image helps me understand the message of John the Baptist when he said to the crowds out in the wilderness, "Prepare the way of the Lord, make straight paths for him" (Matthew 3:3). John wasn't advocating for a new highway project in Israel. He was basically telling people, "You have the potential to be a road for the Messiah. Clear the path for him!"

God has designed me to function best when I'm available and faithful. When I do that, He'll travel on me.

That's what Ezra did. Again, I'm so amazed by this book. The book is named for Ezra and yet he doesn't appear on the scene until chapter 7. The reason is the book is *not* about Ezra. It's about God.

Ezra appears on the scene and the Bible says, "God's hand was on Ezra, the king gave him everything he asked for … My God was on my side and I was ready to go. And I organized all the leaders of Israel to go with me" (Ezra 7:6, 28).

So here's the deal with Ezra. God was traveling back to Israel in His plan and purpose, and He needed a road for that journey, and Ezra was it! And because Ezra was a flat smooth surface, God could use him to pool resources and people for a journey.

I mean, what kind of road would I rather travel on—one full of potholes or a long smooth surface?

Lord Jesus, thank you today that you're the only way to God. And I'm so thankful that in your sovereignty you allowed me to be saved. Thank you for saving me and my dad and my mother and my sister. Thank you also for the broader family of God—all these wonderful brothers and sisters who pray for me and wade through this blog. Thank you for each and every one of them.

I confess I know where the road is today: I have cancer. But I don't know where the road is headed tomorrow or in the short term. And I'm okay with that, because you're driving. I do know the ultimate destination of the road and I'm thankful for it. Praise your name, Author and Finisher!

Lord, be the car and let me be your road, under you, supporting you, in your journey. You don't need my support, but I need you more than ever. May the most prominent thing about me be not *cancer* but *you*. And Lord, no matter where you make this road go, I want to be a platform for you. Amen.

October 14. "Route John" through Cancerville

Still not done with Psalm 84 … you know, one of the blessings of less activity is more time for meditation. I find I'm better able to roll the Word around in my mouth like a good piece of candy (or better yet, a good sucker). My favorite sucker as a kid was a Tootsie Pop. The candy part lasts a long time and then there's the chocolate part—the best sucker ever.

Tootsie Pops always come to mind when I think about the Jewish concept of meditation. In Old Testament times, Jews believed you received the Word in your mouth. We've focused on the image of taking the Word into our hearts. True. But the Jews looked at it in a different way. I learned this a few years ago when I was studying Joshua 1:8: "Do not let this Book of the Law depart out of your mouth; meditate on it day and night, so that you may be careful to do everything written in it. Then you will be prosperous and successful." How about that?

The picture of meditation is sort of like sucking on a Tootsie Pop. It involves getting every bit of the flavor out of a passage and letting truth be absorbed in my life. I'm not sure I've honestly ever had the opportunity to do this before in my life until now. Thank you again Lord for the blessings that are accumulating because of cancer.

All of that to say this truth about me being a road for God has arrested me. For now, call me Route John through Cancerville! I've been thinking about roads and streets and highways and routes a lot since yesterday.

Do you realize how many names we have for streets in American culture? They're all crucial to us; I'm not sure we realize how crucial. But by their very nature, you don't really think about streets unless they're in bad condition!

The best kind of street or highway or route is the one you don't think about! Streets at their best are innocuous. When they're functioning in the right way (I'm speaking of them in human terms), then I'm able to drive my car and look out the window and see all the scenery.

But when a road isn't functioning well, when it has potholes and detours and road construction, it draws my attention to it and away from my surroundings. In fact, my habit is to avoid those kinds of roads completely, unless I'm four-wheeling.

If you think about it, the normal type of driving we do is difficult enough. We don't need the added headache of dealing with road issues (not to mention traffic jams). I'm trying to get to work or get to an appointment. I want my road to be as free and clear as possible. Get it?

Another thing I thought of yesterday is when someone does go on a driving vacation, you *never* hear them comment about the road itself. "I'll tell you what, I love the asphalt between here and Kansas City. It was such a beautiful shade of black with some grey. And the lines! They did such a good job of painting the lines with such a pretty shade of yellow!" You *never* hear that. You only hear about what they saw *along* the road.

For something so common and so crucial, we never focus on it (unless it's bad).

And do you realize roads make places accessible? I think I'm pretty typical in my aversion to bad roads or no roads. If a mountain town or rural community isn't accessible by a road, I'm certainly a lot less likely to go there, but if I can get there off an interstate highway in a fairly decent amount of time, then I'm more likely to go.

Roads literally create destinations and familiarity! I can tell others about places because a road allowed me to go there, and then others can go there to see it for themselves.

But here's another thing about roads. The very definition of a road is it goes *through* towns and cities and countryside. Right? We have totally different names for cement and asphalt cars drive on that doesn't go *through* a place. We call them driveways, cul-de-sacs, or (how about this word) *dead ends.*

If I see a Dead End sign on the street I'm driving on when I'm looking for the home of a family to visit, I know I'm not going to get anywhere. I have to turn around.

But when I'm lost and I'm driving down a *street* that goes *through,* I know if I keep on going, I'm going to get somewhere somehow.

Okay, had enough of *street* talk? I chewed on all this yesterday like the chocolate center of a Tootsie Pop, and it's deeply convicting.

As I talk about this, don't get me wrong. I'm as thrilled as many across the globe about the miraculous and joyous rescue of the thirty-three Chilean miners. I'm so thankful all those men got out of the mine safely, but still it's distressing to see how quickly in our culture the focus shifts away from the miracle of the rescue and on to the book deals some of the rescued miners are already being asked to sign. And I read today that even now, authorities in Chile are looking for people to blame for the accident. The last man just came up out of that mine only a few hours ago. Can't we just rejoice in the rescue for a little while?

But that's the human tendency. In our sinful nature, we want to be the center of the universe.

Those of us who are part of God's family struggle with the same temptations, and believe me, it persists when you get cancer. And we see it all the time. Michael Douglas appears on Leno or Letterman (I can't remember which one) and the fact that he now has throat cancer increases the show's ratings, I'm sure.

But if you're going to be a road, only the Lord can do that, and no one focuses on or talks about roads unless they're bad. I'm determined to be, for now, Route John through Cancerville, a good road and therefore not prominent. I believe it's a calling. Cancer needs a road, a broad six-lane highway to it and *through* it.

Why? So much about cancer is a remote and mysterious mountain town you can't get to. Just say the word *cancer* and everyone melts with fear, saying in their heart, "Well, that's it for them." I believed that! I remember saying to Mother and Marilyn after my dad died of cancer, "It doesn't matter what they do to treat it, it ends up coming back and it kills you." Okay, for some that may be the tragic truth, *but that isn't everyone.*

Or about chemo—I thought I'd be flat on my back in bed for four months vomiting and weak. That's the case for some, but again, not for me and not for everyone!

But all this presses the issue: Cancerville needs a road!

God is calling me to be a road through Cancerville! What that means is John fades into the background and becomes as insignificant as the color of asphalt, and God grows in significance as He drives through all the hamlets and villages and communities on the way to and through Cancerville. There are some scary places along the way, but they need to be exposed as places where God goes. Let me name a few: Shock of Cancer City, Biopsy Gulch, Bone Marrow Biopsy Canyon, Mount Chemo (a hilly road with deep drops and steep climbs).

The Lord needs a road through all these places for a few reasons. If he can make a road through them, then all the mystery is eliminated. Roads say *someone has been here before.* And if John Talbert, one of the whiniest wimps who ever lived, can be a road for God through there, then so can you!

But here's the most encouraging thing about roads. They aren't dead ends! They go *through.* I want to yell this from the roof of the house today: "Cancerville is not my destination; I'm going through it!" Hooray! Cancer will not be the final word; it's only the road God has made me to be now, as a platform for Him to reveal truth. It's not my final destination, *even if* the Lord chooses not to heal me and I die of cancer. (I believe in Him for a radically different outcome, but it's still in His hands ultimately.)

I'm here today to testify that because *the Way to the Father equals Jesus* saved me, he made me a road that goes through cancer and any other towns this road will pass through in the future.

And because of this, I can rejoice that Jesus is a good shelter in this life. It's interesting that after the assertions about his people being roads (Psalm 84:5), the end of the psalm goes back to talking about God's house: "One day spent in your house, this beautiful place of worship, beats thousands spent on Greek island beaches. I'd rather scrub floors in the house of my God than be honored as a guest in the palace of sin. All sunshine and sovereign is God, generous in gifts and glory. He doesn't scrimp with his traveling companions. It's smooth sailing all the way with God of the Angel Armies" (Psalm 84:10–12). This isn't some Pollyanna dream world. I can testify that even with cancer God's road is smooth sailing because being with Him and His people is the only real destination in this life. And even roads need a solid bedrock foundation, and God is it!

Father, my heart is so full of gratitude today. Thank you for making me and remaking me into a road through cancer for your glory. Shine the light on this dark city! So many are deathly afraid of it! Show people who know you and those who don't that you can go even there and conquer even cancer.

Thank you for all the places and towns and curves and hills and valleys this cancer road has gone through. Thank you for all you've taken me through up to this day, and we're still going!

Thank you for another day to show this world what you can do by means of asphalt like me. May you be prominent today, more than poor little me with cancer, God of the Angel Armies! Amen.

October 15. The illusion of "control"

Yesterday was a rather odd day. It was one of the most beautiful October days I've ever seen—bright and clear and sunny and hot—near eighty degrees. I got to spend some time with a friend. We had a good meal and shared together. I was also able to be outside for a while. What could be wrong?

Me. And here's the weird deal. I can't really figure out why, except to say it's the illusion of control. And all this came into focus for me when I read a couple articles about John Elway.

Yesterday it came out in the news that Elway and a business partner lost fifteen million dollars with a hedge fund manager who was recently arrested for running a Ponzi scheme. Not good. The article referenced another one by Rick Reilly, a famous writer for Sports Illustrated who lives here in Denver.

Reilly listed all the losses Elway has accumulated since he retired from professional football: his father died of a heart attack, most of his business ventures have failed, his wife left him, and three weeks ago his twin sister died of lung cancer. Reilly goes on to detail all these "sacks" Elway has taken, and quotes the former quarterback as saying, "When you're a quarterback, you're in control. The football's in your hand, and it's fourth-and-twelve, and if the wide out doesn't take the right route, I'm going to run around and make things happen. But now, things go wrong and I don't have the football anymore."

Wow, I can't get over that. "I don't have the football anymore." In other words, I'm not in control. My question for John Elway is: were you *ever* in control, even when you had the football?

I think all of us live under the illusion that at certain times, we control our lives. I remember this was reinforced for me after my visit with the surgeon who examined the bulge on my abdomen. It was before the biopsy, but she looked me in the eye in the examining room and said, "This doesn't look like a hernia. You could have lymphoma." Huh?

After that appointment, I called my primary care physician. When I told her what the surgeon said, my doctor said, "It sounds like lymphoma to me too, John." Then she added this little bit of advice: "Just remember, and keep this mind, 'this is out of my control; this is out of my control.'" It was like she was giving me a mantra to recite.

Words—any old words, especially mine—have no power to transform anything! Telling myself something over and over and over has no power either.

Going back to what my doctor said about a potential cancer diagnosis: "Tell yourself that you're not in control." I remember my immediate thought was, "I've always believed that!" Of course I'm not in control, and I never was!

But that statement is more easily believed in the head than lived out in life. I found that out yesterday.

Let me see if I can explain it. I really felt yesterday was going to be a good day because the weather was nice (right or wrong, good or bad—and I know it's wrong and bad—the weather has an effect on my disposition), and I seemed to be feeling better physically. I'm learning that the cycle of chemo means the first ten days are the *feeling bad or at least more fatigued* days after chemo, but days eleven (yesterday) up to the next chemo are the *feeling good to great* days.

So in my brain (and I had not realized this until yesterday), I was looking forward to feeling better and not thinking about cancer. Because I felt better, I was more *in control* of things. Honestly, I wouldn't have articulated it that way yesterday morning. But reading John Elway's comment last night made me realize I was thinking this way.

The tacit assumption is: I feel better, and therefore I'll be more in control of things!

Is that true? *No!*

What the Lord showed me yesterday is whether I feel bad or feel good, I still need Him. Maybe I need Him *more* when I feel good; because my emotions don't fluctuate as much as they seem to when I'm dealing with all the side effects of chemo, I'm not reminded to pray and depend on Him as much.

It's almost like the mindset is: whew, I feel good and it's a good day so I don't need to think about cancer and about God as much. I can just live a normal life for a day!

Wow, it pains me even to write that. But there's so much truth to it. I'm deeply convicted that when I feel well, I'm tempted to live as if I don't need the Lord as much as I do when I feel sick.

I was talking to Dan on the phone yesterday. He called to encourage me. Both of us were talking about the physical challenges we face, and in the course of the conversation I remembered someone had said to me: "I wonder why we just can't learn what God wants us to learn when things are going well." My response (as I told Dan, and he agreed wholeheartedly) is "there are some things we can never learn until we are flat-on-our-backs sick. This is the only way."

Now I'm realizing the truth of what I said.

So where does this leave me today? I feel good, better than I ever imagined, really. But here's the truth: I need God more today than I ever have. And I'm determined to depend on Him fully today, just as much as I do when I'm lying on this couch feeling sick. Amen.

It's all about learning to be sensitive to the Holy Spirit's conviction of sin. When the Lord points out error in my life, I must turn away from it, no matter how insidious it is. Shortly after Ezra arrived in Jerusalem, he found out the Israelites were intermarrying with the pagan people of the land. He wasn't doing it himself; others were, but it didn't matter. Here's his testimony: "When I heard all this, I ripped my clothes and my cape; I pulled hair from my head and out of my beard; I slumped to the ground, appalled" (Ezra 9:3). The rest of the chapter is his prayer.

Here's a man who's so sensitive to sin and compromise that He responds immediately to the Lord. Father, give me that kind of sensitivity to any move of unbelief away from you, no matter how subtle it may be. And I affirm sin is never subtle to you.

This is why the prayers of Psalm 85 are so appropriate. "You lifted the cloud of guilt from your people, you put their sins far out of sight … Help us again, God of our help; don't hold a grudge against us forever … Why not help us make a fresh start—a resurrection life? Then your people will laugh and sing!" (Psalm 85:2, 4, 6).

Lord, you have the football today and always. I've never had it and never will, no matter how good I feel. I affirm you're in control of the good times and the bad, the sick times and the well times and every time in between.

I confess I wish I didn't have cancer and want my normal life back. Lord, this is so wrong.

Thank you again for cancer. Thank you that this life has never been mine at any time. Thank you that "normal" has nothing to do with me but everything to do with you. I choose to depend on you every moment.

Make a fresh start in me today through the resurrection life of Jesus who lives in me. Re-route Route John and get me on track today. I love you and need you, "God of our help!" Amen.

October 17. The call to ministry

I remember the night very vividly—a Friday night. We were having revival services at church. The preacher's name was Allen Buchanek. He shared his testimony and at the close of the service, added this appeal, "I don't normally do this, but I just feel led to say I believe the Lord is calling someone tonight to full-time vocational service and I want to invite him or her publicly to acknowledge it." *Bam!*

That very morning the Lord had done just that in my life, and all day long I struggled with the timing of letting that cat out of the bag. Well, I couldn't keep it under my hat any longer.

I remember standing in front of the folks who were there that night at Beverly Hills Baptist Church and saying, "I need you." And I did, because at that moment, that night, I was scared to death to think the Lord wanted me for something, anything.

It's a vivid memory because that night more than any other in my Christian life up to that point, I realized how crucial the body of Christ is. My fellow believers are vital for me to follow God's call. And they're indispensable in another way. You can't really have preaching if there's no one to hear. In other words, we do need each other in the body of Christ to exercise our gifts.

But here's another thing I've learned since I got cancer: I need the body of Christ *period*.

The weird thing about cancer is the need for affirmation is continual, and the desire to talk about it *again* and *again* diminishes. There still really isn't a day that goes by where it doesn't hit me right between the eyes: "I just can't believe I have cancer, and I wonder if I'm going to die." When that question comes to mind, I have to face the reality of death.

I have to go back and think about what the oncologist has said, what fellow Christians have said, and above and beyond all that, what God has said. Here's what I call it: *rehearsing reality*. And things begin to get on track, but I cannot overstate how important a timely word is.

Yesterday it came from my mother. If you think about it, just on face value, I don't think anyone would argue with the fact that it would be very hard to have both your husband and your son have cancer. If your husband died of cancer, that makes it even harder. And I don't think anyone would fault her for grieving about all that all the time.

But that wasn't my mother even when my dad died, and she's said so. Back in August 1973, she realized she didn't have time to be a weeping widow because she had two teenage kids to rear, and she did it as a single parent.

But yesterday when we were talking about cancer again, she repeated what she's often said before: "When we found out you had cancer, I couldn't get all emotional and cry about it, because I firmly believe this is part of God's plan for your life and you are going to get well." She's said it before, but yesterday I heard it, and I needed to hear it. Not just the words, but also the life that backs them up. I've seen firsthand how the grace of God has carried my mother through some tough stuff, and how He's doing it again.

Mother's an emotional person (she's human after all), but she's demonstrated how the grace of God can help a human trust God even in extremely difficult circumstances.

And I need that, not only from my mother and sister, but also from the body of Christ. It's called *support*. This is one of the major ways I'm learning now that I need people.

The second way is *space*. Even as I write this word, I realize I could write a whole lot on this and I will later.

Space means people don't make excessive demands when you're sick. For example, my pastor friends Bart and Mike called this week just to let me know they were thinking of me and praying for me. They asked for nothing else. In fact, Bart said, "Hey, you can call me back if you want or if you don't want to, no problem." That may not seem like a big deal, but after living in a world where the expectation is always "call me back," (and I have that expectation too), this is refreshing. It's called *space*.

But here's another need the body of Christ supplies: *springs*. This is the amazing affirmation at the end of Psalm 87. The psalm is about Zion, God's city and home of born-again believers. It affirms that all sorts of people will be in Zion because they're born again, even folks from nations that have been enemies of Israel such as "Egypt and Babylon, also Philistia, even Tyre, along with Cush" (verse 4). "Those folks and more will have their names in God's book ... This one, this and this one—born again, right here" (verse 6). But here's how the psalm concludes: "Singers and dancers give credit to Zion: 'All my springs are in you!'" (Psalm 87:7).

"All my springs are in you." *Wow.* In a day and time when water wasn't as available as it is today (an understatement), this is huge. Zion, God's city with God's born-again folks living there, is completely adequate as a source for sustaining life. Of course, this looks forward to heaven, but that type of community is available on earth too—it's called fellowship.

Lord, thank you for allowing me through your grace to be born again into the Zion community. Thank you for saving my mother and sister and taking all of us through my dad's death. Thank you that we'll get to see him again in heaven someday. Thank you for the support, space, and *springs* that my family of origin and my Christian family have provided.

Thank you for the words, cards, email messages, postings on Caring Bridge, and phone calls—every single one of them.

I love you because as a result of all the springs that are in you, I can affirm that my experience has been as Jesus said, "Whoever believes in me, as the Scripture has said, streams of living water will flow from within him" (John 7:38, NIV). As the song says, "Flow river flow." Let those springs flow now and forevermore along with all the Zion citizens and the singers and dancers. Amen.

October 18. Humanity in the Bible

I love the humanity of the psalms. It helps me greatly as I go through these days and encounter people who need help.

Yesterday was a good day. I had a good prayer time before the services with John and Bernard. I'm so grateful to the Lord for these two brothers who are faithful each week to show up an hour early just to pray. It turns out to be more than that, of course.

I gave Bernard my Fatty Taylor rookie card along with a Sharpie and asked him to get Fatty's autograph. Bernard said he and several other guys have been trying for days to reach Fatty on the phone, and no one has been able to reach him. I told Bernard, "Well, he just found out he has breast cancer in his left breast and maybe he's struggling with it." Who knows? But we all prayed for Fatty again, and I'm going to continue to do so.

That's the hell of this disease: it could come back, and when it does, it always seems to be worse.

This happened to a lady in our church—Sharon. Her husband Ray is one of our deacons and Sharon has the greatest attitude ever. She's now undergoing chemo and radiation for breast cancer that has recurred. She wasn't in church yesterday because she's really hurting these days. She finished chemo treatments and is now preparing for radiation.

So Fatty and Sharon are going through tough times.

I met and talked to another individual who's going through a tough time (*not* cancer or an illness). I could see on their face that they were angry. I watched them throughout the sermon, and after the service we talked briefly at the door.

I think I'm getting better than I used to be at reading people's reactions. I could just see it in this person's face: "I'm not listening to what you have to say because I'm mad and I refuse to be comforted." Okay.

All these people—Fatty, Sharon, and the unnamed individual above—and their stories don't fit into neat and clean categories. Neither does God and neither does prayer.

Honestly, I've always chafed against the pop teaching that says, "God always answers prayer and it's one of three answers—yes, no, or wait."

How does Psalm 88 fit into one of those categories?

This is someone who describes himself as being "a black hole in oblivion" and "dropped … into a bottomless pit, sunk … into a pitch-black abyss … caught in a maze and can't find my way out" (verses 5, 6, and 8). He's lost his friends and he cries out to God, "Why, God, do you turn a deaf ear? Why do you make yourself scarce?" (verse 14).

He goes on to further accuse God, "You've attacked me fiercely from every side, raining down blows till I'm nearly dead" (verse

17). And then he concludes with this remark: "You made lover and neighbor alike dump me; the only friend I have left is Darkness" (verse 18).

There you go.

How does that fit into one of the three neat little categories of yes, no, or wait? It doesn't. This psalm starts with the "black hole in oblivion" and ends with "Darkness." And sometimes this is the exact experience of the genuine believer who's earnestly seeking the Lord in prayer.

But how does this square with what I know about God and my belief that He does answer and has answered prayer in my life?

Well, here's what I believe about Psalm 88. This is reality. Times of silence from the throne of God and times of darkness occur. It's what Psalm 23 describes as "the valley of the shadow of death" (Psalm 23:4, NIV).

But it's not death. It's not the end. It's not the final reality. The Christian life is characterized by light and life. This begins now and continues on into eternity. This is the overall picture.

But times of darkness where God gives no answer and it seems like He's not even listening do occur, and we need to affirm it.

I want to be clear: I believe God is going to heal me. And I'm so grateful for all the reminders I get from sincere people who are praying for me. Yesterday Diane said, "I'm sure that God's going to heal you." And I so appreciated that. Here's what I told her: "Diane, I believe as well, but pray for me because I'm not quite there yet."

I do believe in the Lord. And I'm firmly convinced He has me and my cancer in His hands. And He'll always take care of me, whether I'm healed of cancer today, tomorrow, or never.

You see, I think times of darkness are ordained by God. Sometimes cancer comes back, even after you've been healed. Sometimes we go through difficult times where God is silent and the neat little answers don't work. I think God allows those times to show us He's bigger than our logic and His ways are mysterious.

And here's what I'm learning about my situation and about ministering to others. First, I don't think you ever *get over* cancer. I'm talking here about the mental aspect. I've talked to folks who've had cancer and have been cancer-free for years, and they all say, "Every single time I go in for a checkup, I wonder."

It's been ten years between Fatty's first breast cancer treatment and this recurrence. Ten years!

Sharon has gone through this treatment stuff before. Why again?

There are no answers to these questions, but here's where I am with all this. I'm thankful that for the rest of my life I'll have another strong reminder to trust Him *period*. I'll never take my health for granted ever again.

And here's what this is teaching me about the angry person I encountered at church yesterday (I'm going to call him Bitter). When God allows times of darkness, my best approach as a pastor is *not* to try to get someone out of the darkness. If this is God-ordained, then He has a plan and a purpose. And who am I to think I can be one of Job's verbose friends who can talk someone out of a trial? I've tried to do this many times. Now I'm realizing how wrong it is.

I realized this yesterday. And now I'm just going to pray for this person, encourage them to trust God, and be there for them. God is in charge even of the darkness!

The other passage I read provides a wonderful balance to this. I've finished Ezra and decided to move right into Nehemiah, which tells the story of the same time period of Ezra, except from a different perspective. The first two chapters of Nehemiah are a story of God answering prayer.

Nehemiah, who was Artaxerxes' cupbearer, prayed God would allow him to leave Persia and help the exiles by rebuilding the wall of Jerusalem. God answered his prayer. The king sent him back to do just that. Why? "The generous hand of my God was with me" (Nehemiah 2:8).

Same God.

Lord, I praise you today that you defy categorization. I thank you for all the times, too many to count, when you've answered prayer. Thank you also for the times of darkness. Thank you for the times when you're silent and give no answer.

Lord, teach me to hold on to you whether I'm living in the bright light of day or the middle of the night. Help Fatty, Sharon, and Bitter to do the same, *today.*

I confess the sin of trying to explain away who you are and what you're doing with clichés and easy answers. I'll never understand you or figure out what you're doing, and it's okay.

Whatever your plan is for me, Lord, I'm going to trust you and follow you. Teach me how to walk with you, step by step, through whatever comes along this road. Whatever. Amen.

October 19. More sensitive to tragedy

Sobering, that's how I respond. One of the things I'm noticing about myself since I was diagnosed with cancer is I'm much more aware of and sensitive to sickness, disease, and tragedy.

For example, yesterday I came across an article in the Sports section of the Denver Post. Last Saturday in a college football game "Rutgers defensive tackle Eric LeGrand was paralyzed below the neck after making a tackle against Army, and he will remain hospitalized for the near future." I know Eric chose to play football and there are risks that go with that choice, but wow. Paralyzed. I just pray his paralysis is temporary and the Lord will heal him.

I heard about two other guys serving in Southern Baptist Convention churches who are dealing with physical issues. Another pastor in Colorado, Pastor Kim Bearden at Rosemont Baptist Church in Montrose, is undergoing chemo treatments. And Mike Farnham, an associate pastor at Circle Drive Baptist Church, has a terminal neurological disease, according to our state executive Mark Edlund's October 15 prayer update.

Bart called me yesterday. He's president of the pastors' conference at the state convention this week. I asked him about Mike and what *terminal* means when it comes to a neurological disease. He explained the symptoms get so bad that ultimately you die of something else (I can't remember exactly what he said Mike's prognosis was). Bart found this out in corresponding with Mike's wife.

Again I say, "Wow." I asked everyone at church join me in prayer for Eric, Kim, and Mike.

I have and am having several reactions to the news about these three guys since yesterday. First, I referred to myself as a whiner. I am one, but here's what I've learned about that. I need to be careful about whining because there are always folks who are in more difficult circumstances than me.

I don't know anything about Kim's circumstances (and neither did Bart), but the other two guys ... my heart goes out to both and my whining mouth is temporarily closed. I'm having a cakewalk compared to what those guys are going through.

I know comparing tragedies isn't a good thing to do. Each person's situation is tough and unique, but this is one of the ways the Lord sobers *me* up (I'm using the term *sober up* in the spiritual sense here, just to be clear).

Second, tragedy, in whatever form it comes, has a tendency to make you feel distant from God. Every time I've been in the hospital and sat in that chemo room, I've been very aware of the prayers of God's people. That's my strongest impression, but very close to it is the feeling that I'm on another planet. "God, how did I end up here and where are you in all this?" Of course He's never moved, but I have, and it makes me wonder. And sometimes that wonder moves toward despair.

This is the expression of Psalm 89, another one of those incredibly human cries to our God. It starts off in a rather predictable way. The psalmist praises God for His love and His uniqueness: "Search high and low, scan skies and land, you'll find nothing and no one quite like God" (verse 6). He goes on to trace how the Lord has defeated enemies, shown love to His people, chosen the family tree of David as the ancestral line for the Messiah, and been faithful to His promises: "dependable as the phases of the moon, inescapable as weather" (verse 37). Everything is good, right?

Nope.

In verse 38 an abrupt shift slaps the reader in the face. "But God, you did walk off and leave us, you lost your temper with the one you anointed. You tore up the promise you made to your servant, you stomped his crown in the mud" (verses 38–39). And the list goes on as he complains and cries out to God about "the taunting jokes of your enemies" (verse 51).

Everything the psalmist lists from verse 38 on contradicts what he enumerated about God just a few verses before. And like Psalm 88, nothing is really resolved at the end. The story doesn't tie up in a pretty little bow with everything resolved and a "happily ever after" walk into the sunset (the kind of ending we all want). The psalm just ends with, "Blessed by God forever and always! Yes. Oh, yes" (Psalm 89:52).

So what gives? Well again, I'm learning there are times and seasons in the walk of faith where we walk in darkness (Psalm 88) and/or when it seems the Lord has walked off and left us (Psalm 89), and this is part of the gig. This is normal in the life of faith.

This leads to my third reaction or response to all this. As I said yesterday, the clichés and formulas don't appeal to me and don't work anyway, because God is bigger than our flip little descriptions of Him. He defies categorization and explanation and He breaks out of our logical boxes. This is what Isaiah 55 affirms, "'For my thoughts are not your thoughts, neither are your ways my ways,' declares the Lord. 'As the heavens are higher than the earth, so are my ways higher than your ways and my thoughts than your thoughts'" (Isaiah 55:8–9, NIV).

So again, what do I do? Well, the psalm and the verses I read in Nehemiah are helping me greatly with this. I'm learning more about praising God than I ever have in my life.

Praise is most difficult when I'm walking in darkness (Psalm 88) or dealing with the feeling that He's left me (Psalm 89), but it's more necessary than ever because the truth is He hasn't left me! And He never will. Praise affirms truth about God in spite of feelings and circumstances.

It builds trust because instead of focusing on feelings and my perceptions of circumstances and my little whiny problems, I focus on the character of God, and somehow I feel encouraged and lifted deep inside. In other words, I'm learning to *praise* my way into a new way of feeling and seeing.

So a huge aspect of the praise life is refusing to listen to the taunts of the enemy. As Nehemiah led the exiles to rebuild the walls of Jerusalem, Sanballat and Tobiah mocked the builders (Nehemiah 4:1–3), and when that didn't stop the construction they gathered with other enemies to plot "together to come and fight against Jerusalem and stir up trouble against it" (verse 8).

So what did Nehemiah do? Stop the work and crawl into a hole? Pull a John Talbert? Nope. Verse 9 says, "But we prayed to our God and posted a guard day and night to meet this threat." And it isn't stated explicitly in this verse, but I'll add *and they kept on working.*

And again, I love how the Lord pulls things together in the truth of His Word. He's incredible! The books of Ezra and Nehemiah are both about what to do when the bottom falls out of your life. The psalms describe that experience. These two books show how to live through it.

Certainly when the exiles returned to their land after more than forty years under the thumb of first the Babylonians and then the Persians, they came back to a home that in many ways was nothing like what they had left. It was in moral decay (this is what Ezra addressed). It was in physical decay—the walls of the city had deteriorated (this rebuilding was the work of Nehemiah). And enemies were rampant (both men faced this challenge). It was a dark time when it seemed God had left them. Sound familiar?

But they stayed faithful to the Lord through His Word and through prayer, and they exhorted and encouraged one another to stay at the work. Nehemiah 3 describes how they started to rebuild the walls of Jerusalem. Each individual or family took a section. Some worked on the part of the wall right in front of their house. For example: "Uzziel son of Harhaiah, one of the goldsmiths, repaired the next section; and Hanahiah, one of the perfume-makers, made repairs next to that. They restored Jerusalem as far as the Broad Wall" (verse 8). This is the type of work all of us need to do!

And I'm so grateful for the folks who are busy on their part of the *wall,* but take time to pray for and encourage me.

Yesterday I mentioned Diane. She joins a host of others who, undaunted, are praying for me. And I say, "Keep it up, and I'm praying for you."

And I tell others the same thing. I got a note from my friend Pam in Oklahoma. Her family was part of FSBCN for a few years. Then the Lord moved Lou and Pam and their two children Keith and Brittany to Oklahoma, where they've lived for the past several years. We keep in touch, though.

When I was talking to Bart yesterday, he said he was going to lead the other pastors to pray for me in addition to Kim and Mike. Last night Dan Dellinger, pastor of First Southern Baptist Church of Westminster, sent me a photo of that prayer meeting. It meant so much to me that others with their challenges and work on the *wall* took time to lift me up. To all the folks in that prayer meeting, from the bottom of my heart I say, "Thank you."

God, you're amazing! I love you and thank you for all the ways you're pulling things together for me. I acknowledge today that so much about cancer makes me feel like I'm living on another planet, and I'm struggling with this daily.

I praise you because no matter how I feel, you're eminently and supremely always *there*. I bank today on your promise that you'll never leave me or forsake me (Hebrews 13:5). I refuse to listen to the constant taunts of the enemy.

I lift up Eric, Kim, and Mike. I pray you'll heal them completely, Lord.

Thank you for everyone like Diane and Pam and all the folks at the pastors' conference last night. Thank you also for the countless other friends and believers who are praying for me.

Lord, I pray that as all of us continue to work and to encourage one another, you'll build a wall of witness to your power and grace on behalf of your people as all of us, exiles in this world on the way to the next, seek to honor and glorify you. I'm picking up another brick today, Lord. Amen.

October 20. God's work, done God's way ...

I wish I'd learned this crucial lesson earlier, but it's all about the work of God, done God's way.

It's been interesting to visit with folks at church who have walked and worked with me over the past few months and years. Last Sunday as Diane was leaving, she said, "I read on your blog about all the stuff we did last summer, but you left something out. What about all the flyers we passed out in the community?" Yes, I did forget that. One more thing. Gulp.

Tired. There's the operative term, for sure. I know that place.

Yesterday I went to the office at church to get some work done. By the time I was ready to leave, I was already feeling exhausted. As I was getting ready to walk out the door, Betty said, "I think I know the time you first got cancer." I perked up a bit, "When?" I asked. She said, "Do you remember those two times last spring when you got sick? I remember, when you came back to work after the second illness, there were dark circles under your eyes. I knew something was wrong." Really?

So again, more information from others at church about what was going on in the months before my diagnosis. All this goes into the bank of information. I go back to what Colleen the nutritionist said before my first chemo treatment: "John, nothing you've done has caused this cancer." I remember that comment and make note of it often.

But ...

I think one is a fool who doesn't evaluate the way they lived before getting cancer, and how they'll live from here on out. And I'm telling you, I was all about work, work, work, and a lot of effort. I pushed myself from a lot of motives that, looking back, did not honor God. I was all about getting things accomplished *my way*. And the tragedy of it is that as a pastor I involved other people. *They* saw it and *they* knew it long before I did.

And the way I lived, pushing myself doing work my way, tore down my health, as sure as I'm sitting here this morning.

But here's what I firmly believe now: God's work is going on today especially, with me having cancer! I think it's going better than it ever has because the type A, push-himself-and-others, gut-out-get-work-done-in-the-flesh John is out of the way.

My crucial mistake is I didn't learn what Nehemiah taught the laborers on the wall. Yesterday I left the story at Nehemiah 4:9, where he countered the opposition with prayer to God and set up a guard.

Well, in verse 10, more enemies begin to gather. "But soon word [the taunts of the enemies] was going around in Judah. The builders were pooped, the rubbish piles up; we're in over our heads, we can't build this wall." So Nehemiah faced physical exhaustion and discouragement.

I can't tell you how often I dealt with that personally (and I know I'm no exception to the rule here; all of us go through this, especially during times when we're working a lot), but I blindly pushed on and stubbornly refused to deal with these very real challenges.

In addition to exhaustion and discouragement, Nehemiah continued to face the threats of Sanballat, Tobiah, and all their cohorts. "They won't know what hit them. Before they know it we'll be at their throats, killing them right and left. That will put a stop to the work!" (verse 11). That's what the enemy wants. He wants to stop the work on the wall by stopping God's people. They had to listen to these threats over and over.

And the neighbors of the Jews didn't help matters. They chimed in, "They have us surrounded; they're going to attack." Nehemiah added, "If we heard it once, we heard it ten times" (verse 12). There's always someone around with a word of "encouragement."

So what did Nehemiah do with all this opposition? Well, if he had gone to the John Talbert School of work, he would have said, "Just ignore all this and work harder. Just keep working and going." I'm convinced if Nehemiah and the exiles had followed that advice, the work on the wall would have failed.

But instead Nehemiah "stationed guards at the most vulnerable places of the wall and assigned people by families with their swords, lances, and bows" (verse 13). In other words, he alerted the people to the places of vulnerability and he equipped his workers for battle along with this exhortation: "Don't be afraid of them. Put your minds on the Master, great and awesome, and then fight for your brothers, your sons, your daughters, your wives and your homes" (verse 14).

Then Nehemiah went back to work with military officers serving as backup for everyone who was at work on the wall and the common laborers holding a tool in one hand and a spear in another (verses 16–17).

The lesson I didn't learn was the lesson of spiritual warfare. This story reminds me of Ephesians 6. Verse 10 starts this way: "Be strong *in the Lord* [emphasis mine] and in his mighty power" (Ephesians 6:10, NIV). Like Nehemiah who countered the enemies he faced (discouragement, exhaustion, ridicule, and fear) with alertness and a spear, Paul exhorts us to rely on God's strength, know where the battle is (not flesh and blood but the spiritual forces of wickedness), and prepare for it accordingly by putting on our armor and praying.

Looking back on my life, I worked with a tool and no spear, oblivious to all the enemies of God's work.

Never again.

And a crucial element of spiritual warfare according to Paul in Ephesians 6:18 is prayer. "And pray in the Spirit on all occasions with all kinds of prayers and requests. With this in mind, be alert and always keep on praying for all the saints."

I cannot begin to tell how my life has changed over the past couple months because of two things. I've ceased working in the flesh (by necessity; I have no choice! This is no gallant and brave commitment on my part, for sure. I had to get cancer to get to this point) *and* a bunch of people are praying for me.

And every day I learn about more. Yesterday as I was leaving, Betty handed me a card from Anne. On this card are notes from people who work with her at Liberty Mutual Insurance Company, most of whom are cancer survivors. They tell me they're praying for me and exhort me to stay strong. All I can say to that is *wow*.

I'll take God working through prayer in His way over my meager efforts any day, and I'm never going back.

Psalm 90 is also about the work of God. The psalmist prays, "Oh! Teach us to live well! Teach us to live wisely and well" (verse

12). He goes on to ask the Lord to bless His people and to "let your servants see what you're best at—the ways you rule and bless your children" (verse 16). And then he concludes by saying, "And let the loveliness of our Lord, our God, rest on us, confirming the work that we do. Oh, yes. Affirm the work that we do" (verse 17).

Confirm (according to Webster) means "to give new assurance of the validity of." Affirm (again according to Webster) has a similar meaning, but goes a little further. It means "to express dedication to." The psalmist prays the Lord would give new assurance to the validity of and express His dedication to the work of my hands.

This reminds me of a statement Gary, a dear brother in our church, makes often. It's actually a quote from Hudson Taylor. "God's work done in God's way will never lack God's supply." Here's another quote from Taylor I found when I looked up the former: "Do not have your concert first, and then tune your instruments afterwards. Begin the day with the Word of God and prayer, and get first of all into harmony with Him."[7]

How about that?

Lord, I'm so thankful you're so dedicated to accomplishing your plan and your work in this world that you'll even allow me to have cancer to see it is accomplished. Thank you again for all the lessons you're teaching me by way of cancer.

I choose today to depend totally on you and your strength. I choose to put on your armor and to join the many praying folks, even those at Liberty Mutual, to pray for others and stay at it.

Lord, help me to let you do your work in your way and I'll be excited to see you supply. First things first, always. Tune me to you today and let the symphony begin. Amen.

October 21. An army of people praying

I wish everyone could have my experience, and I'm not talking about cancer. I'm referring to prayer. I wish every believer could witness for themselves how it feels to have an *army* of people praying for them.

This is the term used by Ilamarques, pastor of the Brazilian congregation that meets in our building, in an email to me the other day. He told me I looked good and that he was glad to hear I feel good, but commented that neither of those two things is surprising because of the army of folks who are praying for me. I say *amen* to that.

To repeat, I wish every believer could experience having an army of folks praying for them. My first exposure to this thought occurred in a conversation with Troy.

Several years ago, the church I serve sponsored Troy and his family to start a congregation in Brighton. (The Lord has since moved Troy to serve a church in Illinois.) I remember quite vividly a statement Troy made when he was just getting started: "My goal is to enlist 250 churches/groups/individuals to pray for me and this new church plant." Two hundred fifty or more people praying! Wow!

And I'm fairly confident Troy was able to accomplish this. I never asked him, but the church is still there, and I know from experience the vast majority of church plants (at least in the Mile High Association) don't make it. So who gets the credit? God.

So there's an example of the way God works through prayer. And I can vouch for it. I don't know exact numbers in my case, but I'm guessing a lot of people are praying for me—maybe more than 250—and I cannot begin to tell you what it means.

Let me say this one more time: I wish more Christians—all Christians—could have this experience. But it won't happen.

Why? Here's what I've learned in twenty-one years of pastoral experience, for whatever this is worth. Sickness or crisis or *newness* is much more of a motivator for prayer than health or non-crisis or *oldness* (I'm not referring to age here, but to a new project versus an old one in terms of how long it's been going).

Have you ever seen someone stand up in church and say, "I'm as healthy as I've ever been and I need everyone to pray for me"? Whoever would do that would be considered a lunatic, but if you have cancer it's a different story.

This whole issue came to light for me when I called everyone in the church several years ago. I called every family to ask them how

I could pray for them. More often than not, I got this response: "I'm doing well. There's nothing to pray for."

Do you see what I'm saying? The fact is we all need prayer *all the time,* whether we have cancer or have lost a job, or not. But that isn't how we look at it. I'm realizing I needed prayer maybe more so before I got cancer than I do now.

I think good times are a greater test than bad.

Maybe if we prayed for each other when things were good, many of us would avoid bad things. How about that?

This is certainly borne out when you read the Psalms and the letters of Paul. The Psalms show me that when the graph is going up, I should praise God and pray then as well (and it's the same when it's going down or has hit rock bottom).

The prayers of Paul show me this even more vividly. There are four major prayer sections in Paul's letters—in Ephesians (two prayers there in chapters 1–3; many argue it's one long prayer), in Colossians, and in Philippians. In each of the prayers, what motivates Paul to pray for folks in the churches is not a crisis. For example, in Colossians 1:3–8, he points to the faith and love and fruitfulness of the church in Colossae and says, "For this reason ..." (verse 9), and he begins to pray for them. In other words Paul's saying, "Wow, you guys are doing great and I heard about this so I'm praying for you more than ever."

That certainly isn't the way we do things, or let me be more personal—the way I've done things.

But there's no better time than the present to change, and I'm learning how from Nehemiah. Today I read two chapters in his story, 5 and 6. And prayer is the over-arching theme in this story of rebuilding the walls of Jerusalem.

In chapter 5 Nehemiah finds out some of the Israelites are charging their brothers exorbitant interest for the necessities of life, like food. Nehemiah is indignant and exhorts the people to change. Thankfully they confess their sin and turn back to the Lord. Nehemiah describes the integrity of his own walk with the Lord. "I had work to do; I worked on this wall. All my men were on the job to do the work. We didn't have time to line our own pockets" (verse

16). The chapter concludes with this prayer: "Remember in my favor, O my God, everything I've done for these people" (verse 19).

In chapter 6 Nehemiah continues to deal with intimidation from his enemies. Sanballat, Tobiah, Gesham the Arab, and the others send him messages over and over. How did Nehemiah respond? "They were trying to intimidate us into quitting. They thought, 'They'll give up; they'll never finish it.' I prayed, 'Give me strength'" (verse 9).

They even cajoled a false prophet named Shemaiah to get Nehemiah to hide in the Temple. Did Nehemiah fall for that retreat trick? Nope. "I sensed that God hadn't sent this man" (verse 12) and he prayed, "O my God, don't let Tobiah and Sanballat get by with all the mischief they've done. And the same goes for the prophetess Noadiah and the other prophets who have been trying to undermine my confidence" (verse 14).

So Nehemiah continued to have conversation with God (pray) and as a result, he led the people to finish the work on the wall as the intimidation continued. This is how chapter 6 concludes.

What does all this tell me? Nehemiah lived his entire life in conversation with God through prayer, and I believe the foundation for this was laid during the good times of his life before he ever came to Israel. It was a habit with him, as natural as breathing.

Praying, talking to God, in good times as well as bad. Praying for healthy people as well as sick people—this is what I'm learning.

In fact I'm so grateful for the folks who are praying for me—*you*—that I'm now praying with fervor for you and for all healthy people who are praying for me. How about that?

This is all about developing a new default mode. My good friend Kenny Moore has encouraged me greatly in this regard. We often talked about prayer before I got sick, but it took me getting cancer to understand more fully what the Lord was teaching me about prayer through him. One of Kenny's great statements goes something like this: "We start with prayer for a while and when it doesn't 'work' immediately or as we want, we default to activity." That describes me exactly.

Well, I'm praying I'll allow the Lord to get into the default settings of my life and turn a switch so that like Nehemiah I might default first and always to conversation with Jesus *equals* prayer.

This is what it means, I believe, to abide in Jesus. That old KJV word *abide* (and I love it) actually means to settle down and make myself at home. I want to learn to make myself at home in my relationship of communication with Jesus.

This is what Psalm 91 is all about. The psalm begins with an affirmation of the Lord as our refuge (verse 2) and a listing all the things the Lord protects His people from. The psalmist then cites this promise from the Lord: "'If you'll hold on to me for dear life,' says God, 'I'll get you out of any trouble. I'll give you the best of care if you'll only get to know and trust me. Call me and I'll answer, be at your side in bad times; I'll rescue you, then throw you a party. I'll give you a long life, give you a long drink of salvation'" (Psalm 91:14–16). Praise God!

Oh Lord, I thank you for your enduring and abiding presence in my life, during my healthiest days, and now that I have cancer. Thank you for all the help you've given me during the good times and bad.

I need you now just as much as I needed you when I didn't have cancer and didn't realize how much I needed you. Thank you Lord for making sense of what I just said.

Thank you for all the people reading this and all the people praying for me. Lord, I ask you today to expand my prayer life. Grow me so I'll pray for everyone you bring across my path, whether they're sick or not, and especially when they're doing well.

Oh Lord, thank you for being at my side as the enemy even now wants to intimidate me to stop me from writing and keep me silent. Rescue me, Lord. And I can't wait for the party. It's good with you all the time. Amen.

October 22. Crisis versus conversational prayer

I learned more about prayer as I walked yesterday.

By the way, I'm seeing more and more of the benefits of walking. Here are two: I'm better able to meditate on the Word as I walk, and it gives me more opportunity for conversation with God. I don't know why this is true. Maybe it's because walking gets the blood flowing in my lethargic brain.

But more than that, I think walking, breathing in fresh morning air, looking at the leaves changing color, watching mothers usher their kids down the street to the bus stop, and observing people hurry off to work—all this shows me prayer and the Word work in those settings as well. Until I got cancer, my time with the Lord was usually spent in a quiet room, alone and in isolation. But I'm learning that God is relevant and prayer and the Word are enhanced when I'm outside walking in the world as well.

All this fits into what the Lord taught me about prayer as I walked yesterday. I'm now firmly convinced there are two major philosophies of prayer. The first is *crisis prayer,* the approach I've followed most of my life. And as I realized this, I was reminded of a man I studied during my Ph.D. days at seminary. His name is Dietrich Bonhoeffer. Bonhoeffer lived and served as a pastor and professor during the rise of Nazism in Germany. As a matter of fact, as Hitler emerged, Bonhoeffer joined the underground movement to depose him. Unfortunately the Nazis found him out and he was executed in front of a firing squad in 1945. His life story is incredible.

One of Bonhoeffer's chief works, written at the end of his life, is *Letters and Papers from Prison.* This book is great because of his observations about the state of Christianity in the twentieth century. I think these perspectives are quite relevant for us here in the United States in the early part of the twenty-first century. Bonhoeffer argued that more and more, God was being pushed out of the center of life. He likened people's perspective of God to a part in Greek theater. In many Greek plays, when the actors had a problem or crisis, they called out to *God.* God swooped in, solved their problems, and swooped out. This was called *deus ex machina,* God of the machine.[8]

Now, I don't know all the particulars of how this works in Greek theater, but the phrase *deus ex machina* came to mind yesterday. That's our view of God! How do I know this? Well, it was confirmed several years ago. We had the highest attendance at prayer meeting on a certain Wednesday night in 2001. Do you know which one it was? The Wednesday after 9/11! My mother and others have told me that during World War II, the churches were full day and night with folks praying. Great! There's nothing wrong with this, nothing at all, but if I only talk to God in times of crisis and don't need Him at other times, something is desperately wrong.

But *crisis praying* is one philosophy and theology. The other is *conversational praying*. I'm not talking here about the technique of prayer, but the philosophy and theology of prayer.

This term came to mind as I read Nehemiah and observed how he told what happened when he led the exiles to rebuild the wall. All along, all the way through this tremendously challenging project, he talked with the Lord.

This kind of lifestyle always leads *to* God's Word, not away from it. After the wall was completed, Nehemiah found Ezra the scribe and asked him to stand in a public square on a raised platform and read the Word from dawn to noon (Nehemiah 8:3–4). When the people heard it, they fell on their faces in worship and weeping.

But Nehemiah called on them to stop weeping. "Go home and prepare a feast, holiday food and drink; and share it with those who don't have anything: This day is holy to God. Don't feel bad. The joy of the Lord is your strength" (Nehemiah 8:10). Nehemiah walked so closely with the Lord that he was able to discern what the Lord was saying to the people as Ezra read the Word.

As the chapter unfolds with Ezra continuing to read, the people were convicted they had failed to observe the Feast of Booths, so they stopped everything, "made booths and lived in them." While they were doing this, "Ezra read from The Revelation of God each day, from the first to the last day—they celebrated the feast for seven days" (verse 18).

When I see God at the center of everything, then it forces me to look to Him and to obey Him every step of the way, not just in crisis. The people of Israel needed to be jarred into seeing that even though they were back in their land, they still needed the Lord! And so do I.

I wonder if I'll pursue the Lord with as much fervor as I do now if the Lord chooses to heal me from cancer? This was the issue on my heart as I finished my walk yesterday: when I don't *need* God to heal me, will I still need Him?

Psalm 92 is all about someone who recognizes the work of God and how much he needs Him. And when he sees it, he realizes what will happen to God's enemies. He compares these enemies to mowed grass. "When the wicked popped up like weeds and all the evil men and women took over, you mowed them down, finished them off once and for all" (verse 7).

In contrast to the mowed-grass-and-weeds enemies are the people of God. "'Good people will prosper like palm trees; grow tall like Lebanon cedars; transplanted to God's courtyard. They'll grow tall in the presence of God, lithe and green, virile still in old age.' Such witnesses to upright God! My mountain, my huge, holy Mountain!" (verses 12–15).

So I'm one of God's hothouse trees in His greenhouse—*all the time.*

Lord, I thank you for being in the middle of and relevant to every situation in life—in the good times as well as cancer. I thank you for the greenhouse in which I live every moment of life.

I confess the sin of trying to relegate you to the role of my servant, my personal problem solver.

You're so much bigger than that. So much. Thank you for what you've made me—a substantial tree in your garden. Thank you for allowing me to see in these recent days and weeks that you're a constant companion and friend who walks with me and in whom I live, and that you're solid. I love you *my mountain,* my huge, holy mountain. Amen.

October 24. The playbook

Before I get to the playbook, I have to say I always feel weird on Sundays when I'm not at church, whether I'm on vacation or sick. I decided it would be best for me just to rest and prepare for chemo treatment number three. The past couple Sundays when I preached, my energy dropped off the map in the afternoon and I felt tired most of the day Monday. I don't want to go into chemo tired. So I felt this was the best way to approach it.

A good brother in our church, John, will be preaching today. He and his wife Mary lead our discipleship group that meets on Sunday mornings. Mary is struggling with cancer herself, but you'd never know it. She's always smiling and so gracious.

John and Mary served as missionaries overseas. When the Lord brought them back to the States, they were involved in student work, eventually in Canada. I've shared some good fellowship with this couple and their kids, particularly their son Matthew who's now serving as a pastor in Georgia. So I have no worries about how the preaching will go today. It's great to see people step forward to serve the Lord in my absence. That's what it's all about, isn't it?

Throughout all of this, I'm learning more and more about what the church should be. It's *not* a one-man show with the pastor gobbling up the entire ministry and preaching. It's about the pastor equipping the saints for the work of ministry so the *body* ministers. It took me getting cancer to finally learn this—I mean really learn it. And I'm never going back to the one-man show ever again. *Ever.*

Enough about that; now back to the playbook. One of the things I've been doing to keep my brain occupied on the days when I'm sitting on the couch is go through old papers I've accumulated. My family jokes (and rightfully so) that I'm the ultimate pack rat. I have a hard time throwing anything away. I still have papers I wrote in elementary school!

But one of the interesting things I came across is a playbook. My sister Marilyn and I spent a lot of time as kids playing football in the back yard. Marilyn never liked prissy girly things like dolls. She liked and excelled at sports, just about any she got involved in. And I was glad because on our team, I was the quarterback and she was the receiver.

Marilyn was a great receiver for two main reasons: she was a fast runner and a fierce competitor. We spent hours in the back yard throwing and catching and devising plays. And to keep track of them all, we wrote them down on notebook paper with numbers and descriptions for each play. I have to laugh as I flip through the pages.

At the back of the playbook there's a list of the symbols we used in our little book, and the last page is a list of audibles (a number I called out at the line of scrimmage if we wanted to change the play, just like the pros who play today).

It wasn't long after Marilyn and I started our team that the boy next door, David, joined us. He was a scrawny little kid. I don't remember much about his role on the team except he snapped the ball to me and tried to get in the way of the pass rusher. That's about all he did, as I recall.

Our big game day came about when another kid down the street named Grant challenged our three-*man* team to a game. Grant had two buddies who were both pretty good-sized kids. Now remember, these three boys challenged a girl, a scrawny kid, and me. Who do you think was going to win?

At the start of the game they kicked off to us and Marilyn ran it back all the way for a touchdown. I'm not exactly sure what happened after that. I think they got the ball, marched down the field, and scored.

They kicked off again and Marilyn ran it back for another touchdown. They couldn't catch her! I think we stopped them the next time they got the ball and when they punted to us, Marilyn ran that one all the way back!

As you can imagine, these three boys were getting frustrated because a girl was taking them to school. It was hilarious! As I remember, after that last kick was returned for a score, the game ended. They just couldn't take it any longer. Grant started arguing and challenging me and before he knew it, Marilyn jumped on him with fists and feet flying. He was on the ground before he knew what hit him!

And of course, here was the big bad quarterback who'd really done nothing the whole day—we didn't need the playbook or the audibles because Marilyn kept running kicks back for touchdowns. I just stood there watching Marilyn take care of business! Ha!!!! I laugh whenever I think about it.

I remember all three of us walking away with Grant and his buddies yelling at us. The Quarterback, the Girl, and the Scrawny Kid had won. Of course, David and I had done little more than stay out of Marilyn's way, but we claimed victory nonetheless! Not long after that my glory days in football ended when Marilyn injured her knee while we were playing football in the back yard. She moved on to tennis after that, and I was on my own.

All that came to mind when I found the playbook, and it reminds me of the unfolding story in Nehemiah and the way God works, if we let him.

At the end of chapter 9, Nehemiah led the exiles to draw "up a binding pledge, a sealed document signed by our princes, our Levites, and our priests" (Nehemiah 9:38). Chapter 10 describes it further as "a binding oath to follow The Revelation of God given through Moses the servant of God, to keep and carry out all the commandments of God our Master, all his decisions and standards" (Nehemiah 10:29). In other words, Nehemiah led the people to follow God's playbook.

All the plays we need to run are contained in His Word—*the Playbook.*

Beginning at verse 30, the Bible tells which "plays" they needed to run. The first one concerned intermarriage with foreign neighbors and goes back to the challenge of Ezra. The next involved keeping the Sabbath, and the final series centered on tithes, sacrifices, and worship, to see that the Temple was never again neglected.

The ministries of Ezra and Nehemiah didn't make up new plays. The Lord used these men to bring the people back to the commands and statutes He'd already given hundreds of years earlier via Moses. The Lord's playbook doesn't change, *ever!*

But the Lord does take care of us when life situations demand an audible. I think that's what cancer is for me. Several months ago and most days since then, I come to the line of scrimmage expecting the customary defense and instead find an all-out blitz from parts of the field I never imagined. And all of a sudden I need to call an audible.

I'll be honest, that's where I am today. I'm a little more apprehensive about what's going to happen in chemo number three than I was going into number two. Last time I had more confidence because the doctor told me my experiences will be basically the same every time, except I'll get progressively more fatigued.

But I had some side effects after number two that I didn't have after number one. So what's going to happen this time? What's the defense going to throw at me? Will I have to call an audible and will I be able to do it?

I hear myself ask these questions and realize it is so easy to drift back into the fleshly mode of "how am I going to handle the side effects this time—me, myself, and I?"

But the truth is the Lord is there when life demands an audible. Psalm 94 reminds me of this. "How blessed the man you train, God, the woman you instruct in your Word, providing a circle of quiet within the clamor of evil, while a jail is being built for the wicked" (Psalm 94:13). I love the phrase "circle of quiet within the clamor of evil." This psalm is all about the way God helps His people when they face trouble. "The minute I said, 'I'm slipping, I'm falling,' your love, God, took hold and held me fast" (verse 18).

So many times during these past few months, when I begin to think I'm overwhelmed by the opposing defense as I look at how big *Grant and his buddies* are and how little I am, the Lord takes hold of me and holds me tight. When I wonder, "How am I going to pull this off?" the Lord takes care of things so that, like the big game down the street, I don't even have to run the plays! It's not up to me! I just need to get out of His way and let Him score again!

He wrote the playbook and He runs the plays. He takes care of everything!

Praise God!

Lord, I thank you for the way you're using everything, even crumpled notebook pages written by kids, to remind me of who you are and what you're doing in my life. Thank you for the Revelation. Thank you for cancer. Thank you for being in charge of the game and how it unfolds.

I'm apprehensive as I approach the next chemo treatment. I honestly don't know what to expect this time, but I place the game firmly in the hands of the One who already knows how it's all going to turn out!

May you increase and may john talbert (small letters intentional here) decrease. Win another one today and tomorrow and all the games ahead, Lord. Amen.

October 26. A rainbow!

Praise God—I'm three-sixths or half of the way done! When I was learning fractions from Miss Canon in fourth grade math, I had no idea how useful they'd be for my psyche and outlook on life down the road!

Yesterday was a good day, the best chemo day I've had so far, and it started off in an amazing way. While we were sitting in the waiting room waiting for my treatment, someone said, "Look at the rainbow." Sure enough, to the north and west of the hospital was an incredible rainbow. Marilyn went outside the building and snapped a picture of it. It seemed to get brighter and more substantial the longer we sat there. I've never seen a rainbow last so long. (Of course, I've probably never been in a position to watch one that long.) We were in that waiting room over a half an hour. Marilyn said, "There's God's message to you for today." Amen. Lord, you're as faithful to me as you were to Noah and all generations that came after him. Thank you.

There's more to tell about yesterday and I'll do that later, but first I want to return to a subject I began yesterday. Because I had a lot of time to meditate yesterday (these treatments still take six hours), I was in a position for the Lord to speak with me more about *boundaries,* and it all came about in a rather strange way.

The nurse who attended to me yesterday was Nicole. She's probably the best nurse I've had so far—not only because of the way she cared for me but also in the brief conversations we had. We somehow got on the subject of pets and she asked me if I had any. I replied, "No, I don't have time for pets. You see, I'm a pastor and I pretty much work day and night. I don't have time to take care of an animal. When I want to see pets, I go to their house" (and I pointed to my mother and sister).

Nicole nodded her head. "That's basically the same reason my husband and I can't have pets either." She fixed another pack of medicine on my catheter and hurried off.

But my words, "I'm a pastor and I pretty much work day and night" hit me between the eyes. That statement really is me! *Boundaries.* My mind immediately went back to last summer again, and then back further. And I remembered the times last year when I made similar comments to friends, who politely reminded me that maybe I was burning the candle at both ends a little too much.

As I share all this, please don't feel sorry for me, as if any of this was anyone else's fault but mine. It was certainly not the fault of my church family. Sure, sometimes folks make excessive demands, but are these different than any other job? Come on!

No, the problem is how I respond to those demands. In other words, it's my fault!

The fact is that someone who's adopted the "I-work-day-and-night" mentality is lazy, and that's not my indictment. Eugene Peterson made that comment in one of his seminars I have on tape. I need to dig it up and listen to it again. Anyone who's a slave to the *tyranny of the urgent* (the title of another book I need to find and read) is lazy.

The problem with busy-ness is it seems to be anything but laziness. It appears to be so noble, and people say positive things like, "Wow, you sure work hard." But it's smoke and mirrors.

I'll be honest—when I first heard Peterson call busy-ness laziness, it made me mad. I like Peterson and admire his work as a pastor (he was pastor of the same church for thirty years, and it wasn't a megachurch). But I still thought, "You're out of your mind." However, in recent days I'm realizing he's so right.

It's not a laziness of activity, it's a laziness of mentality. There's a very subtle and dangerous mindset that develops. It seems to be easier to please people than God, *up front.* Rather than wait on God and pray and seek His direction for the day or a decision or an activity, it seems easier just to let other people set your schedule to make them (or keep them) happy. At least that's the rationale, right?

It's so easy to do this, but here's the rub (and all these folks came to mind yesterday while I sat there in the chemo room). Over the years, the people I tried hardest to please were the ones I had the least success in pleasing, and they were the folks who were the quickest out the door when they became unhappy with something at church. And right now I can tick off those names, one after another.

Why has this taken so long to sink into my brain? You can't please people! I've preached it and had people say it to me over and over. It's a carrot on a string.

But isn't that what Paul said? "I try to please everybody in every way" (part of 1 Corinthians 10:33, NIV). Paul said it! There's the John Talbert I-work-day-and-night identity and mentality. All good, right?

Wrong.

Paul also said, "Am I now trying to win the approval of men, or of God? Or am I trying to please men? If I were still trying to please men, I would not be a servant of Christ" (Galatians 1:10, NIV). How about that? This is a rock-solid conviction, foundational to Paul's life and ministry. Every page of his story in the New Testament confirms this.

What about 1 Corinthians 10:33? Well, I only quoted part of the verse (always dangerous to build any theology on partial verses, even though folks do it all the time). This section from chapter 8 through chapter 11 is all about eating meat offered to idols and how to minister to folks who are doing that. And Paul is offering principles of ministry. In an earlier chapter he says, "To the weak I became weak, to win the weak. I have become all things to all men so that by all possible means I might save some" (1 Corinthians 9:22).

The statement in chapter 10 is similar if you look at the context and the rest of the verse. The whole verse reads "even as I try to please everybody in every way. For I am not seeking my own good but the good of many, so that they may be saved." So this verse is *not in fact* a candidate to justify its adoption as the motto for a martyr complex of "I work day and night." It was a principle of ministry in reaching lost folks. Well, okay.

As I said yesterday, this is all about pleasing God first and foremost. And here's the deal with that: *I can please God!* All the running around in the world can't please everyone, but I can please God.

What does this mean? I'm learning that pleasing God involves saying *no.* I can say no because of physical limitations. And I had just as many of those before I realized I had cancer as I do now, but I always swept them under the carpet and drove myself. It was pride and arrogance, and indeed contributed to what I'm going through now. You can only push yourself so far.

I can say no because of concerns for my family. Someone years ago said to me, "John, you are a family. You are a family of one." But I didn't heed that advice. I didn't listen, and so I neglected my "family." And I've done it with my mother and sister as well. But I'm realizing one of my main responsibilities *now,* even though I'm sick, is to minister to them.

After we got home from chemo yesterday, both of them crashed. They were more exhausted than I was. I should have learned this before now because I've observed it in other families in a variety of situations. In dealing with sickness, it's just as hard or harder for the caregivers as it is for the patient—all the time.

Boundaries—factoring in my health and my family—are now in the loop of the decision-making process before the cancer-sponsoring word *yes* comes out of my mouth. I know that's a rather extreme statement, but add up over twenty years of people-pleasing, tyranny of the urgent, lazy *yes* responses, and you have a cancer patient. That's the plain and simple truth.

But after reading Nehemiah 13 today, I'm realizing the subject of boundaries has a crucial vertical dimension as well. Nehemiah went back to Persia for a while after the wall was completed, but in his absence the exiles lapsed in some areas. The whole issue of intermarriage cropped up again and had to be dealt with, and the people neglected the Temple *again.*

Apparently Eliashib the priest allowed an enemy (Tobiah) to use a room in the Temple to store some of his stuff! When Nehemiah heard about this in Persia, he secured permission from the king for a return trip, threw all Tobiah's junk out into the street, and cleansed the temple. And when he learned all the singers had gone home because the people stopped tithing, he brought them back and reestablished the priority of giving. He also shut down all commerce on the Sabbath (verses 13–22).

Nehemiah was responsible for setting a crucial boundary for the nation of Israel when they returned from exile: the exclusivity and priority of the worship of God. He was zealous to remove any hint of compromise.

It all goes back to who runs the show—the Lord or me. "Get out the message—God rules! He put the world on a firm foundation; He treats everyone fair and square" (Psalm 96:10).

This time in my life—from a physical standpoint—is about the eradication of cancer cells from my body through drastic means. Chemo is drastic. They put a lot of medicine in the body—large bags of liquid through a surgically inserted port—and it takes six hours. This isn't just a pill (although I have to take those too).

But I'm learning that on a more important spiritual level, this disease is also about the Ezra/Nehemiah work of unearthing and eradicating sin (even religious sin) from my life.

So be it.

Lord, I do acknowledge your rule today. I pray as you continue to reveal storage rooms in my life that are filled with junk, you'll give me the courage to clean them out. Remove all the clutter of laziness and compromise. Help me not to waste this cancer experience. I want to get well physically, but I also want to be *whole* spiritually— all of me for all of you. Amen.

October 27. Robert

Today I want to tell you about Robert.

Before I do, things caught up with me last night. I started to feel bad and it just seemed to get worse through the night. Today I feel like someone ran over me. This is about the time the aftereffects of chemo and the shot usually hit. This is part of the tough stuff Jon Hardin warned me about.

Even as I start to write, I'm noticing I feel a little better. I guess it reinforces the fact that all these words are mainly therapy for me. Thank you Lord for allowing me to write and thank you for everyone who wades through all this.

Back to Robert ... on Monday, the day of my chemo, this guy came in. He walked very slowly and slumped down in a chair in the corner of the room. He was the epitome of the term *weary*. When the nurses hooked him up to the catheter and the tubes, he leaned a little forward as if he were straining, like a racehorse near the finish line but without the energy.

I felt for him, as I looked his way often. Sometimes he laid his head back on the chair. Other times he shifted to the side. He was obviously very uncomfortable. I think he was the sickest guy I've seen in the chemo room.

We acknowledged one another as I shuffled my way to the bathroom once. There's sort of an unwritten code of camaraderie in that room, the same type of bond I felt with Roger when I saw him during my first two treatments.

But honestly, when we left the chemo room on Monday, I really didn't think about the guy in the corner until yesterday.

After the first and second chemo treatments, Marilyn had to take me to the Rocky Mountain Cancer Center's midtown location just east of Presbyterian/St Luke's Hospital. It's the only location open on Saturday and my first two treatments were on Friday. But this time because I had my chemo on Monday, I was able to get my white blood cell booster shot at the Sky Ridge location, so Marilyn took me there yesterday.

That's when I saw the guy from the corner again. He shuffled into the waiting room, signed in, and then ventured over to where Marilyn and I were seated. I was a little shocked when he said, "Hi,

John!" How did he know my name? He must have picked it up the day before. When I asked him his name, he told me it was Robert.

"Are you just starting?" he asked me. "Yep." "What kind of cancer do you have?" I told him. Then I asked him about his experience.

"Well," said Robert, his voice rather raspy and a little muffled, "this is my fourth round of chemo and it's pretty rough. I've been dealing with this for seven years. They've been trying to find a treatment to curb my cancer, which is rather rare and aggressive. Each time I have to come in for several days in a row."

He could see by the expression on my face he'd just blown me out of the water. All I could get out of my mouth was, "Wow. That's a lot."

He went on. "Well, I wish they'd get to me because I need to go to work." Before I could comment again, he continued, "Yeah, I have to keep working just to keep my mind occupied."

"How do you do it? I asked.

"Oh," he said, "people tell me they think what I'm doing is amazing. It isn't. I'm just doing what anyone would do in my situation. You do what you have to do. You'd do it too."

At that time the nurse came in and called me over for my shot. I told Robert I hoped I'd see him again and we said our goodbyes.

That was my second significant encounter with another cancer patient, and needless to say, it stuck in my mind and started to yank on it.

My encounter with Robert reminded me of a quote I read from Scott Hamilton (the Olympic gold medalist skater) in a chemo brochure I found at midtown after my first shot. He said, "By the time I went through my third round of chemo, I was ready to give up on treatment. I wanted to die. Then a friend asked me a simple question: 'How many rounds of chemo do you have left?' I answered, 'Only one.' That's when I realized I was almost there. Without that voice of reason, I would have quit."[9]

After my brief talk with Robert and my recollection of Hamilton's words, I was searching for some kind of voice, any kind. All the questions came flooding into my mind: "I feel fairly good today, but what if this round of chemo doesn't work, and I have to go one or two or three rounds more? I just don't know if I could do it."

I'm so thankful for my mother and sister when I have those brain floods. They have more than reason at their disposal. They have the wisdom of God. When I shared this with them, they said, "John, that's Robert's experience. Not yours. Who knows what is going on in his life? He's not you. Just take this day and rejoice in it."

Right, right, right.

I'm realizing I have to be very careful when I talk to other folks with cancer. This is the mission field God's put me in. I never would've met Robert or Roger or Dr Jotte or Nicole or Kayla or any of the other nurses if I didn't have cancer. So this is an opportunity.

But I have to be careful not to extrapolate the experiences of other cancer patients into mine. I don't know where Robert and Scott Hamilton are with the Lord, but I do know this. As much as I enjoy my work and appreciate how the church is ministering to me, work is not my answer. And the voice of reason is not my answer either.

My answer for making it through this whole ordeal comes back to the Lord and what He does in the lives of believers. Today's passages remind me of this.

Psalm 97 repeats the affirmation of Psalm 96 in the first verse. "God rules: there's something to shout over! On the double, mainlands and islands—celebrate!" This psalm is all about the way creation itself gives praise to God. And because creation does this, I can and must. "And Zion, you listen and take heart! Daughters of Zion, sing your hearts out: God has done it all, has set everything right. You, God, are High God of the cosmos, far, far higher than any of the gods [the gods of work and reason]. ... So, God's people, shout praise to God. Give thanks to our Holy God!" (Psalm 97:8–9, 12). *Yes!*

I'm shouting in my heart in the stillness of this new day: "You, God, are High God of the cosmos, far, far higher than any of the gods." And I will make it.

Why? Because I have a resource even Olympic champions who don't know you don't have. And John the Baptist preached about it.

After my jaunt through Ezra and Nehemiah (a life-changing reading of those two books, by the way), I'm back in the New Testament in Mark. John shouted this message in the wilderness (I'd shout too if I had to wear a camel hair *habit* as the Message calls it; *girdle* in the KJV—that would cause me to shout right there!): "I'm baptizing you here in the river, turning your old life in for a Kingdom life. His baptism—a baptism by the Holy Spirit—will change you from the inside out" (Mark 1:8). *Yes, again.* That's worth shouting about!

Lord Jesus, thank you again today for being firmly established on the throne and ruling this universe and my cancer. I confess my fears and anxieties about what's ahead. I acknowledge I very quickly lapse into that flood of questions, but the flood can't touch you.

I lift up Robert today and pray that in the course of his cancer ordeal he'll come to know you as his personal Savior and Ruler. Use me to witness to him again if the opportunity presents itself, *but* guard my mind from doubt as I do.

Lord, I'm amazed at how much better I feel just since I started writing today. Thank you for that. Thank you for the power of the Spirit who is even now changing me from the inside out. That's worth shouting about! *Amen!!!!!*

October 31. "God of Earth and Outer Space"

Okay, I'll admit it. This hymn title has always been rather curious and a little quirky to me; hence I've avoided it, *until today.* I searched for it on the Internet to find the tune so I can sing it on God's front porch this morning. Verse three says, "Launch us from complacency."[10] Amen.

I needed this correction today as I approach another Sunday where I won't be preaching or even be at church. I struggled with the decision, but I'm not going. I was a little more active yesterday, and today I'm feeling it again. I ache like I have the flu. It's frustrating because I'd like my emergence from the aftereffects of chemo to take place in a straight line.

It doesn't.

But I have another day to sit and pray and think, and Lord I thank you for this gift. Help me use it wisely for the benefit and expansion of the Kingdom of God.

Yesterday evening I had a chance to visit with my secretary Betty over the phone. She's been such a great help and support and encouragement during all this, especially since I've just not been able to be in the office all that much for the past several months. Much of the day-to-day stuff of the church has fallen into her lap as a result. It's huge. But it's been such a ministry to me *not* to have deal with that stuff.

Last night as Betty shared some of the stuff that's going on (nothing out of the ordinary, just challenges and opportunities), I felt my blood pressure rising and my mind racing and anxiety emerging. I often feel the pull that says "you need to be back in the saddle and take care of these issues," as if my presence is some magic that can solve problems.

If anything is true over the past twenty-one-plus years, my presence and hands-on involvement has gummed up the works. It's an illusion to view oneself as *necessary*.

Eugene Peterson argues vehemently against this mindset. I pulled a series of tapes out of the closet a few days ago. Back in 1999 I attended a pastors' conference at Regent College in Vancouver where Peterson was one of the main speakers. The title of the conference was "The Unnecessary Pastor: Counter-cultural Soul." How about that for a title? I attended the conference and even had a one-on-one talk with Peterson over lunch.

It was an excellent conference and I had a great conversation with Peterson, but as I've listened again to these tapes over the past few days, I realize I didn't learn anything *then*. Maybe *now* I will.

Understand that one of the main reasons I've resurrected these tapes is because I feel so unnecessary, so out of the loop, so helpless to get my hands in there and correct problems/issues—not even able to preach! But after listening to the lectures again, I'm deeply convicted by my false impulses.

Let me pause here to clarify that the name of the seminar is a little deceiving because Peterson is *not* arguing that we should fire all the pastors and that we really don't need them! *No.* He says pastors like me need to recover a biblical sense of their vocation and see themselves as unnecessary in three vital ways: in what culture presumes to be important, in what pastors themselves feel is essential, and in what congregations insist pastors must do—all three areas.

Peterson contends that pastors must resist all worldly forces that push to define the role of the pastor. The models are out there—CEO, rancher, director of operations, manager, and so on. All of these labels contain an element of truth as it pertains to the role and function of the pastor (for example, management is part of the gig at times), making the pastor necessary to the organization. But these aren't always just worldly forces.

Right now I'm fighting the need to be needed because of what I accomplish for the organization. I think the expression is to *earn my keep.* I think there are folks in churches who expect that out of the pastor as well. They might think things like, "Well, we're paying him to do that ministry."

Now let me be clear on this point: I've felt none of this from the church I serve. I've only felt encouragement and affirmation from my church family. They'll miss me today, but they won't criticize me for not being there again.

But all these pressures and forces inside of me are very real, and it all came back last night. When I hung up the phone with Betty, I realized all this is a breaking process. God is breaking me of the urge to be necessary, and maybe for the first time in my life putting me in a position to be a pastor as the Bible defines that role.

Instead of chafing against the fact that I can't be there to preach, manage, correct, and so on, I should be rejoicing that all these roles and functions are being taken care of in the body of Christ. I mean, after all, isn't one of my biblical jobs "the full equipping of the saints that they should do the work of ministering" (Ephesians 4:12, Amplified Bible)?

Shouldn't I be happy? The fact that I'm still struggling shows I have a long way to go in this regard. Lord, I confess the sin of being a ministry hog, the *human vacuum cleaner pastor,* sucking up ministry so others can't do it and then complaining all the time that I have too much to do. Boo hoo, poor overworked John. He's so busy! There's that devilish word again.

And this morning, even as conviction grows in my life about all this, I realize that in my usual routine of preparing for Sunday I'm a lot more concerned about being *prayed up* on the stuff I have to do than about *praying for* God's people who are serving. How selfish!

So today maybe my greatest work is *not* to be there, but to pray for the leaders and teachers and singers and preacher. The truth is that's my greatest opportunity for impact every Sunday, whether I'm there or not.

All of this reminds me of a statement Charles Spurgeon made about *boiler room prayer*. During every service at the Metropolitan Tabernacle (while it was going on), hundreds of folks knelt before the Lord in the boiler room and prayed for the service. And so when someone asked Spurgeon about the secret to his success (there's another word I don't like, but I think what they were asking was why he thought so many folks were saved after listening to his sermons), he replied, "My people pray for me."[11]

Doesn't it make sense that if I pray for God's people who are serving, the Lord will bless them?

All of these very hard lessons I'm learning fit the message of Psalm 101. It starts off with the psalmist talking about what he embraces in his relationship with the Lord. He prays the Lord will help him find his "way down the road of right living ... I'm doing the best I can, and I'm doing it at home, where it counts" (verse 2).

But then he moves very quickly to talking about what he refuses: "corrupting people ... degrading things ... made-in-Canaan gods" (verse 3). He goes on to say, "I can't stand arrogance" (verse 5). But then he affirms, "But I have my eye on salt-of-the-earth people —they're the ones I want working with me; men and women on the straight and narrow—those are the ones I want at my side" (Psalm 101:6).

Lord, I thank you today for being well able to run your church without me. I lift up Jose Tello, pastor of the Hispanic congregation that meets in our building, as he preaches for me today. Give him the words to share as he makes the effort to preach maybe his first sermon ever in English. I pray for Ron who will be sharing his testimony today.

I lift up all our teachers: Al, Nancy, Bill, John, JJ, Patti, James, John/Mary, Jim/Judy, and all those who teach in nursing homes and in the church's other congregations. Give Jorge and Vida strength and grace as they lead worship today. All these folks are serving you today. Fill them with the Holy Spirit and power.

Thank you for the breaking process that's going on in my life. I pray my perspective of and involvement in the pastoral ministry of FSBCN will reflect your standards and your Word, nothing else.

God of earth and outer space, rule, reign supreme in all realms today, especially the *space* in me, and forevermore as your love goes out to a lost world today. Amen.

November 1. A "sneaky" tough day

As I sit here this morning, I'm still flabbergasted. Wow, I can't believe it caught me so off guard.

I felt well toward the end of last week. I was able to get out and be rather active. Going into Sunday, I seriously debated going to church, and then *bam*. The bottom dropped out. My legs ached and I had weird muscle reactions, but mainly my energy was gone. I took a walk yesterday morning and that helped. I got out some in the afternoon, but after that I sat down and conked out totally for a few hours.

Weird. And I guess what made it so hard is I was totally unprepared for it to happen, and it knocked me for a loop emotionally. I just wasn't ready for it, and what dawns on me is I'm not sure I ever will be.

The oncologist told me the main thing that's going to happen as I progress through these treatments is I'll get increasingly fatigued. I guess he was right.

I just sat around again most of the day, and it seems to be getting harder and harder for me to do that (especially on a Sunday, a day when I'd normally be very active and involved and engaged with others).

This whole cancer thing has been such a huge disruption. My life has changed totally. I mean *totally*. And yesterday the realization of that hit me harder than it ever has to this point, and it happened in a strange way.

Just to keep from completely losing my mind as I sit around (and read and pray and look at the computer), I thumb through old papers and documents to weed them out. I came across some correspondence from one of the best friends I've had in my whole life.

His name was Bill Johnson and his family lived across the street from us. He was a few years older than I was. Bill was in a wheelchair, a cripple his whole life who dealt with many physical problems, especially respiratory illness. You might think it was a downer to be around him, but it was just the opposite. He was one of the most upbeat, positive encouragers I've ever met in my life.

I think Bill would have been a professional athlete had he been able to walk, because he was so competitive and loved all kinds of sports. That's what we did when we got together—we played electric football and a hockey game like foosball. We joked and laughed with one another. He was a true friend.

The letters I found from him were dated August 1971, and it hit me that I've kept letters from a friend I had in seventh grade for thirty-nine years. And yesterday of all days, I pulled them out and read them again—two letters in particular. It was obvious as I read them that Bill wrote them to me while he and his family were on a trip. Here's one of his statements: "We swim too. I told my mother that if the Germans had used that cold water on me in the war, I would have talked. It didn't seem quite so cold the second day." That was typical of his humor.

Both letters demonstrate a lot of empathy. He asks often how I'm doing. Bill celebrated my activities even though he couldn't walk. He cared about the sports I played even though he couldn't play. One letter concludes, "I miss you, say hi to everyone for me and all of us. Your buddy—Bill."

Now here was a guy in a wheelchair who faced a lot of challenges and obstacles and barriers just to get through each day, and yet what came through (and came back to me) was his sense of humor and zest for life and friendship. The question I asked myself yesterday was, "What about me in my current set of circumstances?" Hmmm.

Bill died of pneumonia later that year.

There's so much more to say about Bill. I do believe he accepted Christ before his death and that I'll see my buddy again in heaven where we'll both walk and leap and praise God forever. But here's the point: I got down yesterday because I was inactive for one day! And here was a young man who was never down, even though he was never able to walk.

Wow, the Lord has a way of making a point. I think I'm going to keep that correspondence from Bill another thirty-nine years, if the Lord allows me to live that long.

These days I'm noticing that dealing with trying circumstances, whatever they are, is a theme common to the Psalms. Psalm 102 is no exception. Here's one of its vivid images: "I'm like a buzzard in the desert, a crow perched on the rubble. Insomniac, I twitter way, mournful as a sparrow in the gutter ... There's nothing left of me—a withered weed, swept clean from the path" (verses 6–7, 11).

As you read the psalm, it's clear this is a person who's crying out to the Lord from the rubble of his former hometown—Jerusalem— and from the aloneness of his "terminal illness" before God (verse 4). But there's no despair in these words. Instead there's a confident trust in the sovereignty of God. "Yet you, God, are sovereign still, always and ever sovereign. You'll get up from your throne and help Zion—it's time for compassionate help ... 'God looked out from his high holy place; from heaven he surveyed the earth. He listened to the groans of the doomed, he opened the doors of their death cells'" (Psalm 102:12–13; 19–20).

The Lord is always there to help "buzzards in the desert" and cancer patients and people who can't walk.

This truth is reinforced by what I read in Mark 3. Jesus was in a congregational setting and "he found a man with a crippled hand" (verse 1). Jesus found him! Then he said to all his critics who were ready to jump on him for violating some Sabbath rule they made up, "'What kind of action suits the Sabbath best? Doing good or doing evil? Helping people or leaving them helpless?' No one said a word" (Mark 3:4). And Jesus healed the man.

What hits me this morning as I read that story is that nothing—no time (not even the Sabbath), no place, no circumstance, no physical limitation (no matter how severe), can limit Jesus!

Oh Lord, thank you for yesterday, a very tough day. Thank you for using my friendship with Bill of thirty-nine years ago to encourage me. Thank you that he's with you right now.

God, I'm having a hard time adjusting to the more frequent periods of inactivity in my life. I acknowledge this to you and cry out to you today.

Thank you for being ever sovereign, ever in control of what's going on with me, day by day. Lord, however I end up feeling today, I will praise you and worship you and trust you. Thank you for finding me, no matter where I am. I love you. Amen.

November 2. Long, "sharp" days

There's a line from a movie that has been on my mind the past several days: "the days drew out like a knife." This is a description of time.

Somehow things seem harder these past few days as the reality of what I'm facing begins to dawn on me: going through chemo is indeed some tough stuff, as my friend Jon said. There's the physical aspect of course, the main issue being fatigue. But the most difficult aspect of the whole thing is mental.

Yesterday for the first time the couch in the room where I sit in my mother's house seemed like a dungeon. Don't get me wrong—I'm thankful for it. And I'm thankful again for my church family allowing me the space and time to get well (how can you measure the value of a gift like that?). But sometimes I still shake my head and hope I wake up to find out I've been having a bad dream.

Or I just think, "I want to be done with this *right now*." Nope. Not yet. And the days draw out like a knife. Dealing with that, living in that long-day world—that's where I am.

Somehow though, the Lord keeps throwing lifelines my way when I think I'm going to sink. My memories of my paralyzed friend Bill Johnson have led me in a couple directions. First, I'm convinced there's an element of incapacity that goes with all kinds of suffering. It's a feeling that we're caught, trapped, immobilized whether it's paralysis, cancer, or just a difficult situation.

This is the type of thing Paul alludes to in 2 Corinthians in a series of vivid images: "We've been surrounded and battered by troubles, but we're not demoralized; we're not sure what to do, but we know God knows what to do; we've been spiritually terrorized, but God hasn't left our side; we've been thrown down, but we haven't broken" (2 Corinthians 4:8–9). I love the Phillips version of these verses: "We are handicapped on all sides, but we are never frustrated; we are puzzled, but never in despair. We are persecuted, but we never have to stand it alone: we may be knocked down but we are never knocked out." Wow!

Handicapped on all sides? What's that? *Incapacity.* That's a prison wall. That's a life in which, for whatever reason, I'm not able to move around as I want to. In fact, the word *handicap* is derived from a seventeenth century game with forfeits called "hand in a cap," and it has two distinct meanings. One meaning of handicap (according to FreeDictionary.com) is disability or permanent injury, and it refers to some defect that interferes with normal function of the body or the ability to be self-sufficient in society.

Now I'm not sure what a *game with forfeits* is all about, but I do understand what it means to deal with interference with normal functioning or not being self-sufficient. Paul, who wasn't in a wheelchair and didn't have cancer, was in that boat.

At certain times and in certain situations, he was like Rocky Balboa versus Apollo Creed. He was on the mat, incapacitated, for a little while. If you took a picture of all the troubles he faced, those times of being *knocked down* would definitely be a part of the portfolio, but he recognized a greater reality.

Sufferings, incapacities, and getting knocked down are part of the experience, but they're not all of it. And they're not ultimate reality.

I have to remind myself of this more and more. I'm sitting in a room dealing with cancer and recovering from chemo, but that isn't the final chapter of the book.

But on the other hand, what if things don't change? What if I get worse and eventually I'm totally disabled somehow because the cancer spreads? (If that happened it still wouldn't be the final chapter, only the next chapter, but be that as it may …).

In other words, I've also been thinking it could be a lot worse, and for some people it is. Bill was paralyzed.

I've been thinking of Joni Eareckson Tada (no, not the gal who lived a few doors down from us when Marilyn and I were kids who joined with Marilyn in a takeover of the fort in the backyard). She once said, "Jesus was paralyzed on the cross." I found the quote yesterday in a recent book she's written entitled *When God Weeps*.

I'm just starting to read this book. It's an excellent treatise on suffering from the standpoint of someone who hasn't been healed, but is still *not* knocked out.

For instance, in the context of the aforementioned quote, she tells a story about meeting a fireman at a diner. He was angry and bitter because he'd lost both his arms in a fire and as a result, lost his job. When Joni approached him to minister to him, this bitter man replied, "So he understands. Big deal. What good does that do me?" Joni answered back, "I don't know all the answers. And I'm not sure if I did that it would help. But I do know the One who has the answers—and knowing him makes all the difference."

Then she said, "I'd rather be in this chair knowing him than on my feet without him."[12]

Here's someone with a handicap whose circumstances haven't changed, but who still bounces up from the mat to keep boxing Apollo Creed.

So what I'm learning is the key to all this is not hoping my circumstances will change, but placing my faith in the God who doesn't change. How about that?

That's the challenge. That's the demand of discipline. That's where my self-talk needs to go. That's what Psalm 103 is all about. As I read it this morning, I'm impressed again. "O my soul, bless God, don't forget a single blessing" (verse 2). Then the psalmist lists them: forgiveness, healing (God heals every disease—paralysis and cancer included), redemption, reward, blessing, and renewal—all these blessings and more.

And the psalm concludes the way it started: "Bless God, all creatures, wherever you are—everything and everyone made by God. And you, O my soul, bless God" (Psalm 103:22).

This psalm starts and ends the same way—with a stern word to self. "Self, bless God!"

Going back to my original statement about time, "the days drew out like a knife," this psalm answers that as well. "God's love, though, is ever and always, *eternally present* [emphasis mine] to all who fear him" (verse 17).

Even in the longest, hardest days, "self, bless God."

Lord, I thank you for my current circumstances: I have cancer and I'm often incapacitated. I know there are others like Joni who are *permanently* (as humans view it) disabled. I pray you'll heal her and allow her to walk. But I'm thankful for the example of one who, whether she's ever healed or not, knows you, blesses you, testifies about you, and follows you. Give me the grace to do the same.

I certainly don't know what's going to happen to me. Many are joining my family and me to pray you'll heal me. I pray that again today. But Lord, whether you do or not, I'm telling myself again today to bless you and never forget everything you've done and are doing for me.

Bless the Lord, oh my soul! Amen.

November 4. A bulwark never failing

The second phrase of the hymn "A Mighty Fortress is Our God" alludes to the Lord as "a bulwark never failing."[13]

Wow, is it any wonder this hymn has endured for 500 years or so? There's so much to unpack in just those first two verses. Once again, it's incredible how the Lord pulls things together when I take the time to praise Him.

The Lord is a bulwark. I looked that word up in a couple online dictionaries and found out it has a couple meanings. First, it signifies a defensive wall or rampart. The other nuances of the word have to do with water. It can also mean a breakwater, or it can describe the wall or fence abovedeck designed to keep waves from coming over the gunwale.

I praise you Lord for protecting me in so many ways. Thank you for saving me from sin. Thank you for taking care of me via the love of my biological family and my Christian family.

While I'm on the subject, I so appreciate people who take the time to call and just leave messages if I don't answer. I really don't talk on the phone much these days, and it isn't because I don't want to. But the one of the main side effects of chemo that seems to linger the longest is my muffled voice. It's very exasperating because it takes so much effort to talk over what feels like a fist in my throat. As a result, I just don't talk on the phone much.

But I still appreciate the calls and concern and prayers. Dan Tracy called me Sunday to encourage me and I spoke with him briefly. Another gal from church called and I spoke with her for about a minute. Ronnie, a dear brother and former pastor who's helped me with some financial stuff and is always an encourager, called yesterday just to let me know he was thinking of me and to urge me to read Psalm 147.

That's another thing people are doing for me that fits in the category of *bulwark*—giving me passages of Scripture to read. A friend from college, Lynda, recommended Psalm 42 the other day. My mother encouraged me to read Psalm 58. These passages people have shared with me are road signs and traffic signals to keep me on the road. They serve as a breakwater to keep my beach from eroding.

But I thank you Lord because my current circumstances—cancer and chemo and all that goes with them—are protection for me also.

This is dawning on me more and more over the past few days. And reading another biography has helped me discern this.

Yesterday Marilyn handed me her copy of *Peace in the Valley*. It's a devotional guide, but really a biography of sorts of the famous preacher Vance Havner. There's a lot in this little book about birds. I didn't know this about Havner, but he was an avid birdwatcher. He loved to pursue it wherever his preaching travels took him. He loved to take walks in the woods, watching and listening to birds.

One entry in the book affected me more than the others. The title is "My Other Income," and it starts out this way: "I am taking eight weeks out of a busy preaching ministry to stay at home, tramp the woods, meditate and write a little. Since I am not a salaried man there will be no financial income during that time. Some go-getters might raise an eyebrow at a preacher who quits preaching for two months just to be still … I'd rather rest, deep in the woods, and hear the wood thrush sing his vespers than … travel."[14]

These words made quite an impact on me, especially as I read them in the context of the whole book. Here's a busy preacher (aren't we all?) intentionally taking time away to rest, to be still, and to walk in the woods. Here's a man who learned he needed to do that. He embraced it to the point that it was more valuable than the money he could earn (and needed to earn; he says later on in this entry, about the paycheck, "I could use it"). But his time away was more vital than preaching. Hence the title of the section, "My Other Income."

I should have been doing this type of thing during the twenty-one years I've been a pastor, but I didn't. I was too busy to be still, to rest, and to walk in the woods.

So God allowed cancer in my life to catch me up in that regard. I know that may sound rather strange to put it in those terms, but if I believe the Lord is in control (and I do) and if I believe He wants the best for me (and I do), then it makes sense.

These long days and weeks and now months are *not* about God depriving me—big, bad, mean God gave John cancer and disrupted his life. *No!!!!!!!*

This is about God being a bulwark and allowing me these days for my own good. Amen.

It's all about the right Man being on our side. I have to keep that in mind. This is all about Jesus allowing circumstances and even illnesses into our lives for our own good. Isn't that what Romans 8:28 is all about? Does cancer fit in the category of "and we know that *in all things* [emphasis mine] God works for the good of those who love him, who have been called according to his purpose"

(Romans 8:28, NIV)? I think so, but it's hard to translate that knowledge into my life.

That's why I'm so impatient and want to be done with cancer.

But that's why the hymn rightfully says, "Did we in our own strength confide, our striving would be losing." I'm so glad today that Jesus is on my side in all this. It reminds me of something that happened on a church basketball team when I was in seminary.

My church, Arlington Heights Baptist Church, was playing Broadway Baptist Church in the title game. I got in the game for a few minutes, and somehow I did something that caused a bigger player on the other team to get angry. He squared up to me like he was going to punch me.

Well before I could do anything, my teammate Wayne jumped off the bench and got in this guy's face. "Do you have a problem? Let's deal with it right now!" Wayne wasn't much bigger than I was, but he was so angry on my behalf that it caught the other guy completely off guard, and he just turned and walked away.

Wayne stood up for me, and can I say right here and now that I was glad he did? I think that player from Broadway Baptist Church would have cleaned my clock, but the right man was on my side.

That's Jesus always, but especially now that I have cancer.

It dawned on me as I read further today in Mark 3 that Jesus was teaching his disciples this very truth. After the story of the man with the crippled hand, Mark tells about Jesus casting out demons and not allowing them to speak, but then Jesus called his disciples up on a mountain and, "He settled on twelve, and designated them apostles. The plan was they would be with him, and he would send them out to proclaim the Word" (Mark 3:14).

Did I really miss that all these years? Jesus called his twelve disciples *first,* not to an activity, but to a relationship. His primary calling was that these twelve guys would be *with him* every day. Jesus enlisted a team of guys and they were on his side, but more significantly, *he was on their side.*

This is evident through history, as Psalm 105 demonstrates. It gives a brief history of Israel from Abraham through Joseph all the way to Moses and the wilderness wanderings. And all the way through, every step of the way, "He permitted no one to abuse them. He told kings to keep their hands off: 'Don't you dare lay a hand on my anointed, don't hurt a hair on the heads of my prophets'" (Psalm 105:14–15).

This is how God operated all the way to the Promised Land, and to this very day. "He made them a gift of the country they entered, helped them seize the wealth of the nations so they could do everything he told them—could follow his instructions to the letter. Hallelujah" (verses 44–45).

Lord, I thank you for loving us so much that you'll even allow sickness into our lives to bring us to the point where we'll once again value and esteem and spend time on the main thing—our relationship with you.

I know I've been so out of whack for so long that it's hard for me just be still, to rest, to wait on you, and to walk in the woods. But I ask you to help me stop champing at the bit.

Lord, I'm so grateful all this is about you protecting me and being on my side. Thank you for standing up for me, fighting for me, and winning the battle. I'll follow your instructions to the letter. Win another one through me today. Amen.

November 5. Remembering my dad

So much of what's going on with me right now is about remembrance and perspective, and it's coming about in a rather curious way. I'm just trying to keep myself occupied when I'm sitting around.

As I've said, I spend more time praying than ever. I also study for my sermons. I read. I just sit and think. I walk. And I try to find reasons to get in my car and drive somewhere. I thumb through old pictures and documents (like Bill Johnson's letters). And added to that list, I scan old slides.

A couple weeks ago we were weeding through all my mother's books (you can add that to the list also; I now have stacks of books sitting around—I love it). We came across about fifteen carousels of slides, pictures my dad took of family vacations. Wow!

The first carousel was from a trip we took to Hawaii in March 1971. I decided I didn't want these pictures to be lost forever, since we got rid of the slide projector years ago. So I'm taking the time to scan all these slides into my computer. Who knows how long it will take? But I think it's worth the effort.

While I was scanning last night, I came across a picture of my dad. Just seeing that picture struck me. First, there aren't many pictures of my dad because he was always the one taking the pictures on our vacations. But there he was.

I asked my mother what was going on with him in March 1971, and she said he'd just had his cancer surgery. Oh, yeah. I remember the panic we all felt when my dad started to exhibit some weird symptoms late in 1970. The doctors checked him out and discovered he had colon cancer. They operated on him in early 1971, taking out a lot of his colon and surrounding tissue. They *thought* they got it all.

I don't know if they did anything else besides surgery. I do remember how we felt after the operation. We were all jubilant and so we decided to take a trip. It was a blast. I have a picture of Marilyn and me playing in the ocean.

But there was my dad in that picture, age forty-five, thinking he was done with cancer …

Here I am, thirty-nine years later, seven years older than my dad when I was first diagnosed, hoping that with all these chemo treatments *and* the many prayers of God's people, the Lord will allow me to be done with cancer … really done. But I wonder …

1971—what a year. My dad had cancer surgery. My best friend Bill got pneumonia in late summer that year. He was in the hospital a long time as he slowly declined.

I'll never forget the day I ran out of school at the end of the day and saw my dad standing by his car. He was there to pick me up, and he *never* picked me up from school. And the second I saw him, I knew.

Bill had died.

I cried all the way home. When we got home, my dad took me across the street. We knocked on the Johnsons' door and Gordon and Eloise, Bill's folks, came to the door. We all hugged each other and cried.

That happened in 1971 also.

It's weird to me that somehow the Lord is allowing me to go back thirty-nine years *at this point* in my life. What am I to think about all that? Why remember it all now?

Well, Psalm 106 gave me some help today. It's actually a pretty depressing psalm because it chronicles the sins and failures of God's people throughout Old Testament history. God took His people out of Egypt through the Red Sea, but "it wasn't long before they forgot the whole thing, wouldn't wait to be told what to do. They only cared about pleasing themselves in that desert, provoked God with their insistent demands. He gave them exactly what they asked for—but along with it they got an empty heart" (verses 13–15).

It goes on to talk about their unbelief and idolatry and compromise as they moved through the wilderness and ultimately to Canaan. One sin after another. One rebellion against God added to the next. Each time God forgave them and allowed them to have another chance, only to have them to blow it again.

The psalm goes on and on, but how does it end? "Still, when God saw the trouble they were in and heard their cries for help, He remembered His Covenant with them, and immense with love, took them by the hand. He poured out his mercy on them while their captors looked on, amazed. Save us, God, our God! Gather us back out of exile so we can give thanks to your holy name and join in the glory when you are praised! Blessed by God, Israel's God! Bless now, bless always! Oh! Let everyone say Amen! Hallelujah!" (Psalm 106:44–48).

How did this story of sin end? With God wiping everyone out and wiping His hands of the wicked nation? *Nope.* It ended with mercy.

How is my story going to turn out? The same way as my dad's? Will the Lord heal me of cancer or will it get worse? Will it come back like it did for him? Or what? What will the remainder of 2010 hold?

My dad ultimately died of cancer that came back and spread to his liver, but his story ended well. Just like the Israelites, it ended with the mercy of God. My dad has been in heaven for thirty-nine years—can't get much better than that.

Whatever happens to me, my story of sin and failure will end the same way because I'm saved from sin and failure! Amen! Hallelujah.

So today I choose to think the best of God.

It's incredible to me that Jesus was thoroughly misunderstood in his public ministry on earth. Mark 3 chronicles this, and as I continue reading this chapter in the New Testament, one particular statement stood out to me today. The context of this verse is Jesus and his newly chosen group of twelve disciples (verses 16–19) encountering more crowds of people who want him to minister to them and cast out demons.

"His friends heard what was going on and went to rescue him, by force if necessary. They suspected he was getting carried away with himself" (Mark 3:21). Even Jesus' friends were skeptical! His friends!

With friends like that, who needs enemies? But am I that type of *friend* to Jesus?

I ask that because when I saw that smiling picture of my dad in Hawaii, all the doubts and fears came back, and Satan's whisper: "So you really think God cares about you? Your dad died; so will you."

Get behind me, Satan. And as Jesus went on to say to Peter, "You have no idea how God works" (Matthew 16:23). Boy, is that ever true.

Lord, I do praise you today for being at work through this cancer in my life in ways in which I have no idea. I thank you for my dad's cancer. I thank you for your mercy in his life through his illness and through his death. Thank you that he's with you and so is Bill, and someday I'll get to see them both again. Hooray!

Each day is a struggle with this disease. I need help trusting you and following you today. I do believe. Help my unbelief.

Let me serve you and honor you, no matter how my story ends up (but I know ultimately, finally, it will end up the way all the stories of your people end up—mercy). I'm a glad recipient and joyful receiver of your mercy today and forevermore. Amen.

November 6. One of the best days—*ever*

Yesterday I got to spend some extended time outside with a couple of pastor friends. I enjoyed the fellowship with them and thanked both of them, and asked them to thank the churches they serve as well, for praying for me.

When I got home, I jumped in the car with my mother and sister and we headed up to Westminster for Marilyn to meet with a business client. My mother and I waited for Marilyn, and when she was done we went to a pizza joint.

I was out all day! I know that sounds strange, but it's very unusual for me these days. In fact, I can't remember the last time I did that—maybe before chemo started.

Yesterday evening I was tired, but it was a good tired, a rejuvenated tired, if that makes sense.

When we got home, Irene's husband Al called me. One of the first things he said was, "I thought of you tonight and just wanted to call to see how you were doing. I don't know how I can encourage you." I jumped in, "Al, are you kidding? You're a huge encourager to me." And he is.

He told me some fishing stories, from recent times and from his childhood, and I laughed so hard my sides ached. Al is one of the best storytellers *ever*. In fact, a few years ago he typed out some of his stories—classics in their own right. I still have them.

So again I say: it was a good day.

When I finished my conversation with Al, I looked over at the little table that's next to my couch. I have stacks of books on the table representing the various categories of my reading these days: commentaries, Bibles in various versions, books folks have given me, books I'm in the process of reading, and books I want to read in the future. But last night I noticed a new book.

My mother's still weeding out books in her closet and other parts of the house and bringing them to me, so it's not unusual to find new books on the table. This one was a small blue book with a ring binder, with the title "1973."

Then it hit me: this was my dad's appointment book in the last year of his life! I can't believe we had it!

When I learned what this book was, I immediately turned to the month of August. Now, I don't know why I did this. In fact, it's kind of embarrassing to admit. What was I looking for among the appointments pages in August that year? Of course they were blank. Did I expect otherwise? Are you kidding?

My dad died on August 1, 1973. There are no notations after that date, *of course. Duh.*

But as I thumbed back through the book, there were plenty of notations almost right up to August 1. Most of the notes are just people's names under the heading "telephone"—calls to be made each day. Further back in that year, he even made note of friends he was meeting for lunch. Some of the pages were very full.

I'm looking at this book even as I write now. What a lesson!

My dad was very organized, so what I find in this book doesn't surprise me in the least. He would have loved personal computers and all the gadgets I have these days. I remember my dad had one of the first mobile phones that came out. Perhaps it's more accurate to say it was a "briefcase" phone. It was contained in a briefcase and the gadgetry attached to it took up the whole inside of the briefcase! Doesn't that sound strange?

But as we would say in today's vernacular, he was a "type A" personality. He was always racing from one appointment to another, always focused on work. I remember him sitting with a yellow pad of paper scribbling notes when we watched TV as a family.

Even at home, when he wasn't scribbling in his yellow pad, he was busy cleaning up and organizing. He often swooped into a room and gathered up everything that remotely looked like trash to throw it away. Sometimes he threw away stuff that wasn't trash! In fact, last night my mother told Marilyn and me a story about one of those times.

When we were preparing to leave on the trip to Hawaii in 1971, my mother was very upset. She had a habit of taking off her wedding rings to do work in the kitchen. They were sitting on a counter when my dad did one of his swoop jobs through the kitchen. As we were getting in the cab to go to the airport, she told my dad she couldn't find her rings and it was likely he had thrown them away!

So my dad jumped out of the cab and ran over to the trash can sitting on the sidewalk outside our home to look for those rings!

Lo and behold, there they were right on top of all the other trash in the trash can—a miracle! He grabbed them and off we went! Thank the Lord. Of course my mother was very glad, and I bet my dad was even happier.

But that was my dad. Now, I hasten to say his first bout with cancer in spring 1971 changed him significantly. I remember after that he made it a point to tell me he loved me much more often. I always knew he did, but I'll tell you, that's one of the best messages your mother (she was always good at saying it) and dad can leave with you when you go to sleep at night: "Son, I love you."

But anyway, back to the blue book. Here's the thing that hit me about it: my dad still worked pretty much up to the time he died. I'd forgotten this. He was sick in bed a lot in the final months of his life, but he still worked.

That little blue book represents what he focused on daily—his *to-do list* of work goals and appointments. And suddenly, when he died, there were no more *to-dos*. Wow, what a powerful message.

I just can't get over it.

Why? Because I'm like my dad and I approached my work at the church in the same way—daily lists of calls and appointments and things to accomplish. I tried to check all of them off, and at the end of the day I'd evaluate the success of that day by the number of check marks—what I got done.

Somehow now that seems to miss the mark. A focus on doing, doing, doing, going, going, going, calling, visiting, driving, and *doing* more very quickly becomes toxic because it misses the larger priority: *being.*

I'm learning that's quite possible to lose track of who you are in sea of doing. I did, up until July of this year when I found out I have cancer. The Lord knew things had to stop dead in their tracks.

This is what Jesus was talking about in the first and most famous parable in Mark 4. The best name for this parable is the parable of the soils, because this is the crucial element.

The type of soil determines everything. But here's what hit me today as I read Jesus' explanations of the various soils. "The seed cast in the weeds represents the ones who hear the Kingdom news but are overwhelmed with worries about all the things that they have to do and the things they want to get. The stress strangles what they heard, and nothing comes of it" (Mark 4:18–19).

Wow, did Jesus really say that? "Stress strangles what they heard." That describes me to a *T!* But the goal (that needs to be at the top of the daily to-do list) is "the seed planted in the good earth represents those who hear the Word, embrace it, and produce a harvest beyond their wildest dreams" (verse 20).

That's how I want to live! This is a life that sees returns well beyond the time when there are no more to-do lists.

Only the Lord is able to rescue me to live *that kind* of life. That's what Psalm 107 is all about. I think I need to spend more time in this psalm. It presents several different scenarios and describes the Lord's rescue in each.

One of the settings is illness (verse 17), but the Lord is able to deliver. "Then you called out to God in your desperate condition; he got you out in the nick of time. He spoke the word that healed you, pulled you back from the brink of death. So thank God for his marvelous love, for his miracle mercy to the children he loves; offer thanksgiving sacrifices, tell the world what he's done—sing it out" (Psalm 107:19–22). Okay, I will!

Lord, I thank you for the privilege of work. I know you put Adam in the Garden of Eden to work. Work is ordained of you. I thank you for the way my dad worked and the work ethic he taught me. So work is good.

I thank you for my dad and mother—both of whom told me and showed me they loved and love me. It's still happening today. Thank you for the little blue book.

But I confess the fact I twisted something that's good—work—into a weed-like life that choked out the seed of your Word.

Lord, clear the weeds out of the soil of my heart so the seed of your Word can find in my heart a place conducive to bearing fruit.

I choose from now on to place a priority on *being,* to keep my spiritual soil cultivated and ready each day to meet you, hear from you, love you, follow you, and finally and ultimately, do for you. Lord, I want to tell you today, "Father, I love you." Amen.

November 16. Good news—whatever!

My heart is so full of gratitude to Jesus. I'm so appreciative (that's not a strong enough word) of all the prayers that have been offered to God on my behalf, first from my church family and then from everyone in my larger family around the world, the army of people lifting me up to God. Thank you from the bottom of my heart.

I need to give a little explanation before I share today's news. When the doctor first staged my cancer, he based the number ostensibly on the fact that it had spread from my lower abdomen to my chest and neck—three places, hence stage 3. Whenever I go in for a chemo treatment, the doctor makes a point of checking my neck, so I figure he's really concerned about it.

Anyway, my mother and sister and I were sitting in a waiting room yesterday to meet with Dr Jotte. We have this meeting before each chemo treatment. He came in and greeted us as he always does. I tell you, I like him. He's very personable and genuine.

After the greetings he said, "Well, John, are you ready for some good news?" At that moment I felt as if I'd just made a thirty-foot putt for eagle on the golf course. Are you kidding? He went on, "Well, the CT scan showed that your chest is completely better—no signs of cancer. That's one thing. The other is that the *bulge* (he used another word for it) has diminished by sixty percent in the way we measure things, which is kind of different. In actual volume, it's probably closer to seventy to eighty percent. So you're making great progress." *Praise God!*

I asked him about my neck and he said he didn't order the CT scan to look at my neck at this time, but he didn't seem that worried about it. He indicated that when the chemo treatments have been completed, they'll do another PET scan to make more of a determination about how everything is going (including my neck).

Dr Jotte said he'll be attending a conference in the next couple weeks where he'll learn more about the latest treatments for the kind of cancer I have. He said some of the studies he's been reading show that eight chemo treatments may be better than six.

He also added that when I've finished chemo (whether I do six or eight treatments, and this hasn't been decided yet), I could be in maintenance mode for up to five years. Maintenance for me will involve continuing to take Rituxan. This is the first of my four cancer drugs (the *R* in RCVP), and its main purpose is to stimulate my body's attack against cancer cells. According to the doctors and nurses it's not technically a cancer drug.

I think he was just trying to prepare me for what might be ahead, and you know what—even though some of it sounded rather daunting, after hearing the *good news*, I didn't and don't care! Whatever.

And at that point I understood what Robert told me a few weeks ago (he was the cancer patient I met last time I had chemo). Robert said you do what you have to do to get better with cancer. He kept going because his previous treatments had *not* been effective. I'm now motivated for the opposite reason.

Again I say *whatever*. Dr Jotte informed us that the next three chemo treatments might be a little rougher than the first three, and he warned us to be prepared. And I'm noticing that as I type this entry this morning, my fingers feel a little numb. Weird. It may be temporary, but that's one of the symptoms they warned me about at the first. Could just be a bad nut in the cereal I ate this morning! We'll see.

Let me repeat: *whatever.*

As we were winding up the appointment, Dr Jotte said, "Well, think about me. My son just turned sixteen." We all chimed in, "Oh, so he's getting his license." "Yes," said the doctor with a rather disconcerted expression. "I've been driving a 96 Camry, but last summer I decided to get a new car and give the Camry to him. I don't think he's that excited. He came up to me the other day and said, 'Dad, I've been thinking, why don't you buy me a new Camaro? It only has two seats, and that way I'll only be able to take one friend at a time for a ride and I won't get into any trouble." We all laughed.

Dr Jotte's reply was, "Son, I have a better idea. I'm just going to give you the 96 Camry. It's such a duddy car that none of your friends will want to ride with you!" That's such a typical dad's response to the logic of a sixteen-year-old.

His story was so great, it led me to segue to this. As I was praying about the results of this test and trying to keep my focus on trusting Him and not outcomes, I struggled with what to ask Him for, even after everything He's been teaching me about going to Him as one of His children. In spite of all of that, I think I was asking for a 1970 Pinto! "Lord, just a hint of improvement—some little indication that I might possibly be doing a little tiny bit better."

That's what I was hoping, but so many others were asking for a Camaro on my behalf! So many people I've talked to, especially at church, express the confidence that only God can give. "John, the Lord is going to heal you." And in my best moments, my faith in the Lord is strong, but at other times I struggle with unbelief. I'm just being honest here.

Dr Jotte has six kids total. And to carry this analogy out further, it's as if my *dad* listened to my "five" brothers and sisters who were asking for a Camaro, and did what *they* asked on my behalf! And God, much more of a dad than any human father and beyond all human expectations, gave me a BMW Z3!

Above and beyond my wildest dreams! Paul's expression, and one we often quote at church is, "And I pray that you, being rooted and established in love, may have power, together with all the saints, to grasp how wide and long and high and deep is the love of Christ, and to know this love that surpasses knowledge—that you may be filled to the measure of all the fullness of God. Now to him who is able to do *immeasurably more that all we ask or imagine,* according to his power at work within us" (Ephesians 3:17–20, NIV, emphasis mine).

All day long yesterday, a chorus we sang at church Sunday was on my mind, particularly as I was taking chemo and thanking Him: "Evermore I will love you, evermore I will serve you."[15]

Evermore. This praise to God needs to lead to some godly self-talk. That's what's going on in Psalm 116. I love the self-talk in this song and what it leads to. "I said to myself, 'Relax and rest. God has showered you with blessings. Soul, you've been rescued from death; Eye, you've been rescued from tears; And you, Foot, were kept from stumbling'" (Psalm 116:7–8). Amen.

The psalmist declares, "I'm striding in the presence of God, alive in the land of the living! … What can I give back to God for the blessings he's poured out on me? I'll lift high the cup of salvation—a toast to God! I'll pray in the name of God; I'll complete what I promised God I'd do and I'll do it together with his people" (verses 9, 12–14).

As a general rule, I don't like toasts. But in this case I'm lifting a cup full of blessings to God!

Lord, I can't begin to thank you enough today. I praise you for the good report and for answering the prayers of all my brothers and sisters in a way that far exceeds anything I can imagine. Thank you, thank you. *Thank* you.

Even as I do that, I pray for Robert today. I pray for Jorge and Vida's friend Estella and for Fatty Taylor, all of whom are suffering with cancer. Heal them, Lord.

"John, you've received a great blessing from God—you knot head." Help me not to be a knot head. Help me learn from this, Dad. Lengthen my stride today in your presence and give me the grace to live a life of integrity together with all God's people. Amen.

November 18. International Thanksgiving dinner—regardless of me

Yesterday was another one of those days in which the necessity was to push through some tough stuff, to use Jon's phrase again. I honestly don't think I felt as bad as I normally do on day three after chemo, but it's a flu-like body ache and an overall restlessness. I guess it's a combination of the steroid and the shot acting up.

What made it a little more difficult was we had a big event at church last night—our annual international Thanksgiving fellowship. All the congregations who use the building—the English-speakers,

Spanish-speakers, Portuguese-speakers, and Korean-speakers—gather together for a huge potluck to give thanks to God. It's a highlight of the year. In truth and in fact, we're not four churches but one church with four congregations; each group is intertwined with all the others. I'm thankful to be part of a church that's just a little foretaste of heaven.

One of the main reasons I wanted to go was to thank these four congregations for praying for me and to join them as we lift up praise to God Almighty. I was sort of hoping I could sneak in last night for a few minutes, but as the afternoon progressed I knew there was no way.

Instead I continued to read some poetry I've come across. Once again I discovered a gem of a book in our den as I was scouring through more books. In all my studies of Dietrich Bonhoeffer, I'd never seen this little book entitled *Voices in the Night: The Prison Poems of Dietrich Bonhoeffer,* edited and translated by Edwin Robertson.

As I've mentioned before, Bonhoeffer was part of the resistance movement against Hitler, but the Nazis found out about his clandestine activities and threw him into prison. He was there for a few years, and while in jail, he wrote quite extensively. I knew about his theological writings, but I never knew he wrote poems as well.

This little book of poems isn't for the faint of heart. They're hard to digest because they're so raw and poignant, especially when you think of the context. The one that arrested me yesterday afternoon is "Nachtliche Stimmen" or "Voices in the Night." The following stanzas begin and end this rather long poem and say everything. "Stretched out upon my prison bed, I stare at an empty wall. Outside a summer morning, regardless of me, goes rejoicing into the country. Brother, while the long night waits, until our day dawns, we shall hold our ground."[16]

It's hard for me to avoid being very emotional as I read those lines, especially the phrase "regardless of me." What an exquisite translation by Robertson. Here's a man trapped in a cell looking at the four walls around him as life, time, and summer went on *regardless of me.* He's restless through the night anticipating the execution of another "brother," another fellow prisoner, in the morning. This ultimately was Bonhoeffer's fate.

Here I am sitting in a nice house with all the freedom in the world, restless and frustrated because I can't go to a dinner at church, and I'm reading this. I can relate to Dietrich. I really can, but there's no comparison between our experiences. It's very convicting, but I'm learning more and more about the way the Spirit works.

The day before yesterday I was just trying to put myself somewhere for a while, so I sat on my mother's back porch. It was bright, sunny, and rather warm, but the wind was howling. A deep growl preceded each gust of the wind's force as it whipped up the last remaining leaves. As I sat there, I was reminded of Jesus' words to Nicodemus: "The wind blows wherever it pleases. You hear its sound, but you cannot tell where it comes from or where it is going. So it is with everyone born of the Spirit" (John 3:8, NIV).

Tuesday afternoon bore this out. I went inside after sitting on the porch, became occupied with something, and then all of sudden it was snowing—*big time.* You just never know with the wind or the Spirit of God.

In the same way, God was doing a great work through Dietrich in that prison cell, and on a much less significant scale, God is doing something through me right now.

I know He's blowing me somewhere, cooking up something beyond my wildest dreams. I sincerely believe that, but that's the work of the Holy Spirit.

The praise hymn I came to this morning reminds me of this. I don't know the hymn, but the title is "The God of Abraham Praise." The second verse begins with the beautiful phrase, "His Spirit floweth free."[17]

Amen. *His Spirit floweth free,* and He does this in all types of situations and settings.

The Holy Spirit is never confined to a prison cell. Think about Paul. Think about Dietrich. Think about Richard Wurmbrand—all preachers in jail, but their lives and messages weren't. Think about sickness and confinement. He is not limited.

It's hard to keep this in mind as time passes *regardless of me*. But there's no circumstance or situation that can limit God.

That's what Psalm 118 is all about. I love the psalm's rhythm and repetition and cadence, which Peterson brings out so well. Triplet statements predominate. For example: "Hemmed in by barbarians, in God's name I rubbed their faces in the dirt; Hemmed in and with no way out, in God's name I rubbed their faces in the dirt; Like swarming bees, like wild prairie fire, they hemmed me in; in God's name I rubbed their faces in the dirt" (Psalm 118:1–12).

Here's another triplet: "God's my strength, he's also my song, and now he's my salvation" (verse 14). This psalm is a testimony to the way God can bring His people through tough times. "God tested me, he pushed me hard, but he didn't hand me over to Death" (verse 18). "Thank God—He's so good. His love never quits" (verse 29).

Amen. I can honestly say these days in the toughest part of the chemo cycle, His love never quits.

Lord, I acknowledge that the wind of your Spirit is howling. It's strong and powerful. I certainly can't trace where it's going, but today I set my sail. Blow, Spirit of God, blow. Blow me where you want me to go.

Thank you for these days of restless confinement. I admit it's hard to be on the sidelines as life and ministry go by, but I know this is your plan for me *for now*.

I have no idea what's going to happen in the future, but I know *who holds* the future—*you*. I know you'll take care of me just as you took care of Dietrich fifty-five years ago. In life or in death. You flow free! Amen.

November 21. Trust the Lord, not solutions

How about this for a title? "God, Who Stretched the Spangled Heavens." Is this the same *spangled* as "The Star-Spangled Banner?" I'd imagine so. Again, I don't know this hymn, but the first words of the third verse captured my attention today: "As thy new horizons beckon, Father, [g]ive us strength."[18]

What an encouraging prayer for believers! That pretty much sums up the adventure and goal of faith. Good word!

Well, another Sunday in which I won't be preaching and won't even go to church. It's weird, but I'm thankful for another day of rest. I just haven't been sleeping well and feel particularly tired this morning. Again (and I know I sound like a broken record), fatigue is the main thing I'm dealing with these days. I did some things yesterday, but then I came home and sat on the couch, and I was out like a light for over an hour.

There's another reason it probably isn't a good idea for me to be at church today. Betty told me the other day a lot of people have been getting sick. We had a movie night at church a couple Fridays ago and several of the folks involved in this ministry came down with a flu bug. Betty herself was one of them. It's just that time of year, I suppose.

But I just don't need to be exposed to that kind of thing, and neither do my mother and sister. It's hard for all of us to be away from the fellowship of the body of Christ. Very hard. Again, this situation won't last forever, and we're trying to keep the ultimate goal in mind—to get through chemo without being delayed because I picked up some sort of virus or influenza. But I'm still having trouble dealing with all this. It's getting tiresome.

Mother and Marilyn and I finished watching a Bonhoeffer documentary last night. Of course the Nazis eventually did capture and imprison him. He was in jail in Berlin for about two years, if my memory serves me correctly. While in prison, he continued to write. Many of his letters and papers and poems are preserved. (I mentioned the book of his poems the other day. I'm making my way through that book very slowly. It's just so deeply convicting that someone who's in prison can write poetry, knowing he probably isn't going to survive.)

Bonhoeffer was also working on a book entitled *Ethics*. He actually never finished the book before his martyrdom, but after Bonhoeffer died his biographer Eberhard Bethge pulled his notes together into a book. One of Dietrich's main points in *Ethics* was a definition of doing the will of God. He contended it wasn't about rules; it was about abandoning oneself to God. That's what Dietrich did as he continued to serve the Lord in prison while opposing the Nazi regime.

Doing the will of God isn't about rules. If only it were! It would be a lot easier.

So much of what goes on in contemporary teaching and preaching in churches is the *formula-izing* of Christianity—easy platitudes for solving all life's problems, that fit into a neat little five-part sermon series or a brochure for mailing: "Five Steps to Conquering Worry," "How to Affair-Proof Your Marriage," and so on. Somehow these little prescriptions turn my stomach. And I've used them myself, so I'm just as guilty as anyone. But they limit God or give the illusion of doing so. No one, including and especially a preacher, can *actually* limit Him!

God doesn't operate with rules and formulas. If He did, we could figure Him out! But He is above and beyond all that. Two passages come to mind at this point.

"'For my thoughts are not your thoughts, neither are your ways my ways,' declares the Lord. 'As the heavens are higher than the earth, so are my ways higher than your ways and my thoughts than your thoughts. As the rain and the snow come down from heaven, and do not return to it without watering the earth and making it bud and flourish, so that it yields seed for the sower and bread for the eater, so is my word that goes out from my mouth: It will not return to me empty, but will accomplish what I desire and achieve the purpose for which I sent it'" (Isaiah 55:8–11, NIV).

"Oh, the depths of the riches of the wisdom and knowledge of God! How unsearchable his judgments, and his paths beyond tracing out! 'Who has known the mind of the Lord? Or who has been his counselor? Who has ever given to God, that God should repay him?' For from him and through him and to him are all things. To him be the glory forever! Amen" (Romans 11:33–36, NIV). We can't figure God out!

Can you imagine Bonhoeffer trying to do that? What would the title of his sermons series from the Berlin prison be? "Four Ways to Live for Jesus and Assassinate Hitler"? I can't imagine what he went through, but his task, like mine right now with cancer, was to do the will of God when there are no easy explanations or immediate fixes.

That's why right now my mind and heart gravitate toward encouragements to trust the Lord and not *solutions.* For example, this chapter in Jack Taylor's book *After the Spirit Comes* caught my eye the other day: "When God Doesn't Come Through." I love this title, even though it's a little misleading. Taylor asserts that God *always comes through,* but not always in the way I desire or in my appointed time. And he cites story after story from Scripture that confirms this.

After listing some examples, Taylor makes this great point at the end of the chapter: "What about all the others we haven't taken time to explain? They need no explanation because God can't be explained. Neither do his works need to be defended or justified. His ways are not up for votes. He works all things after the counsel of his own will."

He continues, "Yes, there are times when God does not come through in our timing and yet he always will come through. We need to give him such a free hand with ourselves that he could mind his business in us in his own way and not ever hear a murmur from us."[19]

Wow, not ever hearing a murmur from me would be a miracle! But He defies explanation, so why should I try? But I do try, even on a day like today.

This is why the words of Psalm 119 are so crucial for me right now. Because I can't explain what God is doing right now, what do I do? Here are some verses that made an impression on me this morning: "I can see now, God, that your decisions are right; your testing has taught me what's true and right … And let me live whole and holy, soul and body, so I can always walk with my head held high … I watch my step, avoiding the ditches and ruts of evil so I can spend all my time keeping your Word" (Psalm 119:75, 80, 101).

I may not be able to figure things out, but I can stay on the path of God's Word and trust it will not return *void* (the KJV term used in Isaiah 55:11) without accomplishing God's plan and purpose.

Lord, I thank you again for what you're doing. I thank you that your ways are above my ways; your thoughts are way above my thoughts. You're the Counselor, not me.

I confess I'm struggling with just plugging along, another Sunday out of the saddle. But I lift up JJ as he preaches for me today, and the services at the church. You certainly don't need me there to do great works. In fact, thank you for all you're doing without me in the loop as much as I was before I got cancer.

God, I choose to give up the futile effort of trying to figure you out. I choose instead to abandon myself to you like Bonhoeffer did and spend my time keeping your Word. I love you today. Amen.

November 25. Thanksgiving 2010—the best *ever*

This is the thought that's been rolling around in my head in anticipation of this holiday.

Now that the day's arrived, I don't feel well from a physical standpoint. I ate some crazy food yesterday (spicy jalapeño chips at lunch and barbecued beef for dinner), and it's affecting my stomach *big time*. It was indeed stupid.

But in spite of that, my heart is so full of gratitude; so many things come to mind that I just have to list them in no particular order. Lord, I thank you for:

Your great faithfulness
Jesus
Saving me at the age of nine
My dad and his cancer
My mother
My sister
My home
Cancer
The power of God through the prayers of many folks
The good report from the CT scan a few days ago
The way you've helped me *not* to feel as bad as I thought
    I would
Dr Jotte

The nurses who've helped me—Connie, Kayla, Jean, Nicole, Diane, Terry, and all the others

The Rocky Mountain Cancer Center

Roger whom I met the first day of chemo

Miracles

Robert whom I met later

Donnie in Louisiana

Ladies in the church who've had cancer and are now recovering: Linda and Kay

Everyone else I know who's had cancer and been healed by God

Doug, Al, JJ, John, and Jose—the guys who've preached for me since I've had cancer

Betty, Mary Ann, and Barb—the ladies on staff at church who've taken on extra work these past few months

Bernard and John—the guys who pray every Sunday morning whether I'm there or not

Caring Bridge website and the technology that makes what I write immediately accessible on the Internet

The grace and desire to write each day

The Word of God

The inspiration and illumination of the Holy Spirit

Everyone who takes the time to read the blog and comment on it

Every prayer offered on my behalf these past few months

Every text message from Dan and Dan and Rob and others

Every email sent my way

All the cards and notes from Lettie and everyone else

Those like Richard who take the time to write in the guestbook, whether just once or every day

Those like Al and Ronnie who leave voice mail messages to tell me they're thinking of me and praying for me

My pastor friends James, Mike, Allen, Steve, Dan (and Dan), Bart, and Rob

The support from Bob and others in the Mile High
    Association
Mark's email prayer messages
Everyone who's praying for me in the State Convention of
    Colorado
Rick and his church in Louisiana
Bobby and Barbara's church in Jacksonville and the ladies
    who made the quilt
Cindy's church in Georgia and their public prayers for me
Mark and Sam's special prayer meeting
Jon and Lynda—their counsel and prayers
Those who've cooked food for my family and me
The people around the world who're praying for me
The love and support and prayers of my church family
These days and weeks and months out of the loop of the
    daily operation of the church
Time to pray
The walks
The books you've led me to read
Your daily love and mercy, morning by morning ...

I could go on and on and on—so many more names (I've left
out so many) and examples (I could list so many more) of the
demonstrated love of Jesus ...

Praise God!

After writing this list, I regret I don't do this type of thing more
often. So much of my praying is about me—how I feel and what I
want from God. I think that *me* focus blinds me to the Lord and
what He's already done. Hello!

It's so easy to focus on myself and take my eyes and ears off Jesus.
This is the lesson of the transfiguration. In Mark 9, Jesus took Peter,
James, and John up on the mountain where he was transfigured
before their eyes: "his clothes shimmered, glistening white, whiter
than any bleach could make them" (Mark 9:3). And all of a sudden,
Jesus was talking with Elijah and Moses! Never at a loss for words,

Peter blurted out, "Rabbi, this is a great moment! Let's build three memorials—one for you, one for Moses, one for Elijah" (verse 5).

In other words, Peter wanted to put these three on the same level of recognition and honor. Nope.

All of sudden, a voice from the cloud spoke. "This is my Son, marked by my love. Listen to him" (verse 7). Translation: Jesus is *not* on par with Moses and Elijah. He's God's only Son. *And* instead of talking and blurting out nonsense (Peter and John Talbert and all the rest of us who do that over and over), listen to God.

At the end of chapter 8, as Jesus was teaching the disciples about the cross, he concluded with "the Son of Man when he arrives in all the splendor of God, his Father, with an army of the holy angels" (Mark 8:38). This is no ordinary coming because Jesus is no ordinary human, and he gave the disciples a glimpse of this glory on the mountain.

He has no peer; he's the unique Son of God and Son of man.

And I pray today I won't make Peter's mistake of trying to lower him to my level. I pray my praise and thanksgiving will exalt him to the level he alone occupies as Savior and Lord. And because he is Lord, I pray I might spend more time listening than talking.

And there's one other aspect of thanksgiving … I stumbled across another hymn today as I cheated (instead of progressing through the hymns in numerical order as I've been doing the past couple weeks, I went to one of the indexes in the back of the hymnal to find the thanksgiving section). I don't know what I was looking for, but when my eye landed on the title of one particular hymn, I knew I'd found it.

Here's the title (one of the best *ever*): "Thanksgiving/Thanks-Living." How's that? Wow! *I love it!*

I don't know the tune, but I'm going to learn it. I guarantee you. Here are some of the lyrics: "A life of living thankfulness moves lifeless words to willingness."[20]

Words only go so far. Living is what counts.

Again I say, "Wow." Amen. Thanksgiving leads to Thanks-Living.

Oh Lord, from the bottom of my heart I thank you today. I'm so glad you've allowed me to have cancer so I can learn to praise you and thank you. Teach me to turn this gratitude into attitude and act-itude!

It is not and never has been about me. It's all about you. As I've prayed before, make me a road for you to travel on.

You are without peer or equal. You are high and lifted up. Be exalted by my life, and may my living for you *never* be the same—Thanks-Living. Yes! Amen!

November 30. Expanding praise time

With the songbook Jim gave me Sunday (he said we have them at church), I'm getting to sing some choruses as well. "We Will Glorify" is one. "He is Lord of heaven, Lord of earth; He is Lord of all who live."[21]

Lord Jehovah, Lord of heaven, Lord of earth, Lord of all—these are titles for my Savior that I need to remember today.

Going back to the hymnal, I found a song we sang Sunday. One of the things I love about what the Lord's doing in our church is the increased number of testimonies. Jim gave a good word from 1 Peter 5:7 in the New Living Translation: "Give all your worries and cares to God, for he cares about you." How about that? Good word, Jim.

At the end of the service, Helen got up to make an announcement about a women's ministry event this weekend. Lorraine was prepared to give one as well. In the little moment of awkwardness as both women stood to speak at the same time, Lorraine said to Helen, "Age before beauty." We all broke out laughing. Helen did too, but she turned to Lorraine and said, "I'm going to take care of that after the service." It was hilarious—two buddies giving each other a hard time. *I love it.*

But we had another testimony also. Belle shared a word about her experience at a single adult conference at Glorietta Encampment in New Mexico. Belle and her husband Chuck are *mature adults* (Helen's new term for *seniors*) in our church, *huge* encouragers. I've often shared fellowship with them in their home. They were a part of a home Bible study group I led and were always positive participants. That's just the way they are. I appreciate them so much.

Belle shared that the Lord touched her with the hymn "Holy Ground"—at the conference, and still. After she mentioned it, we sang this hymn together, chorus and verses. It was memorable.

Anyway, the Lord is pulling together the chorus book, the hymnal, and the encouragements from corporate worship to enhance my daily worship time with Jesus. I'm learning praise is a spark plug that gets the motor going. It's something that helps me tie together the Bible passages I read each day. And here's another thing. The words of these songs stay in my mind throughout the day, particularly if I know the tune. It's beautiful.

One of the things that happened to me in my quiet time before I got cancer was a truncation of my walk with the Lord. Let me see if I can explain this. When I was in a hurry (and I seemed to be hurrying *all the time*), I'd get up with a distracted mind. I struggled with reading the Bible, finishing, and then not remembering anything I just read. This would go on for days and weeks, and instead of dealing with it, I just quashed it and went on.

My prayer time suffered as well, and I notice this in my journal entries before July of this year. They consisted of gripes and complaints followed by selfish prayer requests. Before I go further, I want to clarify what I mean by *selfish prayer requests*. I certainly believe it's okay to ask God *anything*. He puts no boundaries on prayer requests. I can go to Him with any need or concern or request that's on my heart, absolutely.

But I classify a request as selfish when I don't get around to praying about anything or anyone else *except me*. That's what I was doing! I might mention others in a perfunctory way, but I wasn't really praying for them as I should. I know this now.

I confess all this to you, Lord. I was actually moving away from you while doing things that should have drawn me closer to you. As I write this I'm reminded of something that happened to me my first year in seminary. I lived alone in an apartment on Forrest Ridge Circle East. I was studying one day at my little kitchen table, reading James 5:5. In the NIV, it reads this way: "Or do you think

Scripture says without reason that the spirit he caused to live in us envies intensely?" This is one way to read this verse: small *s* spirit (our human spirit) in its proclivity to envy. This is a viable option for translation.

But I learned that day there are two ways to take the words in the Greek, and the Amplified version brings out this second way: "Or, do you suppose that the Scripture is speaking to no purpose that says, 'The Spirit Whom He has caused to dwell in us yearns over us and He yearns for the Spirit with a jealous love?'" So this verse can also be talking about the Holy Spirit (capital *S*) and the way God yearns over us to be His friends (the contrast in verse 4 is between God's enemies and God's friends) with His jealous love. So you can read this verse as making a statement about God.

Wow. What a statement it is.

Sitting alone in my apartment that day, it hit me. *God actually yearns for me.* He yearns for communion with the Spirit He caused to dwell in me. And honestly, that day I felt God yearning for fellowship with me, and my initial reaction was to push Him away, just as I'd been doing before getting cancer this year. "God, I'm too busy. Don't you know I have to study?"

But the more I pushed, the more He pushed back. "John, I want to spend time with you now." I felt Him yearning for communion with me right then and there. And finally (and it embarrasses me to think how long it took me to get to this point) I just pushed my books away and *stopped* just to be with Him.

Even as I remember that and write about it, it overwhelms me that the God of the universe yearns for communion with a worm like me. He's jealous for time with me! And not just that day. But every day. Today. Now.

Oh Jesus, I'm sitting in your lap and I just want to hug you.

I'm sorry. I'm so wrong. I acknowledge all the times I've pushed you away in the very act of doing a religious exercise like quiet time, and all the other times I pushed you away.

I want to experience what Psalm 125 talks about: "Those who trust in God are like Zion Mountain: Nothing can move it, a rock-solid mountain you can always depend on. Mountains encircle

Jerusalem, and God encircles his people—always has and always will … God will round up the backsliders, corral them with the incorrigibles. Peace over Israel!" (Psalm 125:1–2, 5). Gulp. I want to be surrounded by dependable God and His love instead of being in the corral with the incorrigibles!

Oh Abba Father, thank you for the hugs that surround me this morning. I need your help and strength for another day. Thank you for these early morning times you're providing for me, now that I have cancer.

It's still hard for me not to think about and worry about what's ahead for me. It does get scary at times, still.

But thank you for the gifts of praise and songs and testimonies and laughter and God's people and prayer and the Word and everything you, Abba Father, have given us to help us commune with you. Thank you for your jealous love. I bring you close, right now. I embrace your pierced side. Oh Abba Father. Oh Jesus. Oh Spirit. I love you. Amen.

December 3. Questions, questions, questions

What is it about us as humans that we ask so many questions? Oops, there's another question!

At the end of Mark 11 and just about all the way through Mark 12, various groups (religious groups, I might add) asked Jesus questions. The narrative in these chapters makes it look like an inquisition, a parade of questioners, one after another, with wrong motives.

As I read these chapters, I've been thinking of all the questions that have come to my mind over the past couple months since I was diagnosed with cancer. Of course there are the *why* questions: Why me? Why cancer? Why now? But honestly, I've been around enough and have seen enough sick people in my life and ministry that those types of questions don't predominate, and it isn't because of any extra spirituality on my part.

It's just that I've heard those questions so often. People have asked me as a pastor, "Why did God allow this to happen?" And so many times I've had to answer, "I have no idea." And really there are no answers to those *why* questions.

As far as I'm concerned, I have some *guesses* about those *why* questions, but that's the best I can offer. And I have another response: "Why not me? Why not cancer? Why not now?" And how about this question: "Lord, why have you blessed me so much, even during cancer?"

It's easy to turn the *why* question around, but I rarely hear the flip side of these questions, especially coming out of my mouth! So the *why* questions are there for me, but they aren't prominent.

Here are the questions that *are* prominent: how did I get cancer? What's going to happen to me? What do you want to teach me by way of this? Am I going to make it? When will I be done with treatments forever? Where are you leading me in all this? I'm not asking one category of question all that much (the *why* questions), but I'm asking all the others (the *how, what, when, and where* questions). Great.

And it's interesting how the Lord is dealing with all these questions. Once again, I can hazard *guesses* at the answers to some of these questions. I can only guess about the future as I read and respond to what He shows me in His Word, in prayer, through others, and by the Spirit on a day-to-day basis. But looking at the questions I wrote above, most of them have to do with the future and with the eternal counsel of God, and those are *way* beyond me. But I still ask them, over and over.

Questions.

It's interesting to see how the Lord handles questions. As I read these two chapters of questions in Mark, I'm reminded of another significant section of questions in the Bible, in the story of Job. Job asked the Lord a ton of questions about his suffering, especially on the heels of all the advice he received from his so-called friends.

His buddies were trying to help, but they only muddied the waters because basically they were telling Job, "Hey listen, pal, you must have done something really bad to lose your whole family and end up on this trash heap. Confess your sins to God." (See Job 11:13–20 for an example of this advice).

This type of thing happened to my mother after my dad died of cancer. One her friends came by a few days after his death and said, "Mary Louise, if you had had enough faith, Jerry would not have died." Can you believe that? It still makes me angry even to write those words.

But now that I have cancer, I do understand that comment a little better simply because it reflects our human tendency to find something or someone to blame for calamity and tragedy. And it goes into the loop of the whole questioning mindset. We have to try to find reasons and explanations. That's just what we humans do.

Well Job doesn't tolerate his friends' accusations, but toward the end of the book he still seeks explanations through his questions of God. There's so much verbiage in the book of Job, so much talking and asking and inquiring. Job is like a windup toy, the Energizer Bunny, but he finally winds down and shuts up, at least long enough to allow God a chance to speak.

What does God do? It's rather abrupt. "Why do you confuse the issue? Why do you talk without knowing what you're talking about? Pull yourself together, Job! Up on your feet! Stand tall! I have some questions for you, and I want some straight answers. Where were you when I created the earth? Tell me since you know so much! Who decided on its size? Certainly you'll know that! Who came up with the blueprints and measurements?" (Job 38:2–5). In other words, God answers Job's questions by asking him a whole bunch of questions Job can't answer! How about that?

That's what Jesus did in Mark 11 and 12. Some of the high priests, religious scholars, and leaders came to ask him, "Show us your credentials. Who authorized you to speak and act like this?" (Mark 11:28). Jesus answered, "Sure, I'll be glad to answer your question if you answer mine: The baptism of John—who authorized it?" (verses 29–30, my paraphrase). He answered their question with a question they couldn't answer (because they worshiped human opinion).

And at the beginning of Mark 12, Jesus turned the finger of accusation on them with his story of the wicked farmhands and the vineyard. Of course from Isaiah 5 onward, the vineyard in Scripture is a metaphor for Israel. And this story points to the cross and the Jews' rejection and murder of the landowner's son. Jesus told this story, and again the leaders had nothing to say, but they didn't learn their lesson.

Beginning in verse 13, various groups of religious folk came to Jesus with questions. What do you believe about taxes? What about marriage in heaven? What about the greatest law? All these questions were accusative, trying to trap Jesus, trying to back him into a corner of self-incrimination. And Jesus answered them all. Perfectly.

It's interesting that after all these questions, Jesus does what God did in Job. *He* asked a question. "How is it that the religion scholars say that the Messiah is David's 'son,' when we all know that David, inspired by the Holy Spirit, said, God said to my Master, 'Sit here at my right hand until I put your enemies under your feet'" (verses 35–36). Well no one could answer his question, and it shut up everyone for good. No more questions for Jesus.

So these passages are helping me. I'm learning about questions. I honestly don't think it's wrong to ask the Lord questions. We're human. He has made us. We're weak and fragile and we struggle. He certainly understands.

But I do think two things. First, God knows the motives of our questions and that's what He's concerned about. Jesus knew the motives of all those religious groups. He saw right through them. For example, he said to the Pharisees who asked about taxes, "Why are you playing games with me? Bring me a coin and let me look at it" (verse 15). And he went on to expose their motive in answering their question.

So he sees our hearts. But also he addresses the real issues. God reminded Job of His sovereignty. Job struggled with this truth. With the Sadducees, Jesus corrected their lack of knowledge of his Word and his power.

I guess what I'm saying is I'd better be ready to receive correction from the Lord when I ask questions. He will not be truncated down to being simply an answer to a question. God is so much bigger than that. He's concerned about life, my life, and has the broad picture in mind.

Here's the way things ended up, both with Job and with all those who tried to pepper Jesus with questions: silence. Maybe I can learn from this.

He is Lord, and thank goodness I'm *not*.

This is reinforced by the songs I came to this morning. I won't write the words out, but the *Magnify the Lord* songbook linked these three choruses together: "Emmanuel," "Jesus, Name Above All Names," and "His Name Is Wonderful." Fantastic! Here's a moniker for the Lord in the final song: "Master of everything."[22] Indeed He is, even Master of every question. Not just answerer of every question. Master.

He's Master of sunrises! What a beautiful orange sky He's making right now! I'm going to just look at it for a while.

Back to the songs. The next hymn is "If You Will Only Let God Guide You." The second verse begins: "Only be still, and wait His leisure [i]n cheerful hope, with heart content."[23]

Wow, God cares so much for us that He sees through our questions to our hearts and meets those deepest needs.

Psalm 128, another pilgrim song, makes this statement, "Stand in awe of God's Yes. Oh, how he blesses the one who fears God!" (Psalm 128:4). I love that! Whatever the question, God has already answered *yes!* Jesus is God's yes. Praise his name!

Lord, I acknowledge today that you are King of kings and Lord of lords, Master of everything. Thank you for your patience with me in all my questions. Thank you for caring so much for me that you address all my questions, even if you don't answer all of them.

I'm glad you don't answer all my questions. If you did all the time, I know I might begin to trust the answer and not The Answer. So I'm better off with The Answer.

And I know I couldn't handle the answer if you gave it to me.

So, I choose today to settle on you, the One who has all the answers. I'll trust you today and thank you for letting me spill out all my questions, but in the end, I'll shut up and trust your sovereignty and love today. Amen.

December 4. Unearthing garbage

That's really the only way to say it. It's one of the main things that's going on with me.

Yesterday, even though it was rather gusty (to say the least), was a beautiful day. The temperature reached nearly seventy degrees, and in December. Are you kidding me?

I'm so thankful for the relatively warm weather we've been experiencing this late fall here in Colorado. And even as I write that sentence, I know I speak out of selfish motives. When it's warmer, I so enjoy getting outside and driving or walking or whatever. Thank you Lord.

I relish more and more the latter days of my three-week chemo cycle when I finally feel well enough and energized enough to get off the couch. And conversely, I dread more and more next week and another chemo treatment just because of the way it knocks me for a loop. But I'm not complaining. I'm thankful this whole process is progressing and I'm getting near the end of this phase of treatment.

Anyway, all that to say I was glad to be able to get out of the house yesterday. *But* I'm noticing more and more the Lord is speaking to me—not in an audible voice. It is, as someone has said, much louder than that. I can just be driving around and all of a sudden, *bang*. The Lord brings something to mind. He's convicting me of sin—unearthing garbage.

This image takes me back to my college days. My sophomore year at Baylor University, I moved off campus to live in an apartment with three other guys—Carter, Chuck, and Scott. The first few months of our new living arrangement were rough because none of us had ever lived on our own before.

I remember we started off the year dividing the cooking responsibilities among us. Well that was disastrous because none of us had ever cooked before. I think we all realized this one night when we were sitting at our kitchen table eating Tuna Helper for the third night in a row. Yuck. Tuna Helper wouldn't be good if the best gourmet chef on the planet prepared it!

We were sitting there looking at each other when I said, "Guys, this isn't working. I'll tell you what. Let's just all eat on our own— every man for himself." That sounds selfish, I know, but at that point in my life it was all about survival. And I'd already decided (and the decision persists to this day) I wasn't a cook and I was going to buy a meal plan at the dorm just so I could eat some decent food. And you know if dorm food was appealing to me, I was in desperate condition! Actually, it really wasn't all that bad. At least they never served Tuna Helper!

So we all shifted gears and it saved the day, especially for me because none of the other guys wanted to eat at the dorm. Fine and dandy. Go for it, *but I survived!*

Well the cooking and eating part of apartment life was only one aspect of the struggle Carter, Chuck, Scott, and I faced. The other part was cleaning the apartment. Again, we made assignments in that regard, but none of us followed through. Who wants to vacuum the carpet when you can shoot hoop with some buddies?

As you can imagine, things quickly got bad in the kitchen and in the bathroom (we only had one for four guys; I'll leave the details to your imagination!).

My sister was also a student at Baylor University at the time, and my mother paid us a visit in the fall of my sophomore year. I invited her to the apartment, and I'll never forget the look on her face as she walked through the rooms! I can laugh now, but it wasn't funny then. I was in trouble! She wasn't happy. And I was tired of living in squalor!

After the walk-through, she kicked us all out and spent the better part of two days cleaning the apartment from top to bottom. None of us complained, of course. The fact is we were embarrassed, but not embarrassed enough to do anything about it! Naturally one of her conditions for the cleanup was changes in the way we operated. We all took her seriously!

Mother found garbage in all sorts of places, and threw out a bunch of old food and cleaned the bathroom thoroughly. It was a Herculean feat, and I'm surprised she didn't end up in the hospital.

But honestly, this is the closest description I can come up with to what the Spirit of God is doing in my life right now. He's going through the rooms of my heart one by one, and cleaning out all the garbage. It reminds me of Robert Boyd Munger's little book *My Heart Christ's Home.* Using this same analogy, Munger traces Christ's *walk-through* of the heart and the cleanup he wants to do.

This is what the Spirit of God is doing. It's *his* house. Me.

As Jesus has been walking through the rooms of my heart in recent days, he's pointed out a couple symptoms of my pre-cancer life: busy-ness and laziness. I know I just pushed the Spirit aside so often, allowing issues to accumulate in the corners of closets in my heart. But now that I have cancer and there's more leisure and space and time for the Spirit to speak, things are coming to light.

I believe this is what Paul is talking about in Romans 8. "But if the Spirit of Him who raised Jesus from the dead dwells in you, He who raised Christ Jesus from the dead will also give life to your mortal bodies through His Spirit who dwells in you. So then, brethren, we're under obligation, not to the flesh, to live according to the flesh—for if you are living according to the flesh, you must die, but if by the Spirit you are putting to death the deeds of the body, you will live" (Romans 8:11–13, New American Standard Bible, hereafter cited as NASB).

This is what the Spirit is doing. He allowed me to have cancer. He led me into this experience of one of life's greatest stop signs. He's bringing sin to mind. And I believe when he does this, it's my responsibility to confess it to him, repent, and turn to him in faith. This is the process of the Spirit "putting to death the deeds of the body." This is reckoning myself dead to sin but alive to him, as Paul states earlier in Romans (chapter 6).

It's all because Jesus sees things at a far more profound level than anybody. At the end of Mark 12, Jesus is observing the religious crowd once again, this time as they're putting money in the offering plate. He's standing in the temple observing. And it's significant that Jesus' insight and knowledge and understanding of every person in that room leads him to know with intimacy about the offering he or she is putting in the plate. "Many of the rich were making large contributions. One poor widow came up and put in two small coins—a measly two cents" (Mark 12:41–42). Jesus saw all this when no one else could see it at his level.

Then Jesus made this comment to the disciples: "The truth is that this poor widow gave more to the collection than all the others put together. All the others gave what they'll never miss; she gave extravagantly what she couldn't afford—she gave her all" (verses 43–44). You can't hide anything from Jesus!

One of the main areas of conviction for me is a reordering of priorities. I need to value Jesus' opinion more than that of any human. I need to care more about what Jesus sees than what others think. Lord, I confess this to you right now.

It should be all about him, not about me or anyone or anything else.

That's what the medley of songs I came across today is all about. I love the combination of songs in the *Magnify the Lord* songbook. In the medley entitled "Call Upon the Lord," the first song is "Unto Thee, O Lord." The fourth verse starts with these words: "Remember not, the sins of my youth."[24]

I'm so thankful today that as the Spirit convicts and I confess, he forgives and forgets the sins of youth and the sins of yesterday.

The second song in the medley is "Day by Day." Yes, Lord. Those three things, that's what I want. I want to see you with the eyes of faith. I want my love for you to grow each day. And I want to follow you, as closely as possible, each and every day. And because I want those things, I will call upon the Lord, who is worthy to be praised. So shall I be saved from my enemies, I will call upon the Lord.

The hymn for today reinforces this as well. It's "Like a River Glorious." I love this hymn. I hadn't sung it for a long time until today. One of my favorite lines of all is the refrain: "Stayed upon Jehovah, hearts are fully blessed."[25]

That's what the Lord is all about.

Psalm 129 affirms the Lord is able to take care of our enemies and lead us to the affirmation, "We bless you in God's name!" (Psalm 129:8).

Lord, I thank you for the ministry of the Holy Spirit. Thank you for his work of conviction. Thank you for the specific issues he's bringing to light in order to allow me to confess and forsake them.

I acknowledge the sin of failing to keep my confession up to date. I confess my *closets* are full of garbage.

Clean out the closets of my heart, Lord. This is hard to go through. As the doctors are putting poison in me to kill cancer cells, at the same time you're taking poison out of me. And this whole process is making me well and whole. It's incredible to see.

I choose today to continue to cooperate with you, Spirit of God, as you put to death the deeds of the body. May the life of Jesus be evident in me today. Amen.

December 13. Gutting it out

That's really the only way I can describe where I am today.

I was trying to explain it to my family last night, but I don't think I understand it myself. Since I was diagnosed with cancer, the Sundays I don't preach feel like they're two weeks long! For the life of me, I can't completely figure out why.

I miss it when I don't preach, of course. That's a big part of it. I miss the fellowship and worship. I know I've said that it's hard for me to rest. That's another aspect of it. But it's more than that.

Even though I try to minimize it in my own mind, the physical aspect looms large. I know I couldn't have preached yesterday even if I'd planned to. In an email yesterday I told Diane during this time in the cycle (between five and ten days after chemo), especially right after I get out of bed, I feel as if I've run a marathon race. Weird, weird, weird. I can just be walking along and it hits me like a ton of bricks.

I can tell my body is fighting this disease, but it takes so much energy to do so. And the chemo drugs are accumulating in my system, so it takes longer for them to be processed. That's my totally nonmedical, unscientific explanation. And as I write this, I realize I'm still trying to explain why I'm struggling.

But enough of that. By God's grace, I made it through another hard day. And He gets the glory for that.

I want to go back to yesterday for a moment. After writing what I did, I thought of all the ways it could be misunderstood and misinterpreted. Maybe that's the pastor in me. I'm used to people coming up to me after sermons and making comments or asking questions. *And I like this.* It shows me they've listened and they're interested. Cool.

One potential misunderstanding of what I wrote yesterday has to do with the concept of total surrender. In my mind it's just another way of describing what the Lord led me to when I prayed, "Do whatever you want to do in my life." This was all about me giving up my fleshly effort to accomplish spiritual goals and purposes.

But I want to be clear about this. I don't think it's a *one and done* deal.

I do resist all two-tiered views of salvation (this is my term; I'll try to explain it). The Holiness Movement of the late nineteenth century taught that salvation was one thing. Sanctification (the process of God making us holy) is another. And I think it's helpful to distinguish between those terms so we can understand them, even though I totally disagree with this philosophy.

Why? Because it inevitably leads to the view that some type of experience signals a believer has arrived at the second tier. I still remember an experience I had at McDonald's when I was in college. I was sitting at my familiar table (it should have had my name on it because I was there so often) and some young men in black suits came in. They were obviously looking for some folks to talk to.

They sat down at the end of the benches where my friend and I were seated (so we couldn't get out easily). They looked at us and asked, "Have you been baptized by the Holy Spirit?" I was a little shell-shocked, but I replied, "Well, I've received Jesus as my personal Savior and Lord."

One of the young men was visibly agitated by that response and said, "That's not what I'm asking. Have you been baptized by the Holy Spirit and do you speak in tongues?" His voice quivered. "Well," I said, "by your definition and distinction of that experience, no." My answer gave this young man all the fuel he needed to try to convince my friend and me to learn more about speaking in tongues.

That conversation led me to study the Bible as I'd never examined it before, and I learned that at the moment of salvation, the Holy Spirit baptizes every believer. In other words, he comes to dwell in them. *And* I learned the difference between being filled with the Spirit (occurs often or should occur often in the Christian life) and the baptism of the Spirit (occurs once at conversion). *And* as I read Acts, I discovered the chief evidence of being filled with the Spirit was bold proclamation, not tongues.

What those young men at McDonald's were trying to tell me was that accepting Christ is only the first tier of salvation. They were trying to make me feel like a second-class citizen because I wasn't baptized by the Spirit (as they understood it to be a second experience of grace) as evidenced by speaking in tongues.

Does this make sense? I hope so.

My point in telling this story is that there are a lot of different two-tier philosophies out there, not just the speaking-in-tongues view.

For most of my Christian life, I believe *total surrender* may have fit in that category. I can't begin to count the number of sermons I've heard that advocate "if you just commit your life totally to Jesus, everything will be all right." The view is salvation is one thing, but you must go further than that. You must totally commit yourself to Jesus.

Now I do believe this is what the Lord is doing in my life, but I want to be clear: it's not some second experience of grace! It's not some badge of honor.

I believe salvation is a once-and-for-all, never-to-be-repeated experience of conversion that initiates a lifetime process of sanctification. It's a point in time *and* a process! Not two points in time!

In other words, total surrender is just another step in the pilgrimage! I'm not more spiritual because I surrendered to Him a few months ago (that's for sure!). And here's another thing: just because I did it back then doesn't mean it's done forever! I believe He wants me to surrender to Him totally *today*. And today's surrender will (hopefully) look different and reflect more growth that the Lord is bringing about in my life than it did a few months ago.

Maybe this is why Sundays when I don't preach are so hard. Maybe He's teaching me to commit myself totally to Him even and especially when I'm not preaching! I don't know …

Mike Ladra's messages on anger are helping me with this. Mike is pastor of First Presbyterian Church in Salinas, California and recorded a series of CDs entitled "How to Break the Anger Habit."

Yesterday I started to listen to Ladra's second sermon in the series, and he used 1 Corinthians 13 as his text. The first part of his message focused on the last part of the chapter. Paul says, "When I was a child, I talked like a child, I thought like a child, I reasoned like a child. When I became a man, I put childish ways behind me" (1 Corinthians 13:11, NIV).

Here's a statement Ladra made that impacted me: "Paul defines spiritual maturity in terms of love, first of all, but the process involves putting childish things aside!"

When he said this in his sermon, it hit me: total surrender is the call of God to put aside childish things and grow up! That's what's going on with me and that's why things are so hard.

It's hard to grow up! I feel like God's weaning me off the high chair into a grownup chair! It's time for me to stop eating Gerber's! It's time for me to stop defining myself by what I do, even if it's preaching on Sunday! My identity in Christ has nothing to do with that, first of all. It has everything to do with Him and Him alone!

He's helping me with this, and I certainly need it. The song I came across this morning is "Our Great Savior." I love this hymn! The second verse is particularly relevant: "Tempted, tried, and sometimes failing, He, my Strength, my vict'ry wins."[26]

Wow! Yes! Amen!

I think this experience of Jesus in the process of the Christian life is what the psalmist is praying for in Psalm 138 when he says, "The moment I called out, you stepped in; you made my life large with strength" (Psalm 138:3).

John D. Talbert

Lord, I thank you for the way you're leading me and helping me every step of the way. Thank you for the call to total surrender.

I confess I'm having a hard time letting childish things go.

But today I choose to let go of every baby thing I've been holding on to. I want to grow up. Grow me up and out of my narrow little nursery rhyme patterns of life into the largesse of who you are *today*. I love you, Jesus. Amen.

December 14. "For just such a time as this"

This phrase literally jumped off the page of my Bible this morning.

Yesterday I drove up to the church to spend some time. I was able to visit with Betty and catch up on what's going on these days. First, I'm so thankful again for Ilamarques preaching for me. I wish every church in the United States could house at least one other congregation whose folks speak another language! I can't believe the Lord has blessed us with three! I wish we could have ten.

Lord, I pause right here and now to thank you for the blessing of New Generation Christian Community Church and Pastor Ilamarques Morais, Encuentro Con Dios and Pastor Jose Tello, and Korean Comfort Baptist Church and Pastor Dong Lim. Bless these congregations. Fill these pastors with your Holy Spirit and power.

I'm excited about the fact that this coming Sunday night we're all going to meet together for our annual international candle lighting service. Each congregation will participate and then we'll eat together (after all, we're all Baptists). I plan to preach this coming Sunday, morning and evening. It'll be a challenge for me, but I just can't miss either service.

Anyway, back to my conversation with Betty. We talked about where we are as a church and one comment I made was, "I know the Lord has a reason for me to get cancer—not only for me personally but for this church, and it seems now that the Lord is clearing the decks." In addition to wishing every church could house at least one additional congregation in the same building, I would hope every church could see what it's made of when their pastor is taken out of the loop. I'm serious!

I know we've done a lot of things I've pushed for just because I thought they were good ideas. Now I'm not around to do that, and I think it's good! What's left these days is what the *body* thinks we need to do, and it's considerably less activity. And that's not bad! This is different for us.

We're a relatively small church, but we've had a lot of activity over the years. Whew. When I think of all we've done, my head spins! I'm sure we're not unusual in this regard, but cancer has pushed me to question the philosophy that *more is better*. Now I don't think that tenet is necessarily true, especially for churches. I'm coming to believe less is better. When I say that I don't mean fewer people (nor am I alluding to any *numerical* measurement of success; I've already written extensively about that). I'm talking about activity for activity's sake.

Less ineffective activity is more. Betty said it: "I think it is better to do one thing well than a number of things poorly." Amen.

But of course that's easier said than done. Most folks (including pastors) don't like change. And it's just easier to limp along and do what we've always done rather deal with the fallout that transpires when something changes.

I can't do that. I won't.

So we talked about shifting gears in a major ministry area of our church. I need to pray about the particulars more and make sure this is God's idea, not another one of *John's fixes*. (This is another lesson cancer has taught me. He can take care of His church! He doesn't need my help, but He does use people.)

I don't question the timing and the impetus for change. And I know God has a purpose when He changes things. It's not just change for change's sake. The purpose is to save folks.

That brings me to the quote at the beginning of today's entry. In my Bible reading plan I've finished the gospel of Mark. So it's time to go back to the Old Testament, and the book I'm now reading is Esther. What an amazing story! God used the rebellion of Queen Vashti to bring about the selection of a Jewish woman named Hadassah (otherwise known as Esther) for the Persian king Xerxes' harem. (This is a brief summary of chapters 1 and 2 of Esther).

Sometime after that, Haman rose to power in Xerxes' kingdom and issued a decree to massacre all the Jews. Esther's cousin Mordecai, a leader among the Jews, heard about this decree and mourned before the Lord. He went and told Esther about Haman's plan. Then he sent her this message: "Don't think that just because you live in the king's house you're the one Jew who will get out of this alive. If you persist in staying silent at a time like this, help and deliverance will arrive for the Jews from someplace else; but you and your family will be wiped out. Who knows? Maybe you were made queen for just such a time as this" (Esther 4:13–14).

When I read that verse, I thought of Moses, saved as a baby to grow up in Pharaoh's household. Why? He did it to save Israel. I thought of Joseph and his imprisonment and his dreams. Why? To save God's people.

I thought of Paul in prison. Why did the Lord allow him to be imprisoned—the greatest missionary in the history of the church? The Lord slowed him down so he could write most of the New Testament. God is adept at bringing disaster, unique circumstances, and one person together for the deliverance of many. *Wow!* And Esther is another example.

Certainly that's the case with me, and it's *not* because I'm anything special. But that's what He does! And it's overwhelming and awesome to think about it.

The fact is God doesn't *need* any of us to accomplish His purposes, but in His sovereignty, He *uses* us. And Mordecai reminded Esther that God was the one who put her in the position she was in! God. Not Xerxes.

God knows everything, and He knows us. That's what Psalm 139 is all about. God has intimate and detailed knowledge of me that far surpasses that of the smartest biologist on the face of the earth. The understanding of God's knowledge leads the psalmist to pray, "Investigate my life, O God, find out everything about me. Cross examine and test me, get a clear picture of what I'm about; See for yourself whether I've done anything wrong—then guide me on the road to eternal life" (Psalm 139:23–24).

Therefore the circumstances of our lives (whether cancer or appointment to a Persian king's harem) have a dual purpose. God uses them to mold us so He can use us as an instrument of His salvation purposes.

It isn't just about me! I don't have the right to be selfish and passive with the Lord's tests!

David Platt echoes this in his chapter in *Radical* entitled "The Multiplying Community: How All of Us Join Together to Fulfill God's Purpose." He classifies Christians in two categories: receivers and reproducers. Receiving is easy. We go to church and passively listen to a sermon or Bible teaching and walk out. That's receiving.

But reproducers listen so they can share what they learn with someone else. Wow, what a huge distinction.[27]

This is where God has put me. I've said this before, but I feel that right now God has introduced me through cancer to this crash course. I used to write a daily journal just for me. But now God won't let me keep things to myself.

I have cancer, but He won't allow me the luxury of dealing with it on my own or keeping quiet about it. He gave me cancer *for such a time as this.*

As a result, "I will serve Thee, because I love thee."[28] I love that song and I sing it to you, Jesus.

Lord, you're incredibly amazing. Thank you for creating this universe and for making me. You know about everything that's going on in this world and with me. You know me more intimately than I know myself.

I confess the sin of forgetting that and thinking you don't know things. You *know everything,* especially when it comes to me, your plan for me, and your will for that church in Northglenn.

Father, thank you for taking broken pieces and weaving them into the tapestry of your salvation plan. Lord, this cancer isn't just for me. Use it to save many people. Amen.

December 16. Psalm 141: cancer is a hearing aid!

More stuff coming to the surface. That's really the only way I can describe it.

Yesterday I felt the Lord bringing me face-to-face with two new things, and I'll talk about them in a moment.

I'm realizing I've lived the past few years (and maybe more than just a few years) keeping God at arm's length. I think that's what happens when your life is in overdrive and you're busy, especially with *religious things*. My life has become a parable of a parable.

In Luke 10 Jesus tells the story of a man beaten, robbed, and left for dead at the side of the road. And I think it's significant that the first two characters who have an opportunity to help are church people—a priest and a Levite. When they saw this urgent and pressing need, they both made a wide berth in their journey and passed by on the other side of the road (Luke 10:31–32). What a visual! They both avoided an opportunity to be a neighbor to that wounded man.

Now I want to be careful to interpret and apply Scripture properly at this point. This parable is Jesus' answer to a question posed to him by an expert in the law. This expert was trying to justify himself by asking Jesus the snide question, "And who is my neighbor?" (Luke 10:29). So it's about man's responsibility to his fellow man as a disciple of Jesus: love your neighbor as yourself. That's what this parable is all about.

But it comes to mind as a picture *for me* of how I've been treating God the past few years. I've been on my way to *doing* ministry, and in the process *missed* ministry!

What did Will Rogers say? "The government builds roads and Baptists use them up going to meetings." (Something like that). I've been like the priest and the Levite in this story, only in my case I've been making a wide berth around God and the urgent ministry of my personal relationship with Him! That's the only way I can look at it.

The command is love your neighbor *as* yourself. If I have a wound or cut that's bleeding, what do I do? Let it go? *No.* I attend to it. I approach physical problems that way, but I've not given urgent attention to my walk with Jesus, and as I think about it, it's been years. Our ministry to ourselves is not selfishness! It's vital. And I've neglected it. This is what I'm saying.

And we all have ways of doing this. I know I do. "Yes Lord, I know that's a problem and an issue. I agree with you, but I'll get to it later." Somehow I pat myself on the back that I know what the problem is and agree with the Lord about it. *But*—this is a wide berth!

And I do believe God is a very patient parent. Like my dad used to say, "John, I need you to take out the trash." "Sure, Dad, I'll get on it." Fifteen minutes go by. "Ah John, the trash?" "Right, Dad. I'm on it," as I continue to watch the Bronco game. Like my earthly father, God is patient with us in His demands for obedience.

But there's a limit. Finally my dad would say, "I'm not going to say it again. Take out the trash and do it *now*." I knew by the tone of his voice I was in trouble if I didn't do it immediately. The time for procrastination was *over*. It was time for obedience.

God's voice has that tone in it these days. And cancer is allowing me to hear it.

I've often wondered over the years, "What's it going to take for me to get serious with the Lord?" Cancer.

I know some of the physical definitions of cancer, but here's my *spiritual* definition: cancer is a hearing aid! And I wish I didn't need it, but now I know it was God's relentless love that allowed it to happen so that finally (hopefully) I will now hear. Kris Perkins is a wonderful Christian lady and great mother who was a member of our church years ago along with her family, and taught kids in our church. I'll never forget her definition of obedience: doing what God says the first time. That's the goal. Right? When God says something, we jump. But when we don't, He gives us hearing aids! Anyway ...

I'm convinced we don't do any of this on our own. Conviction about specific sin comes from the Holy Spirit, not us. And repentance is a gift from God! If I don't accept that gift in a timely way, then I lose the opportunity.

That's the tragedy of the story of Esau. This verse in Hebrews makes me shiver: "Afterward, as you know, when he wanted to inherit this blessing, he was rejected. He could bring about no change of mind, though he sought the blessing with tears" (Hebrews 12:17, NIV). The context of this statement in Hebrews is the Lord's discipline of His kids. It's not about losing salvation (the Bible doesn't teach this anywhere); it's about lost opportunity.

I don't want to miss any opportunity these days.

The story of Haman reinforces this. I love the book of Esther. What a great story! We left the story in chapter 4 with Esther consenting to risk her life to talk to King Xerxes about the fate of her people, the Jews. Haman, one of the top men in the king's court, had it in for the Jews and Esther's cousin Mordecai.

In chapter 5, Esther met the king and he said, "And what's your desire, Queen Esther? What do you want? Ask and it's yours—even if it's half my kingdom" (Esther 5:3). That question in and of itself was a gift from God!

In reply, Esther invited the king and Haman to supper one night and then invited them back again. Meanwhile, Haman was plotting the death of Mordecai and even built a gallows near his home upon which to hang him.

Between the first and second dinners, the king remembered Mordecai had helped him in the past and he decided to honor him. Well, things turned on Haman and he found himself leading a parade to honor his bitter enemy Mordecai! Haman was humiliated, and when he shared his humiliation with his wife and friends, they said, "If this Mordecai is a Jew, your bad luck has only begun. You don't stand a chance against him—you're as good as ruined" (Esther 6:13).

In chapter 7, at the second dinner, Esther tells the king of Haman's decree to kill all the Jews and the king decides to hang Haman on the gallows he built to execute Mordecai! What an amazing turn of events and solemn lesson!

You don't mess around with God or His people.

This is even further incentive to avoid sin and evil. It's what Psalm 141 is all about. In the first few verses the psalmist says, "Don't let my mouth get me in trouble" (Psalm 141:3, my paraphrase); "don't let me so much as dream of evil or thoughtlessly fall into bad company" (verse 4); and "Don't let sin anoint my head" (verse 5). That last phrase is intriguing. *Don't let sin anoint my head.* Anointing in Scripture sets someone aside for a task. I don't think anyone wants to be set aside for the task of sinning. This may be a description of what happened to Esau.

So this psalm is about avoiding sin at all costs, and it ends with this prayer: "But God, dear Lord, I only have eyes for you. Since I've run for dear life to you, take good care of me" (verse 8). Amen.

I mentioned there were two things the Lord brought to my attention yesterday. One was a spiritual issue. The other was physical. And as I was talking with my mother yesterday, I told her I needed to put this on the blog just so those of you who are faithfully praying for me can pray for this (and again, I don't have words to tell you how much I appreciate your prayers).

Here it is: I'm having increasing problems with *sleep*. I'm just not sleeping at night. I'm sure chemotherapy is a major cause here. They warned me about this at the start. But honestly, I've had sleep problems for years. And for those of you who can relate to this, it's now to the point where it's getting in my head and I'm almost paranoid. So this is also something I need to address *now;* I can't keep sweeping it under the rug like I have for years, really.

It's just time to deal with it. So I'm starting with Dr Jesus—the best sleep expert ever!

Yes, I'm starting with the Great Physician, but I'm also talking with Dr Jotte and my general practitioner, and we'll go from there. Thanks. So much.

Father God, thank you for loving me so much that you're leading me with urgency to deal with issues in my life. Thank you for the conviction of your Holy Spirit.

I confess my sin to you and ask you to grant me the gift of repentance. I accept it and turn from sin and choose to trust you in new and deeper ways.

Thank you for the prayers of your people—this is the greatest thing in all the world and I know I wouldn't have made it to this point without your people praying for me. I'm so grateful for the technology that allows me to share all this, and the way people can read it online and respond instantaneously. *Wow* Lord. You're awesome.

Lord, I'm excited to see what you'll do as I continue to go down this cancer road. Again, let me be a road for you. Amen.

December 18. Purim: tables, somersaults, and boomerangs

I'm so excited to be able to learn more about the ways the Lord works. He's incredible!

I'm not going to give a sleep update every day on this blog, but when I ask for prayer, I feel it's necessary to share what the Lord does. First, I did sleep better last night. And I attribute it to the Lord answering prayer. I want to thank everyone for praying for me in that regard, but something funny happened yesterday.

For some reason these days, I'm just not able to talk on the phone as much (maybe it's the weakness of my voice that seems to plague me for long periods of time after chemo, or just my overall lack of energy). I so appreciate everyone who calls. Rob calls me, especially on the Sundays when I'm preaching, just to let me know he's praying for me. Thanks, Rob. Bart Poole calls often to let me know he's thinking of me. Dan Tracy does the same. Guys, I get your messages eventually and really appreciate the expressions of concern and prayer.

But sometimes just the fact that I'm not around my cell phone gets me into trouble. I've been calling my oncologist about my sleep problems. I talked with Dr Jotte's head nurse Terri about some things on Wednesday night. She was going to talk to the doctor and call me back. It didn't happen Thursday, but she did call me back last night. The only problem was I missed the call! Yep. And Terri didn't leave a message.

When I first realized this, I went into a panic. "Great! I've got this really busy Sunday, and I'll have to face it with no sleep! And I've got to wait until Monday to hear what the doctor says." I was tempted to freak out, but I didn't. It's just the Lord doing His usual *thing*.

I think one of the main things I'm realizing you have to guard against with cancer is extreme self-absorption. There's a kind of arrogance attached to this disease: woe is me. Look at me. I'm so sick. I'm sicker than you are. Nah, nah nah nah, nah. World, know I'm sick and care about me. Me, me, me.

Yesterday was good because it helped me get my attention off myself, and I was glad to help two people who've helped me significantly.

And I'm also thankful I haven't lost my hair. What a blessing! It enables me to get by on certain occasions without even telling folks I have cancer. Some people don't need to know that. I want every Christian on the planet to know so they can pray—don't get me wrong. But I'm learning I don't have to tell every stranger I meet (I did at first, for some reason!).

Anyway, I wanted to share those answers to prayer and thank everyone *again* for praying. Through those answers and through the Scripture passages for today the Lord revealed an amazing truth about Himself. Let me explain.

In chapter 9 of Esther, Esther's proclamation leads the Jews in all of Persia to exact vengeance on the enemies of the Jews. They killed a whole bunch of folks. It wasn't about booty. Over and over in this chapter the Bible says when the Jews killed their enemies they "took no plunder." They were obedient to the Lord, following His instructions to the letter and taking nothing extra. This is all about the protection of God and the triumph of His people.

Out of this, a new holiday emerged in Israel. It's called *Purim*. The word *pur* in Hebrew means *lot*. In the early part of the story, Haman cast the lot to decree the massacre of the Jews in Persia (I'm not sure exactly what that means, but I think it has to do with an irrevocable decision). But after conversing with Queen Esther, the king issued another proclamation that overturned Haman's decree in favor of the Jews. As a result, the Jews instituted a new holiday called Purim to be celebrated on the fourteenth and fifteenth of the month of Adar every single year thereafter!

I was interested to discover this morning that the month of Adar is the equivalent of December on the Jewish calendar. Jews today still celebrate Purim. It's a happy holiday in which people celebrate and give each other gifts. I know a little about Hanukkah, but this sounds like Christmas (not the birth of Christ, certainly, but the celebration part!).

Interesting. But as you read Esther 9, you realize Purim is more about a significant characteristic of God, and in the Message Version Peterson uses three key expressions in this chapter to explain it.

The new edict of Esther occurred on the very day the original proclamation from Haman ordering the massacre of the Jews was supposed to take effect, but "the tables were now turned: the Jews overpowered those who hated them." What an expression: "the tables were turned." I looked this expression up. It's an old one, but it basically means one's "undesirable position was turned into an advantageous position." Wow.

Here's the second expression in this chapter: Purim calls for "an annual celebration on the fourteenth and fifteenth days of Adar as the occasion when Jews got relief from their enemies, the month in which their sorrow turned to joy, *mourning somersaulted into a holiday for parties and fun and laughter*, the sending and receiving of presents and of giving gifts to the poor" [italics mine]. I love the phrase "mourning somersaulted into a holiday."

Those are two incredible statements about what God does. The third is the king "gave written orders that the evil scheme that Haman had worked out should boomerang back on his own head." The picture of a boomerang as it soars out in the sky, making a huge circular arc that brings it right back to the person who threw it is very vivid. So there you go. God turns the tables on His enemies, somersaults mourning into a holiday, and boomerangs evil back on those who instigate it!

In other words, our Lord is an expert in turnarounds! He's deft at taking undesirable situations and turning them around, like a somersault and a boomerang, into desirable situations for His people!

I know that's what He's doing by way of cancer in my life right now! This disease is making a huge arc in God's sky and coming back around to be the greatest thing that ever happened to me! I honestly believe that.

And He's showing me that in other ways as well. Last night was a case in point. When I missed the doctor's call and was poised for another sleepless night, somersault! Boomerang! The Lord turned things around, and now I trust the Lord will turn the tables on this sleep thing somehow, some way. That's His thing.

And He did it all the way through the Bible! Put His people in slavery in Egypt so He could turn the tables to deliver them in spectacular fashion. Put His greatest missionary in prison with God's worked stopped, right? Nope. His gospel spread even more.

Or how about this one? Hang His son on a cross to kill him and put him in a grave. He was dead and finished, right? The ultimate turn of the table somersaulted into Easter with death and the grave—the biggest enemies ever—defeated forever! Purim lives on!

Lord, today I'm so thankful for the amazing ways you win victories on behalf of your people. You're the ultimate expert in dealing with so-called hopeless situations. Thank you for turning the tables on cancer, and I believe you'll do the same for sleeplessness and every other enemy that rears its head in my life. I celebrate the Christian version of Purim today!

I'm an expert at snatching defeat from the jaws of victory through my own weak and frail human efforts, but it's exactly the opposite for you.

May everyone who's reading this today and praying for me and my family experience the kind of somersaults we used to be able to do when we were kids! Turn the tables on the enemy today and win another victory, oh Jesus who died, was buried, and boomeranged back to life! Amen.

December 23. "The pathless air"

This is a phrase in a song I came across the morning. The title of it is "My Father Watches Over Me." I don't know the tune, but the words are particularly poignant and relevant for me today: "He guides the eagle through *the pathless air*"[29] [italics mine].

This song covers all types of situations: land, sea, and air. And as far as air is concerned, He guides the eagle through *the pathless air*. What an image!

If you think about it, most if not all human and spiritual pilgrimage occurs in pathless air. It's not as if there's a clearly marked, actual physical path for any of us. We have indicators. God gives direction, for sure, but it's not something we can see, handle, taste, or touch. It's real. Make no mistake. We just can't see it! But, that having been said, there are different kinds of paths for different kinds of creatures.

My first house backed up to a broad expanse of farmland. It was an empty field with a huge, dead tree in the middle of it. Every morning I'd look out my back porch window while I had my time with the Lord. One day I noticed a rather significant brown dot in the top of that tree. What was it?

As I squinted and stared, I realized it was a bird with a white head! A bald eagle—are you kidding me? His huge wings lifted him off the tree to soar in the sky, around and around. I watched as that magnificent bird hunted its prey.

One morning as I was working on a sermon in my study upstairs (it also had a window facing the direction of that tree), a huge bird flew right by my window. Hey buddy! It was that eagle!

It's hard to imagine how large full-grown eagles are, and they have a huge wingspan.

After I'd lived there for a while, Betty gave me a pair of binoculars. With that focused help, I was able to study that bald eagle—up close and personal—with his white head and yellow beak.

When the eagle wasn't perched in the tree, he lived in the pathless air. No one, including me with my binoculars, could see the path that he flew. But in reality, although it may have appeared to be pathless, he did indeed have one! It was just in the air, for sure. That eagle flew on a path every day of his life. He went up and around and down. But it was a path. And God guided and protected that magnificent bird each day of his life.

I'll never forget that eagle.

This song reminds me of the features of the pathless path. Sometimes we encounter people along the path who give us perspective on what's really going on. In chapter 2 of Luke, Simeon was just such a person. The Bible says the Lord had told him he wouldn't die until he had seen the Messiah.

And one day as he was worshiping in the temple, his path crossed the path of Joseph, Mary, and the baby Jesus. I don't know how he knew this was it. I think the Holy Spirit told him. It was a mid-air collision, but he met the family, took Jesus in his arms, and said, "God, you can now release your servant; release me in peace as you promised. With my own eyes I've seen your salvation; it's now out in the open for everyone to see: A God-revealing light to the non-Jewish nations, and of glory for your people Israel" (Luke 2:29–32). That was news to Joseph and Mary!

They knew their son was special and that the Lord was going to use him among the Jews. But a "light to the non-Jewish nations"— that was beyond incredible!

That's how the Lord has used people in the course of this cancer experience for me in so many ways. Here's one way. I can't tell you how many people have encouraged me to write a book as they've read this blog. Barbara reminded me of this in an email the other day. My mother and sister mention it all the time. Carol said it while she was still in the church and exhorted me shortly after I found out I had cancer (she and her family are great buds and former members of our church whom the Lord moved to Texas).

For years I've believed the Lord wanted me to write, but these folks serve as Simeons in the pathless air of my life.

And we need Simeon and his descendants when we get discouraged and lose sight of the direction. I need them. I certainly struggle with getting off the path, daily.

Another resource the Lord provides along the pathless path is His promises. There's a great statement in Psalm 147 I read today. "He launches his promises earthward—how swift and sure they come" (Psalm 147:15). Maybe it was just because I was thinking about eagles, but this statement reminds me of the swift descent of that bird to nab a meal.

Most of the eagle's life is sitting in a tree and circling in the air, around and around and around, but then there's the moment of truth. All of a sudden, the bird darts down! It's stark and quick. He drops swiftly out of the sky like a dive-bomber and just as suddenly bounces back into the air with an animal in his claws!

God's promises and His delivery of them operate that same way, if you think about it. His promises are real. They're soaring around and around, and all of a sudden, He shoots them to earth. It sometimes seems to take a long time for Him to fulfill His promises, but in reality, in *God time*, it's swift and sure.

Back a few months ago when I started chemotherapy, it seemed like I had the longest road before me. Back in August I wondered if it would ever end. But I had God's promise in Philippians 4:19. "My God will meet all your needs according to his glorious riches in Christ Jesus" (NIV).

Back then I was worried about so many things, like being really sick and how was the church going to make it without indispensable me and how was I going to pay for everything. God promised to meet all my needs and that promise came swift and sure in each one of these areas and in so many more. The eagle has landed!

Philippians 4:19 is familiar, but we don't often quote verse 20: "To our God and Father be glory forever and ever, Amen" (NIV). Amen. It's all about Him. Praise and honor and glory go to Him!

Lord, I thank you today for watching over the eagle and for watching over me. Thank you for the way you ministered to the human parents of the Son of God as you led them down the pathless path.

I need help today as I take another step on this path. I thank you for every Simeon you've brought my way via this blog, email, timely notes, and phone calls. Each one has been so valuable to give me the perspective I need, not just in writing, but in making it day by day.

Thank you also for your very great and precious promises through which you graciously allow me to become a partaker of the divine nature, as 2 Peter 1 affirms. "His divine power has given us everything we need for life and godliness through our knowledge of him who called us by his own glory and goodness. Through these he's given us his very great and precious promises, so that through them you may participate in the divine nature and escape the corruption in the world caused by evil desires" (2 Peter 1:3–4, NIV). Amen to that.

Lord, you have indeed met every need, above and beyond my wildest dreams. Your promises are swift and sure, always there, always true, but they've darted down into my life in so many key ways. I trust you to do it again today. You indeed do watch *over* me. Amen.

December 28. A match play mindset

Wow, I love writing that. When I found out back in August that I was going to have six chemo treatments three weeks apart, it seemed like it would take forever. I felt like I'd be done in 2025. But the Lord has brought me to this point, and I'm grateful.

More than one person has told me based on their experience with someone else who had cancer that this last treatment was really going to be rough, much rougher than all the others. I'm prepared for that possibility, but I haven't thought and will not think about it all that much.

Honestly, what weighs heavily on the *other side* of that possibility is the *fact* that this is the last chemo treatment I'll have in this phase of the process. And there's a lot of hope and encouragement in that.

I'm not saying definitively this is *the* last chemo treatment I'll have. Others have told me they believe that, and I'm thankful for their prayers and encouragement, but that may not be the case. I'm ready for that possibility as well. We'll just have to see.

From my own standpoint, I'm looking at further treatment as I did my opponent's putt in match play. Let me explain what I mean.

There are basically two types of formats for golf tournaments: stroke play and match play. In stroke play, it's simple. Everyone competes against the field, and at the end the player with the lowest score wins.

Match play is different. It's a one-on-one competition. And it's played hole by hole, so the player who gets the lowest score on a hole wins that hole and goes one up. Even if his opponent scores a ten and he scores a three, he only goes one up. So at the end of the day, the player who wins the most holes wins the match.

Match play has a different mindset from stroke play because you're playing your opponent and not the field. But here's a cardinal principle in match play. When you're standing on the green and both of you have a putt, you assume your opponent is going to make his putt every time.

I learned the truth of this early on in some tournaments I played in as a kid. The reason is if you assume otherwise, it's too devastating and too much distraction for you then to concentrate on your putt. I lost a match that way once in my glory days as a junior golfer.

So the match play mindset is focused on the present, a determination to play your own game, and a way of thinking about your opponent. The fact is you can't ignore the person you're playing against, but you can adopt a perspective about what he does so your game isn't adversely affected no matter what he does, good or bad.

This analogy is helping me think about today and put it in context. I'm assuming a match play mindset on the issue of further treatments. I'm trusting God to take care of me today and joining others who are praying I'll be healed, but I'm going into chemo number six not placing my faith in outcomes. This takes me back to something Lynda said a few weeks ago: "Some of the most difficult things about cancer are the *not knowing* and the waiting. The enemy whispers in these times, and we do well to run to the truth of the Word when he does (as you're clearly doing). We're praying that God will give you faith and his peace as you wait. That faith is simply faith *in Him* rather than in a particular outcome."

I'm going into today thinking my opponent is going to make his putt. Translation: I'm fully prepared for the possibility that this isn't my last chemo treatment. And hey, if it is, praise God. If it isn't, praise God! Either way, all ways, make or miss, praise God! At this point, fully trusting the care of the Lord and the fact that I believe He led me to this doctor and the Rocky Mountain Cancer Center for treatment, I'll do anything they tell me to do. Dr Jesus is the head physician!

I've thought a lot about this analogy. I don't think the match play mindset is incompatible with faith. Going back to Lynda's comment, my faith is not in outcomes. It's in the Lord, and believing in the Lord opens you up to many contingencies. You just never know what the Lord's going to do and how He's going to do it. If I end up needing eight chemo treatments or six or fill in the blank, any way, He'll get the glory.

The difference between my golf experiences and this cancer process is I know who's going to win the match, without any doubt. Ultimately the Lord will triumph, whatever the details are.

The passages I read today have helped me in this regard. I've finished Psalms, so today I started reading Proverbs. The book begins with a very familiar and striking statement. I love how Peterson translates it in *The Message*. "Start with God—the first step in learning is bowing down to God; only fools thumb their noses at such wisdom and understanding" (Proverbs 1:7). Bowing down to God—isn't that an acknowledgment that He's in control?

I'm learning in the course of this whole process of treatment that when I assume control, it gums up the works and makes me a fool. Only fools believe they're in charge of their own lives. And I've played the fool so often!

The rest of chapter 1 of Proverbs is all about that. When I listen to the advice of bad companions, I get into trouble. But Lady Wisdom stands "out in the street and shouts" (verse 20). When I follow her advice, it makes me smart (smart in the eyes of God). This first chapter ends with a great statement: "First pay attention to me, and then relax. Now you can take it easy—you're in good hands" (verse 33). The original All State ad! In good hands with the Lord!

Luke 4 reinforces this principle as well. After Jesus' temptation experience in the wilderness, he leaves in the power of the Spirit (Luke 4:14) to preach his first sermon in his hometown of Nazareth. You would think things would go well, huh? But they didn't.

Jesus picked up a scroll and read from the prophecy of Isaiah. He read a passage that refers specifically to him and said, "You've just heard Scripture make history. It came true just now in this place" (Luke 4:21). However, the folks who heard him say this couldn't bring themselves to view him as the Messiah. "Isn't this Joseph's son, the one we've known since he was a youngster?" (verse 22). Jesus replied, "No prophet is ever welcomed in his hometown" (verse 23).

Then Jesus mentioned two incidents—the healing of a widow in Sarepta in Sidon and the healing of Naaman in Syria. These are two significant Old Testament miracles. Out of all the widows in that area, God healed only one. Out of all the lepers in that region, God cleansed only one. I think it's significant that Jesus mentioned this in his first sermon. I need to ponder these references further, but I'm convinced they were an answer to the rejection he experienced from folks in his hometown. Jesus is saying, "You don't know who I really am because you don't understand how God works. He's in charge here, not you."

Well, everyone got extremely angry (as all of us do when first we learn we aren't in control) and tried to push Jesus off a cliff, but he "gave them the slip and was on his way" (verse 30).

No one understands God's sovereign plan and purpose, and today I affirm that and bow to the Lord. He's smarter than I am! Much smarter.

So, as a result of that, I'm going to do what a song I came across encourages: "So forget about yourself and concentrate on Him."[30]

Okay Jesus, thank you for bringing me to this point today. I'm so thankful for all you've done in my life. I worship you right now, oh Lord.

I bow my heart to you today. I choose to listen to your voice and take your advice.

Admittedly, I don't understand your ways and your plans, but I know you. And today, with chemo number six, I trust you.

I place myself in your hands today and I will rejoice, whether my opponent makes his putt or not. The *match* is well in hand, in good hands, your hands. Amen.

December 29. The first day of a new adventure

That's how I felt as we drove away from the Rocky Mountain Cancer Center yesterday. The western sun hit my face, and I thought of Abraham.

It was very busy at the center yesterday. We waited a long time even to get started. The normal routine is Connie or Jennifer takes me back to get weighed (it was Jennifer yesterday); to get my blood pressure, pulse rate, and temperature. They ushered me into a room where they take lots of blood samples via the port. After I'm done I still have a tube sticking out of the port when I visit with the doctor or his assistant. Dr Jotte wasn't there, so we got to talk with Kathy, Dr Bashi's assistant. Dr Bashi was my surrogate doctor yesterday for the chemo treatment. Kathy was very encouraging, said I was doing well, checked the area where the bulge had been, and said she saw no indication of it. So I praise God for that.

We then stopped at a desk to make some more appointments. Of course I had to get my customary $8,000 shot today to help my white blood count. But we also scheduled the next major test—a PET scan for Tuesday, January 11. This will help the doctor know where to go from here. Either I'll be done with chemo or—if they feel I need to continue—I'll have two more treatments. And they went ahead and scheduled the next chemo treatment for Monday, January 17, just in case I'll need it. As I said yesterday, whatever!

After making these appointments, we went into the chemo room. It was crowded and very busy. I wasn't able to sit in my customary seat, but we found a chair in the corner. I was interested to observe what went on, when I was awake. The woman next to me had a scarf on her head. She and her husband were very friendly. They seemed to know a lot of folks in the room and laughed a lot with the nurses. Another lady with a scarf sat across from them. Her husband was in and out. He left for a long time at one juncture, but he returned with an older woman who was the lady's mother, I assume. They had a good conversation.

Right across from me a younger man was receiving treatment with his schoolteacher wife sitting next to him. (I surmised she was a schoolteacher because she was grading papers as she held them in her lap.) The man nodded and smiled at me once as he left to go to the bathroom, and did the same when he departed.

Shortly after this, one of the ladies got up to leave, her treatments finished. One of the nurses gave her a present. I couldn't tell exactly what it was, but I think it was a new scarf. Kayla hugged the lady and her husband. It was a great sight to see.

When my treatment was done, my nurse Diane (the same one who helped me in chemo number five) said, "So, we will see you in three weeks?" I said, "Maybe, but maybe not. This is my sixth treatment." She replied, "So you may be done?" I said, "Yes, but I will be back in to say goodbye if I am."

And I do want to do something for the nurses in that room. I may take them some cookies. I think they do a fantastic job.

When we were done we walked out of the center and got into the car, and it hit me: "Welcome to a new day." I thought of Abraham in Ur and the Lord telling him to leave. "God told Abram: 'Leave your country, your family, and your father's home for a land that I will show you' … So Abram left just as God said" (Genesis 12:1, 4). When you read those words, it seems too simple, but when you live them, that's another story.

These past eighteen weeks have been very regimented and comforting. Progress is evident. I can count the treatments. They've moved in predictable cycles of three weeks. There's a lot of support, not only from the doctors but also from the incredible nurses. They're readily available and quick to respond to phone calls. I know some smart person thought of doing chemo treatments this way. I believe all these things help people to recover from cancer.

And I know this whole setup makes it easier for people to pray. It gives folks benchmarks and predictability. That's good.

But when I walked out of the center yesterday, all that changed. The regimen may be gone (unless I have more chemo treatments) and predictability is out the window. And I'm left with uncertainty. What's going to happen now? I know I'm going to get another PET scan. I do know that, but beyond that, who knows?

But I'll take it.

I'd rather have a new adventure with God than the alternative. Proverbs 2 talks about what happens when you forsake Lady Wisdom and Good Sense (he does personify wisdom in this book—all the way through, as a matter of fact). When someone turns away from the Lord, he ends up "traveling paths that go nowhere, wandering in a maze of detours and dead ends" (Proverbs 2:15). What a nightmare—been there, done that, too many times.

Walking west with God as Abraham did is different. I may not know exactly where I'm headed *but I know He does.* And like Abraham, I'm not responsible for knowing the destination. In fact there isn't one, this side of glory. I just need to be faithful to take each step, each day, and leave the rest to him "as aliens and strangers on earth" (Hebrews 11:13, NIV). This is the gift cancer has given me. I'm never going to take my health or the future for granted again. I can't. It's today and the journey of today.

And responding to His sovereignty is crucial. Going back to Luke 4—the passage I read yesterday—something else hit me. Jesus was preaching in his hometown of Nazareth and wanted to do miracles there as he'd done in other places. Now the text doesn't say this, but I don't think he was able to do much in the way of miraculous deeds there because folks didn't believe him. They couldn't get past the fact that he was the carpenter's son.

Anyway, when Jesus referenced the two miracles of the Old Testament, what I think he was saying is, "You folks have just proven that you are not part of the Elect because you failed to believe in me." *That's why they tried to push him off the cliff.* This whole dilemma of God's sovereignty and man's responsibility has stumped theologians forever, and I certainly have no resolutions. But I do know this: if you believe, you're part of the Elect. If you don't, you aren't. Or to put it another way, no one who truly wants to believe in Jesus is shut out of God's chosen family.

As Spurgeon used to say, these dual doctrines of man's responsibility and God's sovereignty don't come together in our limited minds, but they run parallel like train tracks and ultimately they merge in God's mind.

The point is, I want to make my election sure (I'm not talking about earning salvation; I'm talking about exercising faith) by continuing to trust Him. And through all the twists and turns on the cancer road, I want to trust Him every step of the way, even though I won't understand and won't recognize where I am most of the time, now that I'm out of Ur. But that's what an adventure is, right? There are new vistas, new plateaus, new valleys, new roads … same God.

"El Shaddai," a wonderful song written by Michael Card and John Thompson, has as its setting the Abraham story. As the nomad Abe and his family traveled along, they learned new names for God, but His essential character does not change: "Age to age you're still the same."[31]

Lord, I thank you for bringing me this far in the journey. Thank you for sustaining me through six chemo treatments. I know I may still have some rough days ahead, but I place those in your hands as well.

I love routine. I love to know what's going to happen this day, the next day, and eighteen weeks ahead. Now I'm in a different place.

Give me the grace and courage to follow you step by step in the new adventure, El Shaddai, El Elyona, and Adonai. And here's my prayer:

"What's next, Papa?" (Romans 8:15)

Amen and amen.

Endnotes

1. Bo Baker, *Made for the Mountains* (Waco: Word Publishers, 1977), 16.
2. Artur Weiser, *The Psalms: A Commentary, Old Testament Library* (Philadelphia: Westminster Press, 1962), 724.
3. Ibid.
4. Baker, 33.
5. Granger Westburg, *Good Grief* (Philadelphia: Fortress Press, 1962), 30.
6. Jack Taylor, *The Key to Triumphant Living* (Nashville: Broadman Press, 1971), 21.
7. http://christian-quotes.ochristian.com/Hudson-Taylor-Quotes, accessed October 20, 2010.
8. Dietrich Bonhoeffer, *Letters and Papers from Prison: The Enlarged Edition,* ed. Eberhard Bethge (New York: Touchstone, 1971), 341.
9. "Talking Cancer: Celebrities Speak out about how cancer affected them and those they love," *Guide to Chemotherapy*, 11.
10. "God of Earth and Outer Space" in *Baptist Hymnal,* 1975 edition, ed. William J. Reynolds (Nashville: Convention Press, 1975).
11. Arnold Dallimore, *Spurgeon* (Chicago: Moody Press, 1984), 49.

12. Joni Eareckson Tada and Steven Estes, *When God Weeps* (Grand Rapids: Zondervan, 1997), 132.

13. "A Mighty Fortress Is Our God" in *Baptist Hymnal,* 1991 edition, hymn 8.

14. Vance Havner, *Peace in the Valley* (n.p.: Fleming H. Revell Co., 1962), 36.

15. Geron Davis, "Evermore," http://freechristiansonglc. blogspot.com, accessed November 16, 2010.

16. Dietrich Bonhoeffer, *Voices in the Night: The Prison Poems of Dietrich Bonhoeffer,* ed. and trans. by Edwin Robertson (Grand Rapids: Zondervan, 1999), 67.

17. "The God of Abraham Praise" in *Baptist Hymnal,* 1991 edition, hymn 34.

18. Catherine Cameron, "God, Who Stretched the Spangled Heavens" in *Baptist Hymnal,* 1991 edition, ed. Wesley L. Forbis (Nashville: Convention Press, 1991).

19. Jack Taylor, *After the Spirit Comes* (Nashville: Broadman Press, 1974), 48.

20. Terry W. York, "Thanksgiving/Thanks-Living" in *Baptist Hymnal,* 1991 edition, ed. Wesley L. Forbis (Nashville: Convention Press, 1991).

21. Twila Paris, "We Will Glorify" in *Magnify the Lord: Scripture Songs for Choir or Congregation,* ed. Tom Fettke, comp. Ken Bible and Tom Fettke (Kansas City: Lillenas Publishing Co., 1986).

22. Audrey Mieir, "His Name is Wonderful" in *Magnify the Lord: Scripture Songs for Choir or Congregation,* ed. Tom Fettke, comp. Ken Bible and Tom Fettke (Kansas City: Lillenas Publishing Co., 1986).

23. Georg Neumark, "If You Will Only Let God Guide You" in *Baptist Hymnal,* 1991 edition, ed. Wesley L. Forbis (Nashville: Convention Press, 1991).

24. "Unto Thee, O Lord" in *Magnify the Lord* (Kansas City: Lillenas Publishing Co., 1986), 30-32.

25. "Like a River Glorious" in *Baptist Hymnal,* 1991 edition, hymn 58.

26. J. Wilbur Chapman and Rowland H. Pritchard, "Our Great Savior" in *Magnify the Lord,* ed. Tom Fettke, (Kansas City: Lillenas Publishing Co, 1986), 93.

27. David Platt, *Radical: Taking Back Your Faith from the American Dream* (Colorado Springs: Multnomah Books, 2010), 99-103.

28. Gloria Gaither and William J. Gaither, "I Will Serve Thee" in *Magnify the Lord* (Kansas City: Lillenas Publishing Co., 1986), 98-99.

29. W. C. Martin and Charles H. Gabriel, "My Father Watches Over Me" in *Magnify the Lord* (Kansas City: Lillenas Publishing Co., 1986), 117.

30. Bruce Ballinger, "We Have Come Into His House" in *Great Is the Lord: Favorites for Choir or Congregation,* ed. Tom Fettke, comp. Ken Bible (Kansas City: Lillenas Publishing Co., 1984), 8-9.

31. Michael Card and John Thompson, "El Shaddai" in *Great Is the Lord* (Kansas City: Lillenas Publishing Co., 1986), 13-14.